Children at the Border

Children at the Border

An American Human Rights Crisis

Jo-Anne Wilson-Keenan

McFarland & Company, Inc., Publishers
Jefferson, North Carolina

LIBRARY OF CONGRESS CATALOGUING-IN-PUBLICATION DATA

Names: Wilson-Keenan, Jo-Anne, author.
Title: Children at the border : an American human rights crisis / Jo-Anne Wilson-Keenan.
Description: Jefferson, North Carolina : McFarland & Company, Inc., Publishers, 2021 | Includes bibliographical references and index.
Identifiers: LCCN 2021008643 | ISBN 9781476685427 (Paperback : acid free paper) ∞
ISBN 9781476643342 (eBook)
Subjects: LCSH: U.S. Border Patrol—Rules and practice. | United States. Office of Refugee Resettlement—Rules and practice. | Immigrant children—Legal status, laws, etc.—United States. | Illegal alien children—United States. | Alien detention centers—United States. | Unaccompanied refugee children—United States. | Immigrant families—Government policy—United States. | United States—Emigration and immigration—Government policy. | Refugees—Legal status, laws, etc.—United States. | Unaccompanied refugee children—Mexico. | BISAC: SOCIAL SCIENCE / Emigration & Immigration
Classification: LCC JV6456 .W55 2021 | DDC 323.3/2910973—dc23
LC record available at https://lccn.loc.gov/2021008643

BRITISH LIBRARY CATALOGUING DATA ARE AVAILABLE

ISBN (print) 978-1-4766-8542-7
ISBN (ebook) 978-1-4766-4334-2

© 2021 Jo-Anne Wilson-Keenan. All rights reserved

No part of this book may be reproduced or transmitted in any form or by any means, electronic or mechanical, including photocopying or recording, or by any information storage and retrieval system, without permission in writing from the publisher.

Front cover image © Wasu Watcharadachaphong/Shutterstock

Printed in the United States of America

McFarland & Company, Inc., Publishers
Box 611, Jefferson, North Carolina 28640
www.mcfarlandpub.com

"For all children everywhere and always"
—from the words of Archbishop Desmond Tutu

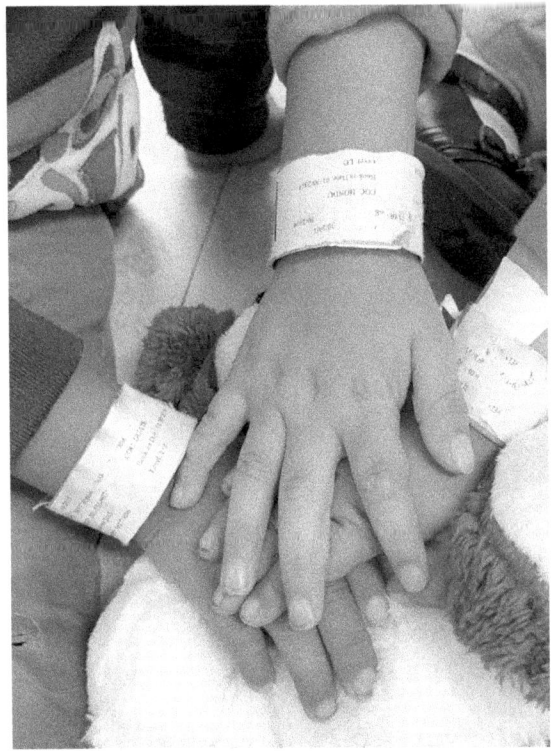

Hands of migrant children (courtesy Marta Vazquez).

The idea that some lives matter less is the root
of all that is wrong with the world.
—Paul Farmer

May God not forget us.
—Christmas wish of a child at the
Hosanna shelter in Mexicali, Mexico, 2019

Table of Contents

Acknowledgments	ix
Guide to Acronyms	1
Preface	3
1. The Dawn of Outrage	9
2. Family Separation	27
3. Increasing Outrage	47
4. The Colossal Failure of Reunification	62
5. Detainment at Border Patrol Stations	74
6. Detainment in Office of Refugee Resettlement Facilities	87
7. A Horrifying Reality	105
8. The Deaths of Children	117
9. Further Harm	128
10. Families in Mexico	147
11. Refugees in the Time of Covid-19	167
12. Seeking Relief Through the Courts	179
13. Seeking Relief Through Congress	206
14. Recommendations	217
The State of Things Today	227
Appendix	231
Chapter Notes	233
Bibliography	237
Index	259

Acknowledgments

Layla Milholen

My deepest thanks to my editor, Layla Milholen, at McFarland. This book would not have been possible without her. I am most grateful to Layla for her believing in my book about the humanitarian crisis of family separation at our southern border. From the very beginning, Layla embraced the project, answered my every question quickly, and guided me through to the completion of the manuscript. Thanks to her suggestion to add photographs to accompany the text, readers will get a firsthand view of the struggles and beauty of the migrant families. I am fortunate, indeed, that Layla was just an email away throughout the entire process.

Dianne Post

This book would not have been possible without the assistance of attorney Dianne Post, the first reader. For months, Dianne helped me understand law cases and legislation that challenge family separation and other government policies and practices that tear migrant families apart. She read and responded to my drafts, added detailed notes to dozens of pages, and returned them to me within hours. Dianne also suggested including photographs, and she pushed my thinking in other ways. I did not understand the depth of the pain of slave children and Native American children who were separated from their families until Dianne led me to compare their lives to those of migrant children today. I am deeply grateful to Dianne for her support.

Friends from Arizona and Mexico

I also offer my thanks to Mary Jo Forman Miller, who invited me to travel to shelters in Mexicali, Mexico, with members of Refugee Aid. Mary Jo founded Refugee Aid in 2018 to support a wave of migrant children and their families who journeyed to the U.S. from Central America. When families arrived in Arizona, they were dropped off at a bus station, but they had to remain outside in a dirt lot while they waited for the bus to their destination. Mary Jo developed a large network of volunteers who created a safety net for the families that included food, shelter, clothing, transportation, and blankets to sit on in the dirt lot. When the Trump administration banned families from coming to the U.S. and they had to remain in Mexico, Mary Jo and Refugee Aid were undeterred. Refugee Aid rented storage units in Calexico, California, and stowed supplies that volunteers transported to shelters in Mexicali, Mexico. Mary Jo reviewed information about Refugee Aid for the book.

Through Mary Jo, I met many Arizona friends—Deirdre Sparling, Craig Campbell, Gloria S., and Martha and Howard Iskyan—and Marta Vazquez welcomed both asylum seekers and me to Phoenix. Deidre shared her beautiful home with me and others who needed a place to rest. Craig took on a night shift at the bus station to make sure that asylum seekers who came in late were not alone in the dark. Gloria befriended volunteers at churches and took care of migrants in heartfelt and wonderful ways. Martha employed her expertise as a Red Cross volunteer and translator to bridge the distances between languages and between need and comfort. Howard Iskyan, Martha's husband, translated words from Spanish to English and back again to make sure the messages were understood. Marta Vazquez purchased a bus to ferry migrants from the bus station to shelters or to wherever else they needed to go. Marta and her husband opened their home to provide shelter, comfort, and safety for many migrant families. All of these people shared their experiences with me for the book.

Reyna Martinez is the director of Caritas/Catholic Charities in Mexicali, Mexico. She often transports goods from Refugee Aid to shelters in Mexicali. Reyna was the leader for our group during our visit to Mexicali. She accompanied us as we crossed the border, drove us to the shelters, and assisted with translation.

Altagarcia Tamayo Madueño is the president of the La Posada, a shelter in Mexicali that houses approximately 300 people. She works to maintain a safe and comfortable home for migrant families. Altagarcia shared her extensive knowledge about how she operates the shelter with us.

* * *

I also wish to thank the following people and organizations who contributed to the book:

Native American Family Advocates

Sisters Kay McGowan and Fay Givens, of Michigan, produced a documentary titled *Indian School: The Survivor's Story*. They shared their knowledge of Native American boarding schools and the resulting intergenerational trauma that has affected countless survivors.

Warren Petoskey, an elder of the *Waganakising* Odwaw and *Minneconjou* Lakotah Nations, appears in *Indian School: The Survivor's Story*. He has written his own book called *Dancing My Dream*. Warren generously shared his knowledge of Native American culture, life in boarding schools, and the intergenerational trauma that resulted from the separation of Native American children from their families.

Human Rights Advocates

United Nations Publications granted permission for the inclusion of material regarding several treaties in this book.

Human Rights First, a nonprofit, nonpartisan international human rights organization based in New York, Washington, D.C., Houston, and Los Angeles, granted me permission to include findings, firsthand accounts, and recommendations from their reports. They interview asylum seekers, immigration attorneys, academic researchers, humanitarian volunteers, and legal monitors to bring the inhumane treatment of asylum seekers to light. Their reports are comprehensive and timely and express the personal trauma of those victimized by current U.S. immigration policies. The information in this book comes mainly from three documents: "The Flores Settlement and Family Incarceration: A Brief History and Next Steps," Kennji Kuzuka, senior researcher; *Orders from Above: Massive Human Rights Abuses Under the Trump Administration Return to Mexico Policy*, written by Eleanor Acer, Kennji Kizuka, and Rebecca Gendelman; and *Pandemic as Pretext: Trump Administration Exploits Covid-19, Expels Asylum Seekers and Children to Escalating Danger*, written by the same team, with Kennji Kizuka as lead author. My thanks to Jim Bernfield, vice president of marketing and communications, Human Rights First, for his assistance in obtaining permission to use this information.

Margo Schlanger, the Wade H. and Dores M. McCree Collegiate Professor of Law, University of Michigan Law School, Ann Arbor, allowed me to use information from summaries of law cases from the Civil Rights Litigation Clearinghouse. Professor Schlanger is the founder and director of the clearinghouse.

Anthony W. Fontes, assistant professor, School of International Service, American University, allowed me to include information from "Migrants' Stories: Why They Flee," from *The Conversation*. For the past ten years, he has done field work in the Northern Triangle of Central America and along migration paths through Mexico, seeking answers to the question of why so many families make the difficult and dangerous journey north to the United States.

Sondra Crosby and George Annas, professors of health law, ethics, and human rights at Boston University, allowed me to include information from "Child Detention at the Border Is Torture," which appeared in *BU Today*. Crosby has evaluated torture victims from throughout the world, including detainees in U.S. detention at Guantanamo Bay. Both she and Annas state, "It is not an exaggeration to say that the current treatment of children in these [migrant] detention centers is torture."

Jaana Juvonen, professor of developmental psychology, and Jennifer Silvers, assistant professor of developmental neuroscience at UCLA, gave permission for me to use information from "Separating Children from Parents at the Border Isn't Just Cruel: It's Torture," which appeared in *UCLA Newsroom*. They state that evidence from neuroscience suggests that the policy of separating children from their families is not just inhumane, it is also, "by definition, torture."

Michael E. Hayden, senior investigative reporter for the Southern Poverty Law Center's (SPLC) Hatewatch blog, allowed me to use information from a six-part series of reports in which he analyzed the content of 900 emails written by Stephen Miller. The emails were exchanged with Breitbart editors from March 4, 2015, to June 27, 2016. Miller's emails regarding immigration focus on severely restricting or terminating nonwhite immigration to the United States.

The Young Center for Immigrant Children's Rights granted me permission to include information from their work in this book. The center's mission is to protect and advance the rights and best interests of immigrant children according to the *Convention on the Rights of the Child* and state and federal law. In 2020, the National Association of Counsel for Children awarded the Young Center their President's Award, which "recognizes excellence in advocacy organizations working to advance the legal rights of children and families."

The Florence Immigrant and Refugee Rights Project allowed me to use information from their newsletters and other online sources. The mission of the Florence Project is to provide free legal and social services to detained adults and unaccompanied children facing immigration removal proceedings in Arizona.

The Kino Border Initiative (KBI) permitted me to use information about how migrant families are surviving in Nogales, Mexico, and how KBI is adapting their services for migrants during the Covid-19 pandemic. My personal thanks to Joanna Williams, director of education and advocacy, and Fr. Sean Carroll, S.J., executive director, for their assistance. The Kino Border Initiative is a binational organization that works in the area of migration and is located in Nogales, Arizona, and Nogales, Sonora, Mexico. The KBI's vision is to help make humane, just, workable migration between the U.S. and Mexico a reality. Its mission is to promote U.S. and Mexico border and immigration policies that affirm the dignity of the human person and a spirit of binational solidarity through direct humanitarian assistance and accompaniment with migrants; social and pastoral education with communities on both sides of the border; and participation in collaborative networks that engage in research and advocacy to transform local, regional, and national immigration policies.

Project on Government Oversight (POGO) is a nonpartisan independent watchdog that investigates and exposes waste, corruption, abuse of power, failures of the government to serve the public, or government silencing of those who report wrongdoing. POGO champions reforms to achieve a more effective, ethical, and accountable federal government that safeguards constitutional principles. Open the Government (OTG) is an inclusive, nonpartisan coalition that works to strengthen our democracy and empower the public by advancing policies that create a more open, accountable, and responsive government. The two organizations allowed me to use the following documents they received through FOIA. The first document is a letter to Sen. Ron Johnson, chairman, and Sen. Claire McCaskill, ranking member, of the Senate Committee on Homeland Security and Government Affairs, dated October 2, 2018. In the letter, Danielle Brian, executive director of the Project on Government Oversight, and Lisa Rosenberg, executive director of Open the Government, submit documentary evidence that Department of Homeland Security Secretary Kirstjen Nielsen may have given false and/or materially misleading testimony before the committee on May 15, 2018.

The second document is a memorandum to Kirstjen Nielsen, secretary of the Department of Homeland Security, from Kevin McAleenan, commissioner of U.S. Customs and Border Protection, L. Francis Cissna, director of U.S. Citizenship and Immigration Services, and Thomas D. (the remainder of his name is redacted). The memo is five pages in length, and parts are redacted. This memo offered Secretary Nielsen three options for the zero-tolerance initiative. In this copy, the signature is redacted, but it is very likely that Secretary Nielsen signed the memo.

The third document is an email dated July 12, 2018. It was recovered under FOIA and instructs border patrol chiefs and deputies to deport families as quickly as possible in order to make room in their facilities for children who had been separated from their parents under the zero-tolerance policy. These families would be reunited under court order by July 26, 2018. This email is written mainly in acronyms. A guide to terminology written by Katherine Hawkins of POGO is linked within the email. I was granted permission to use the guide as well.

Colleagues

I also wish to thank Judy Solsken and Jerri Willett. For many years, we worked together and conducted ethnographic research in schools. When I walked through the shelters in Mexico, my experiences with Judy and Jerri helped me to hear the stories that were being told there and to see the ways in which they were being expressed.

Family Past

I would like to acknowledge my late aunt, Tillie Fredey. When I was a freshman in high school, Tillie sat at her massive Underwood typewriter and typed the first story I ever wrote, as I dictated. It was my entry for a writing contest. When she finished typing, Tillie, who was generally taciturn, complimented my work. That was the moment I began to realize that I was a writer. I did not win the contest, but Tillie's sincere affirmation was a far more valuable prize than any I could have won.

I would also like to remember my mother's cousin Suzanne Nedoncelle, a member of the French Resistance, who deciphered and distributed messages throughout Paris during World War II. Her courage inspires my work.

Family Present

I wish to thank my sisters Catherine Marek, Suzanne Scorzafava, and Mary Arnold for being my best friends. Thanks to my son Noah for answering questions, discussing my work, and challenging my ideas. I am also grateful to my nephew P.J. Scorzafava for his constant support. My thanks to all the other members of my caring family.

I could not have written this book without the assistance of my husband John H. Keenan, who read every word, captured every rogue punctuation mark, and put up with my early-morning writing shift. John's dedication goes beyond reading, editing, and tolerating lost sleep. John's dedication is truly the manifestation of kindness and love.

Families Seeking Asylum

Finally, my deepest gratitude to the families from the Northern Triangle whose temporary homes I visited in Mexico. Despite vast hardships, their faith, strength and joy in being together were clearly visible. The former president called them criminals, bad people and other disparaging names. He ranted that the children were not innocent. In this book, the families share a different story.

Guide to Acronyms

U.S. Government

CBP: Customs and Border Protection
DHS: Department of Homeland Security
GAO: Government Accountability Office
HHS: Department of Health and Human Services
ICE: Immigration and Customs Enforcement
OIG: Office of Inspector General
OMB: Office of Management and Budget
ORR: Office of Refugee Resettlement
UAC: Unaccompanied Alien Children

United Nations

CAT: Convention Against Torture **CRC**: Convention on the Rights of the Child
ICCPR: International Covenant on Civil and Political Rights
ICERD: International Convention on the Elimination of All Forms of Racial Discrimination
UDHR: Universal Declaration of Human Rights
UN: United Nations
UNHCR: United Nations High Commissioner for Refugees
UNICEF: United Nations Children's Fund

Laws

APA: Administrative Procedure Act
FOIA: Freedom of Information Act

IIRAIRA: The Illegal Immigrant Reform and Immigrant Responsibility Act
INA: Immigration and Nationality Act
TVPRA: Trafficking Victims Protection Reauthorization Act

Rights Organizations

ACLU: American Civil Liberties Union
HRF: Human Rights First
SPLC: Southern Poverty Law Center

Preface

Perhaps as is the case with many books, this one has turned out differently than planned at the outset. It did not begin as a book about the human rights of migrant children. My career has focused on children's literacy and ways to collaborate with families as they support their children who are learning speak, listen, read, write, receive information, and express themselves in ever-evolving ways. My previous book, *From Small Places: Toward the Realization of Literacy as a Human Right* (Wilson-Keenan 2015), traces the origins of literacy as a human right and its importance as a means of achieving other rights. My plan was to write a second book that continued to develop ideas that explored ways in which families and community members support children's literacy and other rights.

During the initial stages of the writing, however, my subject changed. A situation was evolving which captured my interest as an educator and a writer. The U.S. government instituted the policy of separating immigrant children from their parents at our southern border. For me, advocating for the survival rights of children moved to the foreground, leading me to write about supporting and protecting the fundamental human rights of children who have been separated from their families or who have been harmed in other ways by our government's immigration policies.

I was a child who lost one of my parents. When I was 7 years old, a second grader, I walked home from school for lunch one spring day and found my aunt and our neighbor at our house. My mother was not home. She was at the hospital because my father had suffered a heart attack that morning. He died. Within moments, my mother's role changed from that of a wife and mother to that of a widow with four daughters, ages 4 to 11. My three sisters' lives changed as well. Life was often difficult. My family's income came mainly from Social Security survivor's benefits and my mother's part-time work as a nurse. Her earnings were strictly limited. If she exceeded the limit, she would lose the survivor's benefits. Despite the challenges, we had our home, and we had each other. My mother has passed away. My sisters remain my best friends to this day. I cannot imagine the horror of a child who has to flee her home country for safety, only to arrive at a place she thinks will be safe and be ripped away from her family.

As a result of the changes in my life when my father died, I came to understand the burdens carried by children whose families experience traumatic events. For nearly 50 years, I have held different positions as an educator, including classroom teacher, elementary school principal, district literacy director, college professor, literacy consultant for school and summer programs, and writer. I am familiar with the intricacies of the learning communities within which young children reside, and I know the depth of thought, work, and caring that goes into designing environments for children that are both physically and psychologically safe. Helping to create places in which children can thrive and learn, places where their families' voices are heard, has been a major part of my work.

The UN defines human rights in the following way:

> Human rights are rights inherent to all human beings, regardless of race, sex, nationality, ethnicity, language, religion, or any other status. Human rights include the right to life and liberty, freedom from slavery and torture, freedom of opinion and expression, the right to work and education, and many more. Everyone is entitled to these rights, without discrimination [United Nations 2020].

As a literacy educator, I have collected hundreds of children's books. One book, sponsored by UNICEF in 2000, is titled *For Every Child*. It interprets rights that are included in the United Nations *Convention on the Rights of the Child* (UN General Assembly 1989b).[1] In this document, a child is defined as a person under the age of eighteen. The foreword to *For Every Child* is written by Archbishop Desmond Tutu of South Africa. Initially, he describes the illustrations in the book as depicting happy children who are healthy and learning. Trusted adults are responsible for protecting children's inalienable rights. Archbishop Tutu explains that these rights, set forth in the CRC, are "the rights of all children everywhere and always."

Archbishop Tutu then contrasts these images with deeply disturbing ones from the twentieth century. The first is that of the young Vietnamese girl, Phan Thi Kim Phuc, who was struck in a napalm attack during the Vietnam War. Her body was burning, so she tore off her clothes and ran down the road screaming and crying. The photo won a Pulitzer in 1973 (Leekley & Leekley 1978). The archbishop remarks that the photo "captures the ghastliness of war," whose victims are frequently women, children and the elderly.

In the next part of the foreword, Archbishop Tutu describes an image from the Soweto uprising of 1976. It is a picture of the lifeless body of a small Black boy being carried by a young man and woman. He was shot by South African police and was the first fatality of the rebellion.

Tutu then tells of the tragedies that destroy the lives of children who are refugees fleeing from those who violate their human rights. These tragedies include "malnutrition, famine, and disease." The young victims are trying to find a secure place to live, a country that they can "call their own" (Tutu 2000). He also writes of the tragic lives of children who are raped and assaulted and of child soldiers who are taught to kill.

In closing, the archbishop calls for replacing the conflict, bloodshed, and strife of the twentieth century with "peace, justice, and development" in the twenty-first century. He explains that with vigilance, a different kind of society can come into being, one that is "more compassionate, more caring, and more sharing where human rights, where children's rights are respected and protected."

In the year 2000, the specific children's rights violations that Archbishop Tutu describes seemed far removed from the United States. Boy soldiers, famine, and accompanying malnutrition were not part of life throughout America. Many believed that violent acts did not take place where they lived and turned a blind eye when they happened. Americans viewed themselves as the guardians of human rights in other places, not perpetrators of human rights violations at home.

As we enter the third decade of the twenty-first century, however, we see that Americans are now facing new realities. Tragically, one of these realities is that child refugees seeking asylum at our southern border have been separated from their parents and detained in the wire cages or cold cement cells called *las hieleras*—ice boxes. These young immigrant children have been traumatized, and many were sexually abused. Others may never see their parents again. Some have died.

In an op-ed in the *New York Times*, Maria Woltjen, executive director and founder of the Young Center for Immigrant Children's Rights, describes a "wish list" of immigration policies that the White House wanted to execute beginning in 2017. The first item on the list was to construct the border wall between the U.S. and Mexico. The second item was to deport children who had traveled to the U.S. on their own. The third thing they hoped for was to dispose of the *Flores* settlement, which prohibits the Department of Homeland Security from holding children in family detention past 20 days (Woltjen 2020).

This book does not follow the administration's attempts to build the physical wall at the border. Rather, it focuses on the administration's construction of a labyrinth of policies and practices that separate children from their parents, that prevent children from being held in safe and sanitary facilities for a reasonable period of time as directed by the *Flores* settlement, and that ultimately prevent them from gaining asylum in the U.S.

Throughout the past two years, I have chronicled events in the lives of immigrant families who have traveled from the Northern Triangle of

Central America to the southern border of the United States. I've explored family separations, incarceration in cages, the deaths of children, and orders from the U.S. government for families to remain in Mexico.

While writing this book, I met members of Refugee Aid, a nonprofit in Phoenix, Arizona, that supports immigrant families, and I visited shelters in Mexico with them. The photographs in this book come from those shelters and also from places on the U.S side of the border. I have networked with other advocates as well. Since the onset of Covid-19 and the nearly complete closing of the U.S. border, I have been documenting the impact on migrant families who are trying to survive in Mexico.

Other sources for this book include dozens of news articles from a wide variety of sources, government documents, and reports from human rights and legal organizations. Two other recent books that tell of the plight of migrant children are *America Is Better Than This: Trump's War on Migrant Families* (Merkley 2019a), by Sen. Jeff Merkley, and *Separated: Inside an American Tragedy* (Soboroff 2020), by journalist Jacob Soboroff. Sen. Merkley's book begins with his experiences when he tried to visit Customs and Border Proection (CBP) facilities in early June 2018. He entered one processing center and found migrant families, some of whom had been separated, detained in locked, chain-link cages. He traveled on to another facility, called Casa Padre, in a converted Walmart. He was not allowed in and was asked to leave by the local police. Sen. Merkley returned to Texas later in June with other lawmakers. He found that 1,500 boys were living in the Walmart. He was the first legislator to pull back the curtain and reveal the treatment of migrant children at the southern border. Jacob Soboroff was one of the first journalists to visit Casa Padre. He was not allowed to take recording equipment into the facility, so he jotted notes in a small "memo book." He later reported on facilities in Arizona and California. Soboroff spent two years writing the inside story of this American tragedy, including documenting the journey of a family from Guatemala that was separated.

Children at the Border: An American Human Rights Crisis relates the story of migrant children who were separated from families. It also tells the parallel story of rights documents that provide protections from discrimination, torture, and racism, and provide special protections for children under the age of 18. Major emphasis is placed on the *Convention on the Rights of the Child* (CRC), adopted by the UN in 1989. Information from the following rights documents is also included: the *International Covenant on Civil and Political Rights* (UN General Assembly 1966a)[2]; *The Convention Relating to the Status of Refugees* (UN General Assembly 1951)[3]; *UN Convention Against Torture and Other Cruel, Inhuman or Degrading Treatment or Punishment* (UN General Assembly 1984)[4]; and *International*

Convention on the Elimination of All Forms of Racial Discrimination (UN General Assembly 1966b).[5]

A more complete description of each of these documents and how they connect to the purposes of this book follow in Chapter 1. Descriptions of law cases filed to ensure migrants' rights are also part of this parallel story. This book also documents congressional legislation that has been drafted to protect migrants and prevent the horrific treatment they have endured from resurfacing in the future. Dianne Post, an international human rights lawyer from Phoenix, Arizona, assisted me with these sections. She was the first reader of this book and continues to provide me with updates on legal decisions.

1

The Dawn of Outrage

1.1 Awareness

On June 18, 2018, one month after the implementation of a Trump administration policy that separated migrant children from parents was announced, Kirstjen Nielsen, secretary of the Department of Homeland Security (DHS), held a press conference at the White House. She stated that the children were provided meals, medical care, and educational services. The last part of her statement caught my attention immediately. There were 2,300 children known to have been separated from their parents since the administration's zero-tolerance policy began. I wondered how the government could have set up quality educational programs, along with all these other services for displaced children, so quickly.

In the days after Nielsen's press conference, I watched, read, and listened to reports. I was appalled by what was revealed. Children who had been separated from their parents were not placed in well-organized facilities and classrooms; rather, they were cold, crying, dirty, and enclosed in crowded, locked, wire cages. As I began to wrap my mind around what I was seeing, my questions started coming. First the practical ones: How could the children escape in case of a fire? Why weren't fire laws being followed? As a teacher and principal, I worked under strict local fire laws and consistent monitoring by the fire department. Fire drills had to be practiced on a regular basis. Egress had to be maintained in assembly spaces, corridors, and doorways. Why weren't those regulations being enforced here? Then the questions about well-being: Were these children being fed and clothed? Were they receiving adequate medical care? How were children possibly receiving educational services under these shocking conditions? Then a question about long-term consequences: What long-term physical and psychological harm would these children suffer as a result of enduring these experiences? Then, the moral question: How could anyone ever treat any children this way?

Large gaps existed between what the American public was being told about the living conditions of the children who had been separated from their parents and what was actually going on in the detention centers.

What started as a zero-tolerance policy that prosecuted adults who crossed the border illegally had drawn the children who accompany them into its vortex. Separating children from their parents was the result of this policy. Children as young as five months old were held in filthy, crowded cages without adequate food, water, or toilet facilities. In these unsanitary conditions, children got sick, and children who were already sick became sicker. One child became seriously ill and died six weeks after being released from U.S. Immigration (Gonzalez 2018). Six children died while in custody (Hennessy-Fiske 2019). Another child drowned attempting to cross a border river (Silva 2019). Three others succumbed to dehydration (McDonnell 2019).

The situation became so horrific that on July 18, 2019, the late Rep. Elijah Cummings, then chairman of the House Oversight Committee, angrily interrupted Kevin McAleenan, acting secretary of Homeland Security (DHS), during a hearing. Cummings had just established that DHS had done a better job keeping track of people's belongings than they did of keeping track of their children. When McAleenan attempted to say that his department was doing their "level best in a challenging—" Cummings broke in and said the following:

> What does that mean? What does that mean when a child is sitting in their own feces, can't take a shower? Come on, man, none of us would have our children in that position. They are human beings.

Cummings continued,

> I get tired of folks saying "Oh, oh, they just beating up on Border Patrol. Oh, they just beating up on Homeland Security." What I am saying, is I want to concentrate on these children. And I want to make sure that they are ok. We are the greatest country in the world. We are the ones that can go anywhere in the world and save people, make sure they have diapers, make sure they have toothbrushes, make sure they're not laying around in defecation in some silver paper.
>
> Come on. We're better than that. And I don't want us to lose sight of that. When we are dancing with the angels, these children will be dealing with the issues that have been presented to them. How do you say to a two-year-old, "Your mother, we can't find your mother, but we can find her keys. We can find her keys. Got your mama's keys?" So, I just think we can do better. And we can go on and on, but I'm hoping that we will see some immediate improvements. I just want to see an improvement [Committee on Oversite and Reform 2019].

Additionally, Sen. Jeff Merkley from Oregon called family separation Trump's "most cruel" law. He emphasized that child separation was not an evil resulting from a civil war or a campaign of genocide initiated by a dictator in a distant land. Merkley states:

1. The Dawn of Outrage

It is here, in America. It is perpetrated by our government, with our resources, on our land. It is the centerpiece of Trump's war on migrant children. Trump's war includes child separation, cages, family internment camps, border blockades, and a network of child prisons on American soil that as of December 2018 held 15,000 migrant children [Merkley 2019, xv].

Historically, child refugees who came to the U.S. southern border were mainly from Mexico, but for the past several years, extreme poverty and violence have been catalysts for migration from the Northern Triangle of Central America, which is made up of Guatemala, Honduras, and El Salvador.

These conditions have been brought about by years of civil war in Guatemala and El Salvador and Honduras's position as a staging area for neighboring conflicts (Speckhard 2018). Many U.S. administrations, both Democratic and Republican, have brought harm to these countries. For decades, U.S. foreign policy played a major role in creating economic and social problems in the Northern Triangle by providing lawless governments in the Northern Triangle with military aid and public support as they undertook actions against their own people (Frerichs 2017).

Toward the end of the twentieth century, after the conflicts ended, thousands of people from Central America came to the U.S. Many of these migrants were men, heads of households in their 20s or 30s, who wanted to work here and send money back to their families. They were economic refugees. In 1996, the U.S. passed the Illegal Immigrant Reform and Immigrant Responsibility Act (IIRAIRA). Subsequently, tens of thousands of convicted criminals were expelled to Central America. As a result, gangs, or maras, flourished there. The gangs had originated in the U.S., not in the Northern Triangle. They included Mara Salvatrucha (MS-13) and the 18th Street gang (Barrio 18) (Martinez 2018).

In 2015, because of the gang-related violence in El Salvador, the murder rate rose to 103 per 100,000. At that time, El Salvador was the most violent not-at-war country in the world. Three years later, that rate dropped by 33 percent, but El Salvador, Honduras, and Guatemala still have the world's highest murder rates.

The ground in Central America was fertile for gangs to take over. In Guatemala, for example, 1.5 million children did not attend school. The UN reports, "School desertion can lead to home confinement, child labour, forced or coerced recruitment, internal or cross border displacement, among other consequences" (UNHCR 2020).

Additionally, Sofia Martinez writes in *The Atlantic*:

> The region's civil wars left behind tens of thousands of young people from broken families. That reality, combined with extreme inequality, policies of mass incarceration of suspicious youth, and weak judicial and security institutions created the new monster that is today's gang problem [Martinez 2018].

The UN reports, "Gang warfare and violence have transformed parts of Central America into some of the most dangerous places on earth" (UNHCR 2020). Gang crimes include rape, robbery, extortion, and murder. Victims are not isolated individuals, but often networks of several family members.

Anthony W. Fontes, a professor at American University School of International Service, has spent the past ten years doing field work in the Northern Triangle of Central America and along migration paths through Mexico. He has been seeking answers to the question of why so many families make the difficult and dangerous journey north to the United States. Fontes states, "The region's extreme poverty and violent impunity are central factors driving this migration." He adds, "Yet every migrant's story is unique." He writes, "Criminal organizations derive much of their power from their deep links with government agents; it's sometimes impossible to identify where the state ends and the underworld begins" (Fontes 2019).[1]

Fontes spoke with Pedro, whose uncle and two brothers were gunned down on a street in Guatemala City. Pedro suspected that his cousin had stolen money from drug traffickers. Pedro, his wife, and two daughters moved away to another part of the city. Despite Pedro's efforts to protect his family, the police found the body of one of his daughters in an alley. She had been raped, burned with cigarettes, and stabbed to death. After that, he and his remaining family members fled Guatemala (Fontes 2019).

Child from El Salvador at La Posada, Mexicali, Mexico (author's photograph).

Fontes also tells the story of Alejandra,

Migrant mother and daughter having breakfast (author's photograph).

a nursing student from another city in Guatemala. She was visiting her family during Christmas break. Alejandra witnessed her uncle being shot to death in his front yard as he was stringing Christmas lights. He would not pay extortion money to a criminal group of former and active police officers. The day after the shooting, Alejandra found threatening messages on her Facebook page. Like Pedro, she also moved away. She says that a few weeks later, a kid with a handgun tried to kill her. She maintains he was sent by the criminal group. Alejandra saved her life by throwing herself off her motor bike. She too, fled Guatemala (Fontes 2019).

As Professor Fontes says, information on how much gangs contribute to the crime rate is "hampered by extremely low prosecution rates and lack of reliable data." He adds, "However, gangs are responsible for the region's most widespread and brutal extortion rackets, which create psychological and economic strife for Central Americans while also causing countless murders. The upshot is that many Central Americans trying to enter the United States are literally 'running for their lives'" (Fontes 2019).

The "runners" include young children, mothers, and their unborn children. The problem of violence in the Northern Triangle is so egregious that it has created an entirely new group of asylum seekers, made up of women, many of whom are pregnant, children, toddlers, and babies. Many children arrive alone.

The UN states:

> Thousands of parents have fled with their families and, in many cases, children have made the perilous journey alone. These unaccompanied children are some of the world's most vulnerable refugees—they have witnessed horrific violence and faced extreme risk [UNHCR 2020].

1.2 *The* Convention on the Rights of the Child *(CRC)*

The United Nations *Convention on the Rights of the Child* delineates children's rights. It was adopted more than 40 years after the Universal Declaration of Human Rights. The following is a brief history of how the convention originated.

The *Convention on the Rights of the Child* (UN General Assembly 1989) developed from the UDHR. After World War II, Eleanor Roosevelt wanted to witness the condition of the refugees in Germany for herself, so she visited the occupied sections there that were controlled at the time by the U.S. Army. She also flew over the bombed-out ruins of Cologne, Frankfurt, and Munich. She stated that she was "stunned and appalled" by the devastation that she witnessed. As she flew home to New York, the faces of women in the black market kept crowding into her mind. She reminded herself, "again and again there was also hope in the air. There had to be hope" (Roosevelt 1958).

Adlai Stevenson said of Eleanor Roosevelt's compassion, "What other single human being has touched and transformed the existence of so many?" She walked "in the slums … of the world, not on a tour of inspection, but as one who could not feel contentment when others were hungry" (Stevenson 1962). Unfortunately, many leaders of our country take an entirely different, cruel stance regarding the support of refugees today.

For children, the hope that Eleanor Roosevelt referred to still exists within the CRC. In 1989, world leaders reasoned, "Children needed a special convention just for them because people under 18 years old often need special care and protection that adults do not" (UNICEF 2016). The leaders wanted to make sure that the world recognized that children have human rights too. In response, in November of that year, the UN General Assembly adopted a separate treaty, the CRC, that is described as follows:

> Built on varied legal systems and cultural traditions, the Convention is a universally agreed set of non-negotiable standards and obligations. These basic standards—also called human rights—set minimum entitlements and freedoms that should be respected by governments. They are founded on respect for the dignity and worth of each individual, regardless of race, colour, gender, language, religion, opinions, origins, wealth, birth status or ability and therefore apply to every human being everywhere [UNICEF 2012].

The convention supports the concept that "children's rights are human rights" (Humanium).

This document is "the first legally binding international instrument to incorporate the full range of human rights—civil, cultural, economic, political and social rights" (UNICEF 2016).

The *Convention on the Rights of the Child* (CRC) encompasses four major principles that have the power to build a compassionate perspective towards children and their rights. The first is the principle of non-discrimination: all children should enjoy their rights without being subjected to discrimination. Another principle is the right to survival and development. A third principle respects the right of children to express their ideas freely. A fourth consideration that occurs throughout this book is "the best interest of the child." These words come from Article 3 of the *Convention on the Rights of the Child* (UNICEF 2020). (The entire text of the CRC appears in the appendix of this book.)

This convention safeguards a child's right to be cared for by his or her parents. It protects a child's identity, including nationality, name, and relationships with family members. It prohibits children from being separated from their parents against their will. Children also have the right to the highest standard of medical assistance and health care and facilities that treat their illnesses and provide rehabilitation services. They must have access to nutritious foods and clean drinking water. The convention states that measures will be taken to diminish infant and child mortality.

The framers understood that ratification alone would not make a difference. "One of the Convention's key strengths is that it recognizes that rights must be actively promoted if they are going to be enforced—awareness isn't enough" (Amnesty International Publications 2012). Strategies for implementation and oversight are built into the concluding articles of the convention.

According to UNICEF, the convention went on to become the most widely ratified human rights treaty in history and has helped transform children's lives (UNICEF n.d.). Until 2015, South Sudan, Somalia, and the U.S. were the only three countries belonging to the UN General Assembly that had not ratified it. Both of South Sudan and Somalia did so in January 2015.

Somali president Hassan Sheikh Mohamud signed it in a ceremony in Mogadishu, and stated what the ratification would mean for the children of his country. He said:

> We have promised you full and equal access before the law. We have promised to make sure that you never have to become a soldier until you are old enough to make that decision for yourself. We have promised to support your families to love and care for you and not to abandon you, or try to profit from you. We have promised to protect you from people who may have bad intentions. We have promised that regardless of whether you are a boy or a girl, you will have equal access to all the opportunities that life will bring you: to have a good education and to get a good job. We have promised to respect your right to thinking independently and to express those thoughts [Aweis 2015].

The CRC is central to this book. The United States government assisted in writing the CRC, and Secretary of State Madeleine Albright signed it on February 16, 1995, but it has not been ratified as a treaty by the U.S. Senate. One hundred and ninety-six other countries have ratified the CRC. The U.S. is the only member state of the UN that has not. For a long time, I have thought of the failure of the U.S. to ratify the CRC as a warning of trouble to come, a "canary in the coal mine" concerning our care of children.

In the past, when I discussed the CRC with others, the response I received was that the U.S. had not ratified it, and that would close down the conversation. Since it has been ratified by every other member state, however, it has become customary international law. Coupled with this fact, since the U.S. has *signed* it, the U.S. is obligated to follow it (D. Post, personal communication, October 20, 2019).

Furthermore, the discussion this time is different. It is important to note that even though the U.S. has not formally ratified the convention, the Northern Triangle countries of Guatemala, Honduras, and El Salvador were among the first countries to ratify it. Guatemala did so on January 26, 1990, the first day it was open for signatures. El Salvador ratified on July 10 of that year, and Honduras, a month later, on August 8.

Tragically, at this moment in history, these countries are extremely dangerous places, and their citizens are forced to seek asylum elsewhere. They are the home countries of the migrant children who have been separated from their parents by the U.S. government. The children's rights under the convention must be recognized wherever they live, but their rights have been eradicated, not honored, by the U.S. government.

1.3 The Purposes of This Book

One purpose of this book is to explore how the Trump administration's beliefs and practices infringe on children's human rights that are set forth in the *Convention on the Rights of the Child* (UN General Assembly 1989) and four other conventions that are part of international law. The book familiarizes readers with these conventions and promotes the understanding that these international law documents protect children's rights that must be honored whether children reside in their home country, in another country, or in countries where they are seeking asylum. Specific rights of children and details of potential violations of those rights are examined. Articles, or sections of articles, from the conventions that relate to specific instances of the cruel treatment of children are included in several chapters.

The following are descriptions of the other four conventions, the *Flores* settlement, and the Trafficking Victims Protection Reauthorization Act. There are many other U.S. and international laws that protect human rights, but due to the limitations of the scope of a single book, these are the ones that are focused upon here.

International Covenant on Civil and Political Rights

The *International Covenant on Civil and Political Rights* (ICCPR) was adopted and opened for signature, ratification and accession by General Assembly resolution 2200A (XXI) of December 16, 1966, entry into force March 23, 1976, in accordance with Article 49.

The ICCPR also protects the rights of children (UN General Assembly 1966a). It is one of two conventions that were part of the Universal Declaration of Human Rights (UDHR). The UDHR was adopted by the United Nations General Assembly in 1948. The ICCPR (UN General Assembly 1966a) was not adopted by the United Nations General Assembly until December 16, 1966, and it came into force on March 23, 1976. It has 52 articles. Its purpose is to ensure the protection of civil and political rights including the rights of children and their families. The Universal Declaration of Human Rights, the *International Covenant on Civil and Political*

Rights, and the International Covenant on Economic, Social, and Cultural Rights are collectively known as the International Bill of Rights (Canadian Civil Liberties Association 2015).

The ICCPR requires countries that have ratified the treaty to protect and preserve basic human rights, including the right to life and human dignity; equality before the law; freedom of speech, assembly, and association; religious freedom and privacy; freedom from torture, ill-treatment, and arbitrary detention; gender equality; the right to a fair trial; and minority rights. The covenant obliges governments to take administrative, judicial, and legislative measures in order to protect the rights embodied in the treaty and to provide an effective remedy (American Civil Liberties Union 2014). The U.S. ratified the ICCPR on June 8, 1992 (United Nations 2020).

Convention Relating to the Status of Refugees

Adopted on July 28, 1951, by the United Nations Conference of Plenipotentiaries on the Status of Refugees and Stateless Persons convened under General Assembly resolution 429 (V) of December 14, 1950, entry into force April 22, 1954, in accordance with Article 43:

> The Convention Relating to the Status of Refugees (UN General Assembly 1951) was adopted in 1951 and is the key legal document that defines the term "refugee" and outlines the rights of the displaced, as well as the legal obligations of States to protect them. The core principle is non-refoulement, which asserts that a refugee should not be returned to a country where they face serious threats to their life or freedom. This is now considered a rule of customary international law. The United States has not ratified this Convention. However, it ratified the Protocol on November 1, 1968 [UNHCR 2015]. The U.S. Refugee Act 1980 "declares that it is the historic policy of the United States to respond to urgent needs of persons subjected to persecution in their homelands."[2]

The Convention Against Torture and Other Cruel, Inhuman or Degrading Treatment or Punishment

Adopted and opened for signature, ratification and accession by General Assembly resolution 39/46 of December 10, 1984, entry into force June 26, 1987, in accordance with Article 27 (1).

When children are subjected to inhumane treatment, the UN *Convention Against Torture* (UN General Assembly 1984) offers protections. It was adopted by the General Assembly of the United Nations on December 10, 1984 (resolution 39/46), and was entered into force on June 26, 1987, after it had been ratified by 20 states (Danelius 1984). The United States ratified signed the treaty on September 28, 1966, and ratified it on October 21, 1994, but included extensive reservations, declarations, and understandings as part of the ratification (UN General Assembly 1984).

International Convention on the Elimination of All Forms of Racial Discrimination

Adopted and opened for signature and ratification by General Assembly resolution 2106 (XX) of December 21, 1965, entry into force January 4, 1969, in accordance with Article 19.

The last document included here, the *International Convention on the Elimination of All Forms of Racial Discrimination* (ICERD), also shields vulnerable children. The ICERD is a treaty, adopted in 1965 by the United Nations General Assembly. The ICERD was adopted in response to growing racial discrimination in the 1960s. Parties to the ICERD "condemn racial discrimination" and commit "to the elimination of racial discrimination in all its forms." States promise to guarantee the right of everyone, without distinction as to race, color, or national or ethnic origin, to equality before the law. States party to the ICERD particularly condemn racial segregation and apartheid. They condemn all propaganda and organizations based on ideas or theories of superiority of one race or group of persons of one color or ethnic origin. The United States signed the treaty on September 28, 1966, and ratified it on October 21, 1994. The U.S., however, "does not accept any obligation under this Convention, in particular under Articles 4 and 7, to restrict those [extensive protections of individual freedom of speech, expression and association contained in the Constitution and laws of the United States], through the adoption of legislation or any other measures, to the extent that they are protected by the Constitution and laws of the United States" (UN General Assembly 1966b).

The full text of the *Convention on the Rights of the Child* is included in the appendix of this book. Links to the other four conventions are also included there.

The *Flores* Settlement and the Trafficking Victims' Protection Act

In addition to the conventions, two U.S documents, the *Flores* settlement of 1997 and Wilburforce Trafficking Victims' Protection Act of 2008 and its amendments, safeguard the rights of migrant children. The Flores settlement resulted from an initial 1985 class action suit filed in California on behalf of unaccompanied alien children who had been apprehended at or near the U.S. border. The children were held in detention pending removal proceedings. The lawsuit challenged procedures regarding the detention, treatment, and release of children (Congressional Research Service 2019).

According to Human Rights First, the *Flores* settlement, which was reached in 1997, imposed several obligations on immigrations. The obligations come under the following three categories:

- The government is required to release children from immigration detention without unnecessary delay in order of preference beginning with parents and including other adult relatives as well as licensed programs willing to accept custody.
- With respect to children for whom a suitable placement is not immediately available, the government is obligated to place children in the "least restrictive" setting appropriate to their age and any special needs.
- The government is required to implement standards relating to the care and treatment of children in immigration detention [Human Rights First 2018].[3]

In 2015, the U.S. District Court for the Central District of California ruled that the federal government's family detention plan violated the *Flores* settlement. The government immediately appealed the decision. In 2016, a ruling by the Ninth U.S. Circuit Court of Appeals upheld that the settings in which detained migrant children are placed should be the least restrictive as possible. Additionally, it upheld that children should be moved to and held in a non-secure, licensed facility within five days of arrest, or "as expeditiously as possible" if there is an "emergency" or "influx" (Human Rights First 2018). The court determined that time can be extended to 20 days in certain individualized situations. Detaining children who are not flight risks or do not need to be detained for their own safety would risk breaching the settlement (Refugee International 2018).

This ruling did not require that the parents would go free. During the detainment, the families were detained together, and children were not separated from their parents. The original lawsuit was brought on behalf of a class of unaccompanied minors who were apprehended at or near the U.S. border and then detained in U.S. custody pending removal proceedings. This appeals case determined that *Flores* applies "unambiguously to accompanied minors" as well as unaccompanied minors (Congressional Research Service 2019). Judge Dolly Gee of the U.S. District Court of Los Angeles oversees the settlement.

Under the Trafficking Victims Protection Reauthorization Act (TVPRA) children from contiguous countries, Mexico and Canada, must be screened for evidence of human trafficking within 48 hours. If there is no evidence of human trafficking, or fear on the part of children

1. The Dawn of Outrage

of returning to their home country or last country of residence, the children can be returned without penalties (Congressional Research Service 2019).

Immigration and Customs Enforcement represents the government in removal proceedings before the Executive Office of Immigration Review (EOIR). To safeguard the welfare of all unaccompanied alien children (UAC), ICE has established the policies for repatriating them, including

- returning unaccompanied alien children (UAC) only during daylight hours;
- recording transfers by ensuring that receiving government officials or designees sign for custody;
- returning UAC through a port designated for repatriation;
- providing UAC the opportunity to communicate with a consular official prior to departure for the home country;
- and preserving the unity of families during removal [Congressional Research Service 2019].

ICE is also responsible for physically transferring UAC from CBP to ORR custody. If children are identified as human trafficking victims, or if they have a fear of returning to their home country or last country of residence, or if they have been apprehended away from the border, they are transferred to the Office of Refugee Resettlement (ORR) (Congressional Research Service 2019). They will then be cared for and given further screening by people who are trained to administer screenings that ensure that children are properly assessed for trafficking and asylum claims. The screeners would also see that the children would not be returned to gangs, cartels, or placed in other perilous situations (National Immigration Forum 2018).

As in the *Flores* agreement, the TVPRA directs that unaccompanied children will "be promptly placed in the least restrictive setting that is in the best interest of the child" (Congressional Research Service 2019). These settings would include placement with a parent, relative or other sponsor in the U.S. The child could also be placed in a foster home or shelter if no sponsor could be located. TVPRA also requires immigration officials to follow special legal procedures for asylum-seeking children, including access to counsel and child advocates (National Immigration Forum 2018).

The TVPRA was passed in October 2000. It combats human trafficking through an established framework of protection, prevention, and prosecution. It was renewed in 2003, 2005, 2008, and 2013. In 2008 it was renamed the William Wilburforce Trafficking Victims Protection Reauthorization Act.[4]

Specific situations in which the *Flores* settlement and the TVPRA protect migrant children, and challenges to the documents, will be examined in this book.

The second purpose of this book is to deconstruct the idea that the migrant children from Central America who seeking asylum in the United States are criminals. President Trump has made cruel statements in an attempt to justify the implementation of policies and practices that do grave harm to migrant children. Hostile words directed at migrants have led to conditions that disregard children's needs, special protection, and care. The president has said that migrant children have exploited loopholes in U.S. laws to come into the country as "unaccompanied alien minors." He tries to associate them with the very criminals in their countries that they are trying to escape. He claims that even though the minors look innocent, they are not innocent and that they will eventually bring gang crime from their countries to the U.S. (Kim 2018).

The children are aware of negative beliefs about migrants, but they do not believe that those ideas are true. In a classroom in a Mexican shelter, I found a two-column poster on the wall that children had composed. In one column were beliefs that the children do not think are true about migrants. In the other column were beliefs that they believe are true. The poster reads:

Column 1—What I do not believe about migrants

- The migrants are criminals.
- The migrant girls, boys, and adolescents are bad guys.
- The migrant girls, boys, and adolescents are lazy.
- The migrants take off from work.

Column 2—What I believe about migrants

- Migrant girls, boys, and adolescents like to learn.
- The migrant girls, boys, and adolescents want to study and learn.
- The girls, boys, and adolescents want to play and have fun.

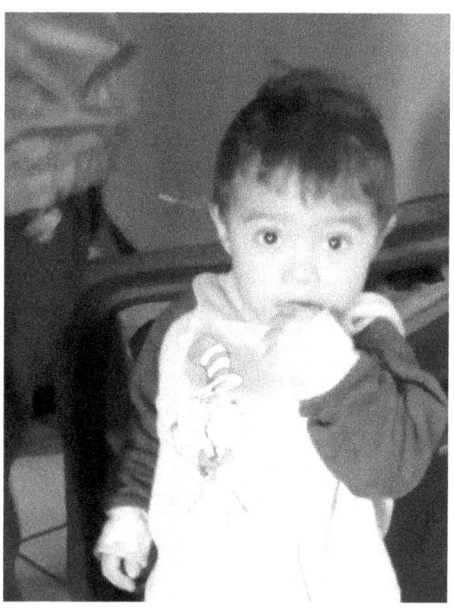

Migrant toddler (author's photograph).

1. *The Dawn of Outrage*

Taking care of baby (author's photograph).

- The migrant girls, boys, and adolescents want to be happy.
- The migrants are looking for better kind of life.
- The migrant girls, boys, and adolescents have hopes and dreams.
- The migrant girls, boys, and adolescents have rights.

A third purpose of this book is to make the ongoing work of legislators, lawyers and advocates visible. Many people are fighting for the dignity

Two friends (author's photograph).

of migrant children and their families. They are working to create laws and set legal precedents so that the inhumane treatment that migrants from Central America have faced during this administration will not reoccur in the future.

This book explores a two-year implementation of immigration policies and practices that have impacted the lives of children and their families at the U.S. southern border and how those policies and practices violate children's rights. Ways in which advocates are working to protect children, families, and their rights, as well as lawsuits and legislation designed to provide relief for immigrant children and their families now and in the future, are also explored. A firsthand view of families who have been struggling to survive for months in Mexico and how they are coping during the coronavirus pandemic is also presented.

In the opening sections, the book explores the zero-tolerance policy under which families were separated at the border. The ensuing outrage against this policy as a violation of human rights, the executive order to reunify families, and the colossal failure of reunification are also taken up.

Next, proposed regulations and inhumane conditions of child detainment in both Customs and Border Protection (CBP) and Office of Refugee Resettlement (ORR) detention facilities are examined. Topics include

1. The Dawn of Outrage

Chart of beliefs and non-beliefs about migrants (author's photograph).

trauma, torture, sexual abuse, forced drugs, and the deaths of six young children. Metering, the policy of limiting the number of those seeking asylum who were allowed into the U.S., is also explained. Throughout this section, specific articles from five UN conventions that detail children's rights and provide protections and special care impugn the conditions the children have endured.

Policies beyond family separation that have caused children and their families harm are the third focus. They include the following:

- Migrant Protection Protocols (MPP) or Remain in Mexico—A policy that requires asylum seekers to stay in Mexico while awaiting asylum hearings in the U.S.
- The Transit Ban—Prohibiting anyone who has travelled through a third country from gaining asylum in the U.S. if they have not gained asylum in the other country they travelled through first.
- Challenges of gaining asylum through deportation courts.
- Public charge—The receipt of public assistance.
- Other actions taken in child detention facilities, such as cutting recreational services and English language lessons, and denying flu vaccines are included as well. As in section two, articles from

the five UN conventions that lay out children's rights contest these policies.

A view of life of children and their families who have remained in Mexico is presented, as is the work of the nonprofit Refugee Aid in Phoenix, Arizona. Information from interviews with migrants served by the Kino Border Initiative in Nogales, Mexico, is included. One focus is how migrant families are coping during the coronavirus pandemic when the southern border is closed and nearly all immigration to the U.S. has ceased. Ways in which the Trump administration's harmful immigration policies have intensified since the onset of the pandemic are also explored.

The last part of the book includes descriptions of laws cases and pieces of legislation that have been drafted in the House of Representatives or the Senate to provide relief and protect the rights of migrant children and their families. These law cases and bills are followed by recommendations from individuals and several humanitarian agencies proposing ways to mitigate the suffering of migrant children and their families.

2

Family Separation

2.1 Child Separation—A Horrifying Legacy

The separation of the children from their parents at the southern border at the hands of the United States government is appalling and shameful, but this is not the first time that Americans have treated children in reprehensible and degrading ways. American history is rife with episodes of the family separations of Black and Native American children that compose the cruelest chapters of our nation's history (D. Post, personal communication, October 20, 2019). Throughout this book, readers will find many parallels between the treatment of African American, Native American, and the immigrant children at the border today.

Slave Children

Code Noir, 1682 to 1803, was an early law that prohibited owners, in the process of selling slaves, to break up a family unit of a husband, wife, and children under the age of fourteen. However, by refusing to recognize slave marriages as legal, owners routinely evaded this section of the code. In other words, they had found a loophole to separate families.

An article in the *Washington Post*, dated May 31, 2018, begins with the words, "A mother unleashed a piercing scream as her baby was ripped from her arms." Over the past few years, incidents like this have constantly taken place at the southern border, but the heartless separation referred to in this quote took place at a slave auction in 1849. Enslaved parents lived in constant fear that they or their children would be separated and sold. In the article, Henry Fernandez, cofounder of the African American Research Collaborative, states that destroying families was one of the worst practices undertaken during slavery. He cites the fugitive slave laws and other rules that categorized slaves as property as the reasons why slave owners could treat slaves in whatever ways they wanted (D.L. Brown 2018).

Fears of sale and separation were not only parents' greatest fears, however. They were also the worst horror that enslaved children could imagine. The threat of separation from family followed them as constantly as their shadows. One of the most frequent catalysts for family separation of slaves was the death of a master. When the master died, his properties—including his slaves—were distributed to heirs, most likely in several distant locations. The sale of children with their mothers was common, but children were also forcibly removed from their parents and sold separately. Often, children who were up for sale were sent naked to the auction block. There in public view, perspective buyers examined their fitness in the same ways they would examine livestock. The children's teeth, bones, and other physical features were evaluated to detect weakness and defects. Slave owners were looking to buy the strongest child of the lot (National Archives UK).

During their lifetimes, some slaves were sold as many as six times. Slave auctions are often thought of as having taken place only in the South. However, they were also conducted in Northern states including Massachusetts, New York, New Jersey, and Rhode Island (Bailey 2020).

The most valuable source of information about the trauma enslaved children experienced is found within their own words. The testimonies included here focus mainly on family separation, but the children also suffered from beatings, whippings, viewing bodies of people who had been hung, scarcity of food, farm accidents, humiliation, the cruelty of their owners, and countless other agonies. The following are excerpts from five interviews of formerly enslaved African Americans that were conducted from 1936 to 1938 by the WPA Slave Narrative Project, Federal Writers' Project, and U.S. Work Projects Administration (Federal Writers Project 1941).

John W. Fields, Enslaved in Kentucky

My name is John W. Fields and I'm eighty-nine (89) years old. I was born March 27, 1848, in Owensburg, Ky. That's 115 miles below Louisville, Ky. There was 11 other children besides myself in my family. When I was six years old, all of us children were taken from my parents, because my master died and his estate had to be settled. We slaves were divided by this method. Three disinterested persons were chosen to come to the plantation and together they wrote the names of the different heirs on a few slips of paper. These slips were put in a hat and passed among us slaves. Each one took a slip and the name on the slip was the new owner. I happened to draw the name of a relative of my master who was a widow. I can't describe the heartbreak and horror of that separation. I was only six years old and it was the last time I ever saw my mother for longer than one night. Twelve children taken from my mother in one day. Five sisters and two brothers went to Charleston, Virginia, one brother and one sister went to Lexington, Ky., one sister went to Hartford, Ky., and one brother and myself stayed in Owensburg, Ky. My mother was later allowed to visit among us children for one week of each year, so she could only remain a short time at each place.

2. Family Separation

Delia Garlic, Enslaved in Georgia and Louisiana
I was growed up when de war come an' I was a mother befo' it closed. Babies was snatched from dere mother's breas' an' sold to speculators. Chilluns was separated from sisters an' brothers an' never saw each other ag'in. 'Course dey cry; you think dey not cry when dey was sold lak cattle? I could tell you 'bout it all day, but even den you couldn't guess de awfulness of it.

John Rudd, Enslaved in Kentucky
If'n you wants to know what unhappiness means, … jess'n you stand on the Slave Block and hear the Auctioneer's voice selling you away from the folks you love.

Katie Rowe, Enslaved in Arkansas
I seen chillun sold off and de mammy not sold, and sometimes de mammy sold and a little baby kept on de place and give to another woman to raise. Dem white folks didn't care nothing 'bout how de slaves grieved when dey tore up a family.

Katie Sutton, Enslaved in Florida
Ole Missus and Young Missus told the little slave children that the stork brought the white babies to their mothers but that the slave children were all hatched out from buzzards' eggs and we believed it was true.

Katie's comment that the slave children believed they hatched from buzzard eggs shows the extent to which children could internalize the message given to them by the women of the plantations. Her mother, however, countered that message by singing a lullaby that declared her love for Katie and told her that she should never be ashamed of who she is.

Native American Children

Native American children were also separated from their families (D. Post, personal communication, October 20, 2019). The government took the lands where their families lived, marginalized them as inferior beings, stole the children from their homes and forced them to live in boarding schools.

On December 3, 1833, in his fifth annual message to Congress, President Andrew Jackson said of Native Americans:

> They have neither the intelligence, the industry, the moral habits, nor the desire of improvement which are essential to any favorable change in their condition. Established in the midst of another and a superior race, and without appreciating the causes of their inferiority or seeking to control them, they must necessarily yield to the force of circumstances and ere long disappear [Jackson 1833].

In 1892, Richard Henry Pratt, a cavalry captain, stated:

> A great general has said that the only good Indian is a dead one…. In a sense, I agree with the sentiment, but only in this that all the Indian there is in the race should be dead. Kill the Indian in him and save the man [Sheridan 1869].

In 1897, Pratt established a boarding school in Carlisle, Pennsylvania, based on this premise. It was called the Carlisle Indian Industrial School, a place where Native American boys and girls endured life apart from their families. It became a model for approximately 150 similar schools that opened in the United States.

In 2011, sisters Kay McGowan and Fay Givens of Michigan produced a documentary titled *Indian School: The Survivor's Story*. The sisters are of Cherokee/Choctaw heritage. Their "Great Grandmother attended the Carlisle School," a life event that had "profound influence on their family" (K. McGowan, personal communication, April 1, 2010). Kay teaches cultural anthropology and Native American studies at Eastern Michigan University. Fay was the director of American Indian Services in Lincoln Park, Michigan, until Covid-19–related budget cuts caused the center to close in July of 2020. They report that over a period of 125 years, 180,000 native American children were removed from their families (Millich 2012). They were sent to 560 Indian boarding schools that were under contract to the federal government.

In the film, survivors and successors of survivors relate experiences from the boarding schools. They describe the schools as places that were emotionally barren, offered no love or support, and were devoid of models for lasting relationships. The schools were militaristic and emphasized discipline, lines, and formations. Physical abuse was widespread. Children were regularly criticized, beaten, and whipped. Sexual abuse was commonplace.

McGowan states that the problems of some Native Americans, such as alcoholism, domestic violence, and suicide, result from growing up in the boarding schools. When children returned home from these institutions, they did not fit in with either tribal or white society. This detachment resulted in a suicide rate of 2.5 times the national average among those who attended Indian schools. Another tragic outcome of not being raised in their own households with their own parents was that Native Americans did not have the opportunity to learn how to become loving parents themselves. Fay Givens reports that survivors of Indian boarding schools often repressed the experience. The sisters see the documentary as a way of helping survivors reconcile with the past (McGowan and Givens 2011).[1]

Warren Petoskey, an Elder of the *Waganakising* Odwaw and *Minneconjou* Lakotah Nations, appears in the documentary. He has written his own book called *Dancing My Dream*. His grandfather and great-aunt are graduates of the Carlisle School. Seven members of his family, including his father, uncles, and aunts, were forced to go to the Indian Industrial School in Mt. Pleasant, Michigan. Although he did not attend the school himself, he grieves for the life his grandparents and parents were denied, and for the effect that loss has had on subsequent generations of his family (Petoskey 2009).[2]

Petoskey explains that children as young as age six were taken to the schools and remained there for several years, sometimes through high school. They were given Anglo-American names. Their hair was shorn. They were deloused with DDT and then given uniforms to wear. Their discolored teeth were extracted without anesthetic. Many girls were sterilized but did not understand how the procedure would alter their lives. The children were stripped of their identity, language, and culture. They were not allowed to practice their traditions or speak their own languages. Petoskey emphasizes that the children lost the knowledge of their natural origins, and of the seasonal and cultural details and routines of daily life (Petoskey 2009).

Petoskey states:

> They came into the house and took the children and loaded them into boxcars and wagons and hauled them away to the boarding schools. And the parents in a lot of cases didn't know where they went. And many of the women it was said when they took the children from the home, they sang the child's death song because they knew that, that the child, when that child came home would never be the same again [McGowan and Givens 2011].

The children seldom if ever saw their parents. At the schools, the children were exposed to deadly infections like tuberculosis and the flu. Some died and were buried in cemeteries at the school and never returned home. Nearly 200 children were buried in the cemetery at the Carlisle School. Their parents may not have been notified that they had died. Kay McGowan states that today, the treatment of the children would be a gross violation of human rights because the parents had no say in what happened to their children.

Anishinaabemowin was the original language of the Great Lakes region. Petoskey writes, "It once was the only language spoken here" (Petoskey 2009, 25). He adds that the rocks, trees, waters, and Mother Earth knew this language. But the "schools were 'designed' to erase all consciousness of Indian language and culture and to 'Americanize' their residents" (Petoskey 2009, 32). The children who went to the schools did not speak the languages. The languages died for them. Future generations of their children could not speak them either.

Petoskey describes "boarding school syndrome" that encompasses trauma, including mental health problems, alcoholism, family abandonment, incarceration, and crime. This trauma ravaged the lives of those who attended the schools and developed into "intergenerational trauma" that permeated generations of Native American families (Petoskey 2009).

The boarding schools themselves closed in the early twentieth century, but Native American households continued to be viewed as "unfit," and children were removed to live with white families. Doug Kiel, a citizen of the Oneida Nation and a professor at Northwestern University, explains that this view was not "an official government policy" but a "racially-biased perception" of Native American families, homes, and mothers (Little 2011). From this false perception, white people drew the power to abduct children from their homes, their original families, community, and culture, and relocate them to the white world.

By 1978, 25 percent to 35 percent of all Native American children were being removed from their homes and 85 percent of these children were placed outside of their families and communities—even when suitable placements with relatives were available (National Indian Child Welfare Association 2020). The Indian Child Welfare Act was passed by Congress that year, and it allowed tribes to designate the residency of their children (Senate and House of Representatives of the United States of America 1978). Beginning in 2017, the U.S. Army began exhuming the bodies of Carlisle students who were buried in the cemetery there and returned them to their families (Gammage 2017). By July of 2019, five bodies had been returned, and six more were scheduled to be returned by the end of the year (Sholtis 2019).

Warren Petoskey has reclaimed his cultural identity by becoming a native artisan, traditional musician and dancer. He is also an ordained Christian minister and a lecturer who teaches others about the history of the nation's infamous boarding school system. He believes that other survivors can also recover their cultural identity through Native American traditions. He adds:

> I'm glad today to say today, to be able to say, that I can go to sweat lodge ceremony and that I can dance with my people, that I can smoke my pipe.... I can play my flute and sing. I can be with my people and ... be accepted [McGowan and Givens 2011].

2.2 Twenty-First Century Child Separation

In 2005, the Bush administration established Operation Streamline, a joint initiative of the Department of Homeland Security and the Department of Justice that supported zero tolerance for illegal border crossings.

Operation Streamline was not a law, but a method of deterring entry into the United States. This method led to the quick prosecution and incarceration of individuals attempting to cross the border (D. Post, personal communication, October 20, 2019). In the past, deportation had been the solution (Office of Inspector General, U.S. Department of Homeland Security, 2015).

Operation Streamline also made exceptions for parents who were traveling with minor children, juveniles, individuals with health conditions, and those who needed immediate return to their home countries for humanitarian reasons (Lydgate 2010).

In 2017, at his confirmation hearing to become the attorney general of the U.S., Alabama Sen. Jeff Sessions praised Operation Streamline and spoke in favor of restoring it if he were to become attorney general.

When Sen. Jeff Flake (AZ) asked Sessions:

> As Attorney General, if you are confirmed, what steps will you take to restore Operation Streamline to a zero-tolerance approach that has been so successful in Arizona, in a portion of Arizona's border?

Sessions answered,

> Like you, I believe that Streamline was very effective. And it was really a surprise that it has been undermined significantly.
>
> The reports I got initially, some years ago, maybe a decade or more ago, was that it was dramatically effective, and so I would absolutely review that. And my inclination would be, at least at this stage, to think it should be restored and even refined and made sure it is lawful and effective. But I think it has great positive potential to improve legality at the border.

When asked by Flake why the program had not been expanded to the Tucson sector, Sessions responded:

> I do not know what reason that might be. It seems to me that we should examine the successes and if they cannot be replicated throughout the border [Committee Hearing on the Judiciary, U.S. Senate (Serial J115-1), 115th Cong 2017].

When the Obama administration came to power, it made changes in immigration policy. This administration focused on releasing parents and then deporting immigrants who committed crimes. Additionally, then-Attorney-General Eric Holder directed U.S. attorneys under Operation Streamline to no longer prosecute first-time border crossers but concentrate on repeat offenders and criminals. When faced with an influx of refugees who were fleeing violence in Central America in 2014, the government kept families together (Khalid 2017).

In June 2014, the administration addressed the increase in the number of children and families seeking protection at the southern border by increasing family incarceration, a policy that had been almost halted. Over the next year, the administration took on an aggressive policy of detaining thousands of families and attempted to prevent their release on bond or parole. They ran into legal roadblocks from the *Flores* settlement (*Janet Reno, Attorney General, et al. v. Jenny Lisette Flores, et al.*, case no. CV85-4544-RJK [C.D. Cal. 1996]), a court settlement that has been in place for over two decades. This settlement places limits on the time and conditions under which children can be incarcerated in immigrant detention (D. Post, personal communication, October 20, 2019).

In 2016, the Obama administration began the Family Case Management Program (FCMP) in five major cities. Priority was given to vulnerable families, including those with pregnant mothers, young children, speakers of indigenous languages, health needs and special needs. These families could stay in an alternative setting, instead of a detention center, while they waited for the decision in their asylum cases (American Immigration Lawyers Association 2016).

Under the direction of President Trump, U.S. Immigration and Customs Enforcement (ICE) closed the FCMP for asylum seekers. Prior to closure, the program housed over than 630 families and was considered the least-restrictive alternative for asylum seekers who came to the U.S. illegally. It cost the government only $36 a day per family as opposed to $319 per person for a family detention center bed (Bajak 2017).

In a statement to CNN, Leon Fresco, a former Department of Justice official in the Obama administration who oversaw civil immigration legislation, said that administration considered family separation, but did not carry out the practice. Fresco stated, "It was never implemented because the idea ... was too detrimental to the safety of the children ... it was always preferable to detain the family as a unit or release the family as a unit" (Diaz 2017).

The Obama administration also implemented the practice of allowing migrants to live in a community while they waited for their hearings in immigration court.

In February 2017, John F. Kelly, then secretary of the Department of Homeland Security, under executive orders issued by President Trump, directed the end of this practice that Trump called "catch-and-release" (Berger 2017). This term is derived from a phrase for catching a fish and then letting it go. It is one of many derogatory references used by President Trump to dehumanize migrants by comparing them to animals.

Despite the order to end this policy, thousands of detainees continued to be freed from detention throughout the spring while they awaited their immigration hearings. They were let out because of the time limits for detention imposed by the *Flores* decision and because of limited immigration detention space (Ainsley 2017).

In a March 2017 interview with CNN's Wolf Blitzer, Kelly verified that his department was weighing the possibility of separating children from their parents. He stated, "We have tremendous experience in dealing with unaccompanied minors. We turn them over to [Health and Human Services] and they do a very good job of putting them in foster care or linking up with parents or family members in the United States." He added: "Yes,

I'm considering [that], in order to deter more movement along this terribly dangerous network. I am considering exactly that. They will be cared for as we deal with their parents" (Blitzer 2017).

The following year in an NPR interview, Kelly was less specific about the placements of the children. He said of the policy of separating children from their parents, "It could be a tough deterrent." When presented with the idea that some people would consider separating children from their mothers cruel and heartless, Kelly added, "I wouldn't put it quite that way. The children will be taken care of—put into foster care or whatever. But the big point is that they elected to come to the United States and this is a technique that no one hopes will be used extensively or for very long" (Burnett 2018).

Kelly added the following statement that includes several reasons for not admitting the people from the Northern Triangle into the U.S.:

> Let me step back and tell you that the vast majority of people that move illegally into the U.S. are not bad people. They're not criminals. They're not MS-13. Some of them are not. But they're also not people who would easily assimilate into the United States into our modern society. They're overwhelmingly rural people in the countries they come from—fourth, fifth, sixth grade educations are kind of the norm. They don't speak English. They don't integrate well. They don't have skills. They're not bad people. They're coming here for a reason. And I sympathize with the reason. But laws are laws. But a big name of the game is deterrence [Burnett 2018].

Kelly's statement deters people from the U.S. based on their national origin. His words discriminate against them based on their rural roots and his assumptions about their skills, home language, education, and ability to assimilate into the U.S. His statement is a violation of international human rights.

Article 1 of the *International Convention on the Elimination of All Forms of Racial Discrimination* (UN General Assembly 1966b) prohibits exclusion and restriction based on national or ethnic origin. It reads:

> In this Convention, the term "racial discrimination" shall mean any distinction, exclusion, restriction or preference based on race, colour, descent, or national or ethnic origin which has the purpose or effect of nullifying or impairing the recognition, enjoyment or exercise, on an equal footing, of human rights and fundamental freedoms in the political, economic, social, cultural or any other field of public life.

Article 2, paragraph 1, of the *Convention on the Rights of the Child* protects children from any kind of discrimination. It reads:

> State parties shall respect and ensure the rights set forth in the present convention to each child within their jurisdiction without discrimination of any kind, irrespective of the child's or his parent's or legal guardian's, race, colour, sex, language, religion, political or other opinion, national, ethnic or social origin, poverty, disability, birth or other status.

During Kelly's tenure as secretary, another district court ruling regarding the *Flores* settlement was issued. In June 2017, the court found that the Trump administration was not complying with its terms. Some children and parents were being detained in secure, unlicensed facilities for up to eight months. This time period was far beyond the three-to-five-day limit, or the 20-day limit authorized for times of emergency or influx. The court also found that Border Patrol facilities were not providing adequate provisions of food or access to clean drinking water. Conditions were unsanitary and unsafe, temperatures were freezing, and sleeping conditions were not adequate. The government was ordered to appoint a juvenile coordinator to oversee compliance with *Flores*. If within one year of the appointment of the coordinator, conditions did not reach substantial compliance, the judge would reconsider a request by the plaintiff to appoint an independent monitor (Human Rights First 2018).

2.3 Opposition to Child Separation

In December 2017, Kirstjen Nielsen replaced Kelly as secretary of the Department of Homeland Security. On the 16th of that month, she testified before the Senate Judiciary Committee and would not rule out the practice of separating children from their families.

Following her appearance at the committee, over 200 child welfare, juvenile justice, and child development organizations released a letter imploring her to give up plans to separate children from their families at the U.S. border (Young Center for Immigrant Children's Rights 2018a).[3] The experts argued that the families were fleeing violence and persecution in their home countries. As a result, the children had already experienced trauma. The letter listed physical illness, psychological distress, depression, and anxiety as both short- and long-term effects of separation. Splitting up families would only deepen the children's trauma and lengthen the amount of time it would take them to return to good health and normal development.

The text of the letter reads:

January 16, 2018

The Honorable Kirstjen M. Nielsen Secretary U.S. Department of Homeland Security
3801 Nebraska Avenue, NW
Washington, D.C. 20016
Urgent Appeal from Experts in Child Welfare, Juvenile Justice and Child Development to Halt Any Plans to Separate Children from Parents at the Border

Dear Secretary Nielsen,

We, the below-signed organizations, have well-recognized expertise in the fields of

2. Family Separation

child welfare, juvenile justice and child health, development and safety. We understand that your agency is considering plans to separate children from their parents when they arrive at or are found near the U.S. border. We fear these actions will have significant and long-lasting consequences for the safety, health, development, and well-being of children, and urgently request that the Administration reverse course on any policies that would separate families.

Countless reports have documented that these families are fleeing persecution and violence in their countries, and come here seeking protection. While many come from Central American countries, the parents and children arrive at our border from all over the world, including countries in Africa, the Caribbean, South America, Asia, the Middle East and Europe. According to recent reports, the proposed plan would require that parents be placed in adult immigration detention centers and/or summarily deported, while their children would be transferred to the custody of the Department of Health and Human Services in facilities across the country—as far away as Illinois, Washington, New York, Florida, and Michigan. HHS would bear the responsibility of caring for the traumatized children and finding suitable, alternative caregivers. These children could remain in government care for months or more than a year, during which time the continued separation from their parents would compound their trauma and the time it would take them to recover and return to a trajectory of good health and normal development. Nor would it make any sense to require those children to participate in a formal legal proceeding about their immigration case while separated from the parent who brought them here, who may have critical information—or the only information—about the child's claim for protection.

There is overwhelming evidence that children need to be cared for by their parents to be safe and healthy, to grow and develop. Likewise, there is ample evidence that separating children from their mothers or fathers leads to serious, negative consequences to children's health and development. Forced separation disrupts the parent-child relationship and puts children at increased risk for both physical and mental illness. Adverse childhood experiences—including the incarceration of a family member—are well-recognized precursors of negative health outcomes later in life. And the psychological distress, anxiety, and depression associated with separation from a parent would follow the children well after the immediate period of separation—even after eventual reunification with a parent or other family. We are deeply concerned that the proposed plan would formalize such harm by taking children from their parents as a matter of policy.

Family unity is a foundational principle of child welfare law. In order to grow and develop, children need to remain in the care of their parents where they are loved, nurtured and feel safe. Thus parents' rights to the care and custody of their children are afforded particularly strong protection under the U.S. Constitution. While parent-child relationships are generally the province of state law, federal law also recognizes the principle of family unity by providing strong incentives for states to keep children with their parents and to provide services to families to prevent separation and maintain family unity. The proposed changes to your agency's policies would eviscerate that principle.

For all of these reasons, we urge you to abandon any plans to systematically separate children from their families absent evidence that a specific parent posed a threat to the safety and wellbeing of his or her child, as required by the laws of all 50 states [Young Center for Immigrant Children's Rights 2018b].

A week later, the organizations sent Secretary Nielsen a second copy of the letter that included the signatures of additional organizations. In June, once the separation policy was officially underway, another letter was submitted to Secretary Nielsen as a renewed appeal. This time there were 540 signatures representing organizations from all 50 states, the District of Columbia and Puerto Rico (Young Center for Immigrant Children's Rights 2018c). The letter pointed out that while in two weeks during May, 658 children had been separated from their parents, the number of their organizations opposed to the policy had grown by more than 300 (Young Center for Immigrant Children's Rights 2018d).

Despite the outrage from the experts that "the administration's plan would eviscerate the principle of family unity and put children in harm's way," reports revealed that the Trump administration was not only considering taking children away from their parents, but had been doing so even before the organizations sent Secretary Nielsen their first letter. In April of 2018, the *New York Times* reported on data from the Office of Refugee Resettlement (ORR), revealing that since October of 2017, over 700 children had been taken from adults who stated that they were their parents. More than 100 of these children were under the age of 4 (Dickerson 2018a). Later, a report from the Government Accountability Office (GAO) showed that the percentage of children referred to ORR who were known to be separated from their parents increased more than tenfold, from 0.3 percent in November 2016, to 2.6 percent by March 2017, to 3.6 percent by August 2017 (Government Accountability Office 2018). Secretary Nielsen denied that these separations were undertaken for deterrent purposes, but Kelly's support of separation as a deterrent repudiates this statement (Hunter 2018).

2.4 *Official Announcement of the Zero-Tolerance Policy*

In a memo dated April 6, 2018, Jeff Sessions, who was now attorney general, ordered all United States Attorney's Offices along the southwest border to implement a new zero-tolerance policy for all offenses referred for prosecution under Section 1325 of Title 8 of the United States Code, "improper entry by an alien," which criminalizes unauthorized entry into the United States. This law has been in effect since 1929. Its counterpart, Section 1326, criminalizes unauthorized re-entry. The directive was to be carried out to the extent feasible and in consultation with the Department of Homeland Security (Sessions 2018a). This section of the law prohibits both illegal entry and illegal reentry into the United States by an alien (Cornell Law School Legal Information Institute).

2. Family Separation

While a senator, Sessions stated,

> The recent increase in aliens illegally crossing our Southwest Border requires an up-dated approach. Past prosecution initiatives in certain districts—such as Operation Streamline—led to a decrease in illegal activities in those districts. We must continue to execute effective policies to meet new challenges [Sessions 2018a].

It is likely that at least in part, Sessions was selected by Trump to be attorney general because of his early support for prosecuting and incarcerating those who crossed the southern border.

On May 7, Sessions gave speeches in Scottsdale, Arizona, and San Diego, California, in which he described the Justice Department's partnership with Homeland Security for the purpose of enforcing this policy. He also conveyed other details of the policy. His statement included the following points.

> Last month, I put in place a "zero-tolerance" policy for illegal entries on our Southwest border referred by the Department of Homeland Security.
>
> Today, the Department of Homeland Security is partnering with us and will begin a new initiative that will result in referring 100 percent of illegal Southwest Border crossings to the Department of Justice for prosecution. And the Department of Justice will take up as many of those cases as humanly possible until we get to 100 percent.
>
> If you cross this border unlawfully, then we will prosecute you. It's that simple.
>
> If you smuggle illegal aliens across our border, then we will prosecute you.
>
> If you are smuggling a child, then we will prosecute you and that child will be separated from you as required by law. If you don't like that, then don't smuggle children over our border [Sessions 2018b].

The separation plan that the Trump administration executed changed the status of *accompanied* refugee and migrant children to *unaccompanied* children, a more vulnerable population. This action required the administration to provide even more support for the protection and care of these children (Cordero, Li Feldman, and Keitner 2020).

Although Sessions stated that children were being separated "by law," the administration was going against international law. As shown below, paragraphs 1 and 2 of Article 3 of the CRC set a high standard for the right of personal liberty of the child that can be denied only as a last resort, if absolutely necessary as an exceptional measure, and then only for the shortest appropriate period of time.

The *United Nations Global Study on Children Deprived of Liberty of 2019* states, "Children may only be deprived of liberty as a measure of last resort, and, if absolutely necessary as an exceptional measure, then only for the shortest period of time." The study continues, "In addition, the principle of best interests of the child in Article 3 CRC requires that States would have to prove that detention of children for purely migration-related reasons is in the best interest of the child" (Nowak 2019, 448).

Article 3, paragraphs 1 and 2, read as follows:

> In all actions concerning children, whether undertaken by public or private social welfare institutions, courts of law, administrative authorities or legislative bodies, the best interests of the child shall be a primary consideration.
>
> State parties undertake to ensure the child such protection and care as is necessary for his or her well-being, taking into account the rights and duties of his or her parents, legal guardians, or other individuals legally responsible for him or her, and, to this end, shall take all appropriate legislative and administrative measures.

A decade ago, the UN Working Group on Arbitrary Detention stated:

> Given the availability of alternatives to detention, it is difficult to conceive of a situation in which detention of an unaccompanied minor child would comply with the requirements stipulated in Article 37 (b), clause 2, of the CRC, according to which detention can be used only as a last resort [UN Human Rights Council 2010].

Article 37 (b) reads:

> No child shall be deprived of his or her liberty unlawfully or arbitrarily. The arrest, detention or imprisonment of a child shall be in conformity with the law and shall be used only as a measure of last resort and for the shortest appropriate period of time.

Additionally, in July 2014, Kofi Annan, UN Secretary General (2014) stated, "Detention of migrant children constitutes a violation of child rights."

In an advisory opinion of 2014, the Inter-American Court of Human Rights found that "the detention of children solely on the basis of their migration status exceeds the requirement of necessity, is contrary to children's best interests, and is incompatible with regional human rights treaties." They concluded, "States should therefore never deprive children of their liberty on the basis of their own parents' or guardians' migration status."

The UN High Commission on Refugees (HCR) defines a refugee in the following words:

> A refugee is someone who has been forced to flee his or her country because of persecution, war or violence. A refugee has a well-founded fear of persecution for reasons of race, religion, nationality, political opinion or membership in a particular social group. Most likely, they cannot return home or are afraid to do so. War and ethnic, tribal and religious violence are leading causes of refugees fleeing their countries [UN High Commission on Refugees 2020].

The *Convention Relating to the Status of Refugees* (UN General Assembly 1951) protects children and their families who have fled their country.

Article 3 of the convention requires that states put this convention into effect without discrimination. It reads: "The contracting states shall apply the provisions of this Convention without discrimination as to race, religion, or country of origin."

2.5 The Trump Administration Perspective

On April 23, 2018, a memo sent to Department of Homeland Security Secretary Nielsen from three immigration officials offered her three options to reduce the number of border crossings, which during the previous week had risen to 700 a day. One option was to prosecute all single adult immigrants caught crossing the border illegally, which would require additional government resources. The second was to work with prosecutors to charge as many adults as possible, using existing resources. The third was to refer for prosecution all immigrants trying to enter the country illegally. Nielsen was pressured to take action so the number would not increase. Although her signature is redacted on copies of the memo, Nielsen probably chose the third option, the one that resulted in children being torn away from their families (Sacchetti 2018).

Even though she most certainly had signed off on this third option, she repeatedly denied that Homeland Security had a policy of separating children from their parents. When questioned by Sen. Kamala Harris of the Senate Homeland Security and Governmental Affairs Committee on May 15, 2018, Nielsen set forth the idea that separations of children from their parents were taking place for purposes of prosecution, not "for purposes of deterrence." Later in the questioning, she added, "We do not have a policy to separate children from their parents" (Nielsen and Harris 2018). On June 17 of that year, she tweeted, "We do not have a policy of separating families at the border. Period" (Nielsen 2018).

If Nielsen, a lawyer, had acknowledged that the administration had a policy of children separation, she would have been admitting a direct violation of international law. Article 9, paragraph 1, of the *Convention on the Rights of the Child* (UN General Assembly 1989) directly prohibits child separation. It reads:

> 1. States Parties shall ensure that a child shall not be separated from his or her parents against their will, except when competent authorities subject to judicial review determine, in accordance with applicable law and procedures, that such separation is necessary for the best interests of the child. Such determination may be necessary in a particular case such as one involving abuse or neglect of the child by the parents, or one where the parents are living separately and a decision must be made as to the child's place of residence.

The following day, Nielsen went to the White House to address the policy and hold a press conference. She made several points: "First, this administration did not create a policy of separating families at the border." She added, "Second, children in Department of Homeland Security and Health and Human Services custody are being well taken care of." Nielsen added, "The Department of Health and Human Services Office of Refugee

Resettlement provides meals, medical care, and educational services to these children" (Sanders and Nielsen 2018).

Next, Nielsen described the parents who enter the country illegally as criminals who put their children at risk. She labeled illegal entry as "a crime as determined by Congress." Finally, she claimed that U.S. Customs and Border Protection (CBP) and Immigration and Customs Enforcement (ICE) officers are trained to care for the minors. She added that DHS and HHS "treats all individuals in its custody with dignity and respect, and complies with all laws and policies" (Sanders and Nielsen 2018), a statement that would prove to be far from the truth.

Nielsen emphasized, "Additionally, all U.S. Border Patrol personnel on the southwest border are bilingual—every last one of them." She added these officers are instructed "to clearly explain the relevant process to apprehended individuals, and provide detainees with written documentation in English and Spanish that lays out the process and appropriate phone numbers to contact" (Sanders and Nielsen 2018). However, a major problem with these explanations and the written documentation is that many migrants speak indigenous languages and do not understand English or Spanish whether written or spoken (D. Post, personal communication, October 20, 2019).

When asked by a reporter if she had intended to separate parents and children or intended to send a message, she replied, "I find that offensive. No. Because why would I ever create a policy that purposely does that." Nielsen then placed the responsibility for ending the separations on Congress. She stated that Congress had to close "loopholes" in the law "and the families will stay together during the proceedings" (Sanders and Nielsen 2018).

In April 2018, the *Washington Post* had knowledge of the confidential memo described above, but the memo was not made public at that time. By October 2018, the Project on Government Oversight and Open the Government, organizations that work to ensure accountability and transparency in the federal government, received a redacted version of the memo through the Freedom of Information Act (FOIA), along with other documents (Project on Government Oversight and Open the Government 2018b).[4] The memo is signed, but the signature is redacted (McAleenan 2018). The organizations had also obtained an unredacted copy of the memo and confirmation from the Department of Homeland Security that the signature was that of Kirstjen Nielsen. They alerted members of the Senate of the discrepancies between this new information and Nielsen's testimony in May.

In a letter to Sen. Ron Johnson (chairman of the Senate Committee and Governmental Affairs) and Sen. Claire McCaskill (ranking member of the committee) dated October 2, 2018, Danielle Brian (executive director,

2. Family Separation

Project on Government Oversight) and Lisa Rosenberg (executive director, Open the Government) proposed that because Nielsen had signed the April memo, her testimony before the committee in May might have been "false and materially misleading" (Project on Government Oversight and Open the Government 2018b).[5]

The letter goes on to state that the committee's unredacted copy of the DHS memo provides further proof that Nielsen knew that the purpose of family separation was to deter migrant families from trying to cross to the United States border. It adds that officials understood "that prosecuting and separating parents would present 'increased legal risk,' based on an attached legal analysis that has never been made public" (Project on Government Oversight and Open the Government 2018b; complete citations in original; for redacted copy see appendix).

The text of the letter reads:

> The Honorable Ron Johnson Chairman Senate Committee on Homeland Security and Governmental Affairs 340 Dirksen Senate Office Building Washington, D.C. 20510
>
> The Honorable Claire McCaskill Ranking Member Senate Committee on Homeland Security and Governmental Affairs 340 Dirksen Senate Office Building Washington, D.C. 20510
>
> October 2, 2018
>
> Dear Chairman Johnson and Ranking Member McCaskill: The Project on Government Oversight (POGO) and Open The Government, organizations dedicated to ensuring a transparent and accountable federal government, are writing to submit documentary evidence that Department of Homeland Security (DHS) Secretary Kirstjen Nielsen may have given false and/or materially misleading testimony before your committee on May 15, 2018.
>
> During that hearing, Secretary Nielsen stated to Senator Kamala Harris, "we do not have a policy to separate children from their parents." Nielsen stated that any separations that did occur were done solely for purposes of prosecution, not "for purposes of deterrence."
>
> Our organizations recently obtained a document in response to a Freedom of Information Act request that demonstrates that Nielsen personally signed off on a policy of separating parents and children to deter others from migrating to the United States.
>
> The document, attached here [see McAleenan 2018], is a memorandum to Nielsen from Kevin McAleenan, the commissioner of U.S. Customs and Border Protection; L. Francis Cissna, the director of U.S. Citizenship and Immigration Services, and Thomas Homan, then the acting director of U.S. Immigration and Customs Enforcement. The memo lays out three options for increasing illegal entry prosecutions, only one of which discussed separating families. It recommends that option, "Option 3," which would "pursue prosecution of all amenable adults who cross our border illegally, including those presenting with a family unit," as "the most effective method to achieve operational objectives and the Administration's goal to end 'catch and release.'" The memo states that Nielsen has the authority to "direct the separation of parents or legal guardians and minors held in immigration detention so that the parents or legal guardians can be prosecuted."

The document contains a redacted signature approving Option 3. The Department of Homeland Security has confirmed that the signature is Nielsen's.2

Open the Government and the Project On Government Oversight have also obtained an unredacted copy of the April 23 memo, which provides further evidence that contrary to her testimony, Nielsen understood that the purpose of family separation was deterrence.[3] The memo acknowledges that prosecuting and separating parents would present "increased legal risk," based on an attached legal analysis that has never been made public. It nevertheless recommends the policy because:

> it is very difficult to complete immigration proceedings and remove adults who are present as part of FMUAs [family units] at the border. In fact, only 10 percent of non–Mexican FMUA apprehended during the Fiscal Year (FY) 2014 surge have been repatriated in the nearly four years since their illegal crossing. Of these options, prosecuting all amenable adults will increase the consequences for illegally entering the United States by enforcing existing law, protect children being smuggled by adults through transnational criminal organizations, and have the greatest impact on current flows.

The memo does not discuss any plan for reuniting separated families, or the harmful effects of separation on children, nor does it reflect any input from the government agencies that would be responsible for caring for the separated children.

Since the hearing, Nielsen has repeatedly claimed that separation was not a deliberate policy; that it was not meant as a deterrent; that parents and children were kept apart no longer than necessary; and that parents were not deported without an opportunity to reunite with their children:

- On June 17, she tweeted, "We do not have a policy of separating families at the border. Period."
- On June 18, at a press conference at the White House, she stated that "this administration did not create a policy of separating families at the border." Asked by a reporter whether she was "intending for parents to be separated from children" or "intending to send a message," Nielsen replied, "I find that offensive. No. Because why would I ever create a policy that purposely does that."
- On July 19, in a public appearance at the Aspen Security Forum, Nielsen was asked about the logistics of reuniting children with parents who had been deported. She replied, "It's complicated because remember all of these adults who left without their kids left based on a decision to leave their children. So now we're saying to them, no, no, no, you have to take the children."
- On July 24, Nielsen told Fox News in response to a question about children deported without their parents that "the way the process works is the parents always have the choice to take the children with them. So, these are parents who have made the decision not to bring the children with them."

All of those statements were false, and provide evidence that Nielsen's misleading testimony in May was not an inadvertent misstatement.

We respectfully request that the Committee take the following steps:

1. Request (by subpoena if necessary) an unredacted copy of the April 23 memo; the legal analysis from the Department of Homeland Security's General Counsel that it references; and all other documents that Nielsen sent or received regarding "zero tolerance" prosecutions and family separation.

2. Require Secretary Nielsen to come before the Committee under oath to provide an explanation for her prior inaccurate testimony, her failure to correct it, and her other false statements regarding family separations.

3. If deemed appropriate after a thorough examination of the factual record by the Committee, make a referral to the Federal Bureau of Investigation for investigation of potential violations of 18 U.S.C. § 1001.

Sincerely yours,

Danielle Brian Executive Director,
Project On Government Oversight

Lisa Rosenberg, Executive Director,
Open The Government

Under the zero-tolerance policy, once parents are sent to federal court and are held under the custody of the U.S. Marshals Service, their children are separated from them because children cannot be held in detention facilities intended for adults (Gore 2018). When children are taken from parents by the Department of Homeland Security (DHS), the law dictates their transfer to the care and custody of the Department of Health and Human Services (HHS) within 72 hours (Office of the Inspector General 2019). Children who cross the border without adults are categorized as "unaccompanied" and become the responsibility of the Office of Refugee Resettlement (ORR), under HHS (Gore 2018). Although Nielsen refused to call family separation a policy, it has had devastating effects on families.

The Office of Refugee Resettlement follows the requirements of the *Flores* settlement, which outlines detailed provisions for ensuring that unaccompanied children are placed in the least restrictive setting appropriate to the child's age and special needs while in government custody. As described above, *Flores* also directs that children are promptly reunited with family members in the U.S. when family members are available and when such reunification is possible and appropriate. The Office of Refugee Resettlement (ORR) and the Division of Unaccompanied Children's Services (DUCS) under the William Wilberforce Trafficking Protection and Reauthorization Act of 2008 also mandate ORR/DUCS to take additional precautions for children in care who meet outlined categories.

More than two years after Nielsen signed the memo described in this chapter, information came to light concerning a secret meeting in May 2018. Two officials who attended the meeting told Julia Ainsley and Jacob Soboroff of NBC News that 11 senior advisors were called to the White House Situation Room by Stephen Miller. He was furious that child separations had not begun. He asked for a show-of-hands vote to decide if they should. Kirstjen Nielsen did not raise her hand because she had growing concerns that children would get lost in a system that was already taxed. A "sea of hands" went up, however. A few days later, Nielsen signed the memo. NBC received the following list of invitees besides Miller and Nielsen: Mike Pompeo, Alex Azar, John Rood, John F. Kelly, Chris Liddell, Don McGhan, and Marc Short. A White House spokesman denied that the vote happened. An HHS spokesman denied that either the vote or the meeting happened (Ainsley and Soboroff 2020).

3

Increasing Outrage

3.1 Powerful Voices

The family separation policy continued to draw attention from the UN and criticism from the professional community that protects the well-being of young children.

In May of 2018, the American Academy of Pediatrics (AAP) issued a statement opposing the separation policy. Colleen Kraft, president of the AAP, authored the statement. She visited the border and saw firsthand the destruction of children and families brought about by the policy. Kraft wrote:

> As a pediatrician, as a parent, as the president of the American Academy of Pediatrics (AAP), I am appalled by a new policy reportedly signed by Department of Homeland Security that will forcibly separate children from their parents, a practice that this Administration has been carrying out for months. In fact, during my recent trip to the border, I saw its impact with my own eyes, and I am not alone in my outrage and dismay at its sweeping cruelty. The AAP is opposed to this policy and will continue to urge the Department of Homeland Security and the Department of Justice to reverse it immediately.
>
> So many of these parents are fleeing for their lives. So many of these children know no other adult than the parent who brought them here. They can be as young as infants and toddlers.
>
> Separating children from their parents contradicts everything we stand for as pediatricians—protecting and promoting children's health. In fact, highly stressful experiences, like family separation, can cause irreparable harm, disrupting the child's brain architecture and affecting his or her short- and long-term health. This type of prolonged exposure to serious stress—known as toxic stress—can carry lifelong consequences for children,
>
> The new policy is the latest example of harmful actions by the Department of Homeland Security against immigrant families, hindering their right to seek asylum in our country and denying parents the right to remain with their children. We can and must do better for these families. We can and must remember that immigrant children are still children: they need our protection, not prosecution [Kraft 2018].

Ravina Shamdasani, a spokesperson for the United Nations High Commissioner on Human Rights, issued a statement calling for an "immediate halt" to the separations. She added that the policy "runs counter to human rights standards and principles" (Shamdasani 2018).

The following is the text of the briefing statement that was issued on June 5, 2019.

> We are deeply concerned that the zero-tolerance policy recently put in place along the U.S. southern border has led to people caught entering the country irregularly being subjected to criminal prosecution and having their children—including extremely young children—taken away from them as a result.
>
> The practice of separating families amounts to arbitrary and unlawful interference in family life, and is a serious violation of the rights of the child. While the rights of children are generally held in high regard in the U.S., it is the only country in the world not to have ratified the UN *Convention on the Rights of the Child*. We encourage it to accede to the Convention and to fully respect the rights of all children.
>
> The use of immigration detention and family separation as a deterrent runs counter to human rights standards and principles. The child's best interest should always come first, including over migration management objectives or other administrative concerns. It is therefore of great concern that in the U.S. migration control appears to have been prioritised over the effective care and protection of migrant children.
>
> Children should never be detained for reasons related to their own or their parents' migration status. Detention is never in the best interests of the child and always constitutes a child rights violation.
>
> Information from various sources suggests that several hundred children have been separated from their families since last October. The practice of separating children from their parents is being applied to both asylum-seekers and other migrants in vulnerable situations, and we note that the American Civil Liberties Union has brought a class action case on behalf of hundreds of parents who have been forcibly separated from their children.
>
> The majority of people arriving at the U.S.'s southern border have fled Honduras, Guatemala and El Salvador—in many cases either because of rampant insecurity and violence, or because of violations of a range of other rights, such as health, education, and housing.
>
> The U.S. should immediately halt this practice of separating families and stop criminalizing what should at most be an administrative offence—that of irregular entry or stay in the U.S.
>
> We call on the U.S. authorities to adopt non-custodial alternatives that allow children to remain with their families and fulfill the best interests of the children, their right to liberty, and their right to family life [Shamdasani 2018].

In connection to the words of Ravina Shamdasani, the preamble of the *Convention on the Rights of the Child* (UN General Assembly 1989) lays out premises under which State Parties agree to sign the convention. It emphasizes that in "the Universal Declaration of Human Rights, the United Nations has proclaimed that childhood is entitled to special care and assistance" (UN General Assembly, 1989).

The preamble also states "the family, as the fundamental group of society and the natural environment for the growth and well-being of all its members and particularly children, should be afforded the necessary protection and assistance so that it can fully assume its responsibilities within the community" (UN General Assembly, 1989).

Additionally, the Preamble recognizes that "the child, for the full and harmonious development of his or her personality, should grow up in a family environment, in an atmosphere of happiness, love and understanding" (UN General Assembly, 1989).

Article 18 of this convention states that parents are the ones who have the responsibility for their child's upbringing. The article reads:

> 1. States Parties shall use their best efforts to ensure recognition of the principle that both parents have common responsibilities for the upbringing and development of the child. Parents or, as the case may be, legal guardians, have the primary responsibility for the upbringing and development of the child. The best interests of the child will be their basic concern.

Article 23, paragraph 1, of the International Convention on Civil and Political Rights also protects the role of the family. It reads:

> 1. The family is the natural and fundamental group unit of society and is entitled to protection by society and the State.

3.2 Turmoil and Secrecy

Communication between the government agencies overseeing the zero-tolerance policy was grossly inadequate. Messages among government officials were contradictory. AG Sessions called zero tolerance a policy, while Nielsen repeatedly denied that DHS had any such policy. Disclosure of what was happening with the children within detention facilities was virtually nonexistent. Journalists and even members of Congress were not allowed into the centers. Those who were finally admitted were not allowed to talk with children. Most workers who spoke with journalists did so anonymously for fear of repercussions including losing their jobs. The following are examples of turmoil that existed in places where children who had been separated from their parents were being held.

Casa Padre, Brownsville, Texas

Casa Padre, run by a company named Southwest Key, was set up in a converted Walmart store in Brownsville, Texas. This shelter housed 300 boys in February 2018, 500 in March, and by June of that year the number climbed to 1,500 boys from the ages of 10 to 17—1,500 boys living in Walmart. Most of the boys were unaccompanied children who had come to the United States on their own, but 70 of them, approximately 5 percent, had been separated from their parents at the border (Miller, Brown, and Davis 2018).

On June 3, 2018, Sen. Jeff Merkley of Oregon attempted to visit Casa Padre. The windows of the building were blacked out. Merkley was denied access although he was live-streaming his visit and had identified himself to the guards as a member of Congress (Tillett 2018). Merkley tweeted, "I was barred entry. Asked repeatedly to speak to a supervisor—he finally came out and said he can't tell us anything. Police were called on us. Children should never be ripped from their families and held in secretive detention centers. RT if you agree this is WRONG" (Merkley 2018). The incident raised serious concerns about the level of secrecy and lack of oversight regarding what was taking place in these child detention facilities.

On June 17, Sen. Merkley returned to Casa Padre. This time, he was accompanied by Sen. Chris Van Hollen of Maryland, representatives Filemon Vela, Vincente Gonzalez, and Sheila Lee Jackson of Texas, Rep. Peter Welch of Vermont, Rep. David Cicilline of Rhode Island, and Rep. Mark Pocan of Wisconsin. The group was escorted by Dr. Juan Sanchez, CEO of Southwest Key. They discovered that Casa Padre offered classroom instruction and recreational activities among other services. But these services were stretched to the limit as the number of boys housed in the facility had risen exponentially. Two sessions of schooling had been set up, one in the morning and one in the afternoon. All of the boys had to share one basketball court and one broken foosball machine. Bedrooms intended for one boy had to be shared by five (Merkley 2019).

The influx of children separated from their parents filled the center beyond its legal capacity. As a result of the overcrowding, Trump administration officials had to quickly open temporary tent cities in various areas of the country. Sanchez suggested that these facilities might not have to be licensed or staffed by trained child welfare professionals if they were set up on federal land. The administration was considering this option (Soboroff 2018).

As a result of the visits by the legislators, negative reports began to surface. In recent years, state childcare facility regulators have cited numerous shelters for dozens of violations, according to data obtained by the *New York Times* from the Texas Health and Human Services Commission and the Department of Family and Protective Services. At least 13 deficiency citations had been filed against Southwest Key's Casa Padre (Fernandez 2018).

Once the spotlight was cast upon Casa Padre, the Associated Press conducted an analysis and found that the detention of "immigrant children has morphed into a surging industry in the U.S., that now reaps $1 billion dollars annually." This figure reflects a "tenfold increase over the past decade." Furthermore, "Health and Human Services grants for shelters, foster care and other child welfare services for detained unaccompanied and separated children soared from $74.5 million in 2007 to $958 million in 2017." Over the last ten years, one of the largest recipients of taxpayer funding for operating these shelters had been Southwest Key, which during this time received $1.39 billion (Mendoza and Fenn 2018).

Although his organization was classified as a charity, in 2018, Juan Sanchez's annual salary as CEO of Southwest Key was $1.5 million. As vice president, his wife Jennifer Sanchez made $500,000. As reported by the *New York Times*, the salaries of eight Southwest Key employees exceeded the salary cap of $187,000. Furthermore, "Southwest Key has created a web of for-profit companies—construction, maintenance, food services, and even a florist—that had funneled money back to the charity through high management fees and helps it circumvent government limits on executive pay" (Baker, Kulish, and Ruiz 2018). By March of 2019, Sanchez was being investigated by the Department of Justice for misuse of federal money, at which time he resigned as CEO of Southwest Key (Merkley 2019).

In addition to the administrative problems, there were other problems at Southwest Key. As a result of a settlement with the Arizona Department of Health and Safety (ADHS), two shelters in Phoenix were closed and a freeze was imposed on admissions to all Southwest Key sites. The facility in Youngtown, Arizona, was closed in 2018 because of allegations that "staff shoved and drugged unruly children." A videotape released to reporters shows staff members "dragging children on the ground and shoving a boy against a door." The charges were investigated but not pursued because authorities decided that there was "no reasonable likelihood of proving" a crime had been committed (Associated Press 2019).

Casa Phoenix, Southwest Key's largest Arizona shelter, also closed within a month of the settlement. ADHS inspectors investigated 77 complaints and substantiated 55 of them. They concluded, "Based on the allegations substantiated and deficient practices found at the facility, a significant risk of harm to the life, health and safety of residents was found." ADHS inspectors also determined that Southwest Key failed to implement changes after previously identifying hundreds of cases of abuse, neglect and other serious incidents at Casa Phoenix (L. Gomez 2019).

Southwest Key paid a penalty of $73,000. A healthcare management professional was hired to vet all of the Arizona facilities, evaluators were hired for each site, and health inspectors monitored compliance. By mid-August, all 11 Southwest Key shelters were reopened without admissions restrictions (L. Gomez 2019).

In 2019, both Casa Phoenix and the Youngstown site renamed their facilities and filed for new applications. Despite the strident objections of child advocates, the shelters were licensed and opened in the fall of 2019 (D. Post, personal communication, October 20, 2019).

Ursula Border Station, McAllen, Texas

On the day of his first attempt to visit Casa Padre, Sen. Merkley also travelled to the Ursula Border Station in McAllen, Texas. He noticed a number of reporters gathered across the street. One approached Merkley and asked him what was going on in the facility. The senator was surprised to find out that no members of the press had been allowed inside. This observation led him to write:

> In America, it's never a good sign when the press has been barred entry to see the basic operations of our government. The press had not been let in for a simple reason: The Trump administration did not want the press, and by extension the American people, to see how they were treating immigrants [Merkley 2019].

Sen. Merkley toured the facility without the press and found dozens of people crammed into what looked like dog cages. People had to sit up because there was not enough space for them to lie down. They were wrapped in mylar blankets and had nothing but the clothes on their backs. They had terrified looks on their faces, and many of the women cried. Merkley was "stunned" and "angered" by what he saw. Upon leaving, he told his distraught communications manager, Ray Zaccaro, "I can't believe what we just saw" (Merkley 2019).

The following day, he told CNN:

> Yesterday morning at the McAllen Border Station, at the processing center, they have big cages made out of fencing and wire and nets stretched across the top of them so people can't climb out of them.... Every time I probed yesterday on the circumstances (of why they were held this way) the response was just basically a generic, "That is what's required for security, this is what is required for control" [Vazquez 2018].

Sen. Merkley, accompanied by the other senators, returned to the McAllen Texas facility on June 17. Media were allowed on this tour, but they were barred from taking pictures or video. Instead, they were given sanitized photos for release from the agency that showed the facility from the government's perspective (Cullinane 2018).

In an interview with Ana Cabrera of CNN, Merkley stated: "We did see the children who were held inside here," he said. "In wire-mesh, chain linked cages that are about 30 × 30, a lot of young folks put into them. I must say though, far fewer than I was here two weeks ago. I was told that buses full (of children) were taken away before I arrived. That was one of my concerns, that essentially, when you have to give lengthy notice, you end up a little bit of a show rather than seeing what's really going on in these centers" (Cabrera 2018).

3. Increasing Outrage

The linked cages that Merkley describe disclose other violations of children's rights documented in Article 3, paragraphs 1 and 2, and Article 20, paragraphs 1 and 2, of the *Convention on the Rights of the Child*. The articles read:

> Article 3
>
> 1. In all actions concerning children, whether undertaken by public or private social welfare institutions, courts of law, administrative authorities or legislative bodies, the best interests of the child shall be a primary consideration.
> 2. States Parties undertake to ensure the child such protection and care as is necessary for his or her well-being, taking into account the rights and duties of his or her parents, legal guardians, or other individuals legally responsible for him or her, and, to this end, shall take all appropriate legislative and administrative measures.
>
> Article 20
>
> 1. A child temporarily or permanently deprived of his or her family environment, or in whose own best interests cannot be allowed to remain in that environment, shall be entitled to special protection and assistance provided by the State.
> 2. States Parties shall in accordance with their national laws ensure alternative care for such a child.

Locking children in wire cages does not provide them with special care or protection.

Despite DHS's denial of the use of cages for incarcerating children, Merkley's revelations raised America's ire against the inhumane treatment of migrant children. Rep. Barbara Lee (CA-13), the Democratic congressional representative to the United Nations and a psychiatric social worker, tweeted that she had called on the UN to look into Trump's zero-tolerance policy. She wrote, "I've asked the UN to investigate President Trump's zero tolerance policy. These practices are a blatant violation of human rights and a stain on America" (Common Dreams 2018).

The following is the text of Rep. Lee's request to UN Secretary-General António Guterres:

> Dear Secretary-General Guterres:
>
> I write today to request your urgent assistance in the ongoing crisis our country is facing at our Southern Border with Mexico.
>
> As the Democratic Congressional Representative to the United Nations (UN), I am formally requesting UN observers travel to the United States to report on the conditions of detention facilities and treatment of children, based on relevant international law and human rights principles.
>
> I am appalled by the reports and images from detention facilities in Texas and other states along the border, where more than 2,300 children have been separated from their parents by border patrol agents.
>
> This weekend, I will be traveling to the border myself, to witness first-hand the conditions adults and children are facing while in detention.

I urge you to send experts from relevant UN agencies to observe conditions in both Department of Homeland Security (DHS) and Office of Refugee Resettlement (ORR) facilities both at the border and throughout the more than 17 states around the country that are now housing children who have been separated from their families.

As a mother, a grandmother, and as a psychiatric social worker, I am most concerned for the physical and mental wellbeing of children separated from their parents at their most vulnerable time. The American Academy of Pediatrics has warned that this practice of family separation "can cause irreparable harm to lifelong development by disrupting a child's brain architecture."

You recently said in a statement, "As a matter of principle, the Secretary-General believes that refugees and migrants should always be treated with respect and dignity, and in accordance with existing international law." And you added, "children must not be traumatized by being separated from their parents. Family unity must be preserved."

I sincerely hope that you will consider this urgent humanitarian request in a timely manner [Lee 2018].

3.3. Faith-Based Responses

As discussed earlier, administration members had sent conflicting messages about whether family separation was a policy and whether it was a means of deterring migrants from crossing the southwest border. Additionally, the president claimed that only congressional action could end the child separation, and had stated, "You can't do it through an executive order" (Shear, Goodnough, and Haberman 2018).

By the third week of June 2018, however, the Trump administration was under extremely intense political pressure to do away with the separations. Laura Bush compared the detention of the children to the internment of Japanese people in the U.S. during World War II (Bush 2018).

In June, 26 Jewish organizations also wrote to Attorney General Sessions and Secretary Nielsen voicing their opposition to the zero-tolerance policy (Twenty-six Jewish Organizations 2018). The text of their letter reads:

Dear Attorney General Sessions and Secretary Nielsen,

On behalf of the 26 undersigned national Jewish organizations and institutions, we write to express our strong opposition to the recently expanded "zero-tolerance" policy that includes separating children from their migrant parents when they cross the border. This policy undermines the values of our nation and jeopardizes the safety and well-being of thousands of people.

As Jews, we understand the plight of being an immigrant fleeing violence and oppression. We believe that the United States is a nation of immigrants and how we treat the stranger reflects on the moral values and ideals of this nation.

Many of these migrant families are seeking asylum in the United States to escape violence in Central America. Taking children away from their families is unconscionable. Such practices inflict unnecessary trauma on parents and children, many of whom have already suffered traumatic experiences. This added trauma negatively impacts physical and mental health, including increasing the risk of early death.

Separating families is a cruel punishment for children and families simply seeking a better life and exacerbates existing challenges in our immigration system. It adds to the backlog of deportation cases and legal challenges in federal courts, places thousands more immigrants in detention facilities and shelters, endangers the lives of more children, and instills additional fear in people seeking safety in our country. In addition, those seeking asylum or other legal protection face numerous obstacles to making a claim, especially from detention. Separating family members at the border would force families into two or more immigration cases instead of a single case for each family, harming their ability to present a successful case.

Our Jewish faith demands of us concern for the stranger in our midst. Our own people's history as "strangers" reminds us of the many struggles faced by immigrants today and compels our commitment to an immigration system in this country that is compassionate and just. We urge you to immediately rescind the "zero tolerance" policy and uphold the values of family unity and justice on which our nation was built.

Pope Francis denounced the separation policy as immoral (Pullella 2018). Catholic bishops from across the U.S. spoke out. Via Twitter, San Antonio's Archbishop Gustavo Garcia-Siller said, "Refugee children belong to their parents, not to the government or other institution. To steal children from their parents is a grave sin, immoral (and) evil. Their lives have been extremely difficult. Why do we (the U.S.) torture them even more, treating them as criminals?"

Bishop Daniel E. Flores of the Diocese of Brownsville, Texas, said via Twitter:

> Separating immigrant parents and children as a supposed deterrent to immigration is a cruel and reprehensible policy. Children are not instruments of deterrence, they are children. A government that thinks any means is suitable to achieve an end cannot secure justice for anyone [B.D. Flores 2018].

Bishop Oscar Solis of Salt Lake City, Utah, described separation policies that "tear at our core values as a nation." He acknowledged the right of the U.S. to "protect its borders," but emphasized "a moral obligation to do so through means that preserve families and the dignity and sanctity of all life." He added, "Refusing asylum to women escaping from domestic violence and separating children from their parents is an unnecessary and aggressive act against human life, and unfathomable from a country with a heart as strong as ours" (Guidos 2018).

A year later, Catholics were still opposing the administration's policies. On July 18, 2019, seventy protestors were arrested at the Russell Senate Office Building, Washington, D.C., in a Catholic Day of Action for Detained Immigrant Children. The protest was organized by several organizations, including Faith in Public Life, Faith in Action and Sisters of Mercy of the Americas. Catholic nuns, priests, and lay members assembled on Capitol

Hill to compel the Trump administration and lawmakers in Congress to end "the immoral and inhumane practice of detaining immigrant children." They were arrested for unlawful demonstrations and were charged under D.C. Code §22–1307, with "Crowding, Obstructing, or Incommoding," according to Capitol Police spokeswoman Eva Malecki (Marquette 2019).

Evangelicals also joined protests. *The Christian Science Monitor* reported that these evangelicals included bible verses on their signs as messages to oppose family separation. When making her poster, Julie Frady from Wichita, Kansas, chose lines from the Book of Obadiah, the Hebrew prophet who condemned the nation of Edom for closing its borders to Israelite refugees fleeing the Babylonians. Frady wrote: "The LORD declares: You should NOT stand at the crossroads to cut down fleeing REFUGEES ... in the day of their ... DISTRESS" (emphasis by Frady) (Bruinius 2018).

Evangelical leaders have also spoken out, but not in highly visible public protests or arrests. The Rev. Franklin Graham, who is a strong supporter of the president, described the policy as "disgraceful." He added, "It's terrible to see families ripped apart, and I don't support that one bit" (Frej 2018).

Members of the Evangelical Immigration Table, including Southern Baptist ethicist Russell Moore and National Hispanic Leadership Conference President Samuel Rodriguez, sent a letter to the president in which they said, "The traumatic effects of this separation on children, which could be devastating and long-lasting, are of utmost concern" (S. Smith 2018). The Southern Baptist Convention is the largest Protestant denomination in the country, and one of the most theologically and politically conservative. At their annual meeting in 2018, however, they passed a resolution that "called for immigration reforms that would include a path to legal status for those here illegally." The resolution stressed that the reforms should preserve "family unity," and "the value and dignity of those seeking a better life for themselves and their families" (Bruinius 2018).

Members of the Trump administration used Bible verses to attempt to deflect criticism of the separation policy. On June 14, 2018, Attorney General Jeff Sessions told an audience in Fort Wayne, Indiana, "Persons who violate the law of our nation are subject to prosecution. I would cite you to the Apostle Paul and his clear and wise command in Romans 13, to obey the laws of the government because God has ordained them for the purpose of order" (Stewart 2018). Sarah Huckabee Sanders, White House press secretary at the time, said that she was unaware of Sessions' remarks. She said, however, "I can say that it is very biblical to enforce the law. That is actually repeated a number of times throughout the Bible" (Stewart 2018).

3.4 Executive Order

The cries of disapproval forced the president to issue an executive order on June 20, 2018, to end the separation of families at the border. There was considerable uncertainty about how the executive order would operate in practice. A new plan included in the order would allow families to be detained together for an indefinite period. The plan did not specify where the families would be detained or where children would be held while waiting for family detention centers to be constructed. White House officials did not have answers to how these issues would be addressed. Confusion ensued about what would happen to these 2,300 children. One statement by spokesman Kenneth Wolfe from the Administration for Children and Families, a division of the Department of Health and Human Services, said that they would not immediately be reunited with their families (Kirby 2018). (See a copy of the executive order of June 20, 2018, in the appendix of this book.)

Refugee International states:

> There is considerable uncertainty about how the Executive Order will operate in practice. Most significantly, the Trump administration is not lawfully able to detain immigrant children indefinitely. Yet, by the terms of the Executive Order, President Trump seeks to do exactly that. The administration's apparent goal is to detain children together with their parents while criminal or immigration proceedings are being resolved [Refugee International 2018].

The separated children's parents were still being held in federal custody awaiting immigration proceedings. Wolfe said, "There will not be grandfathering of existing cases," and added that this decision had been made by the White House. Within hours, however, a statement by Brian Marriott, a senior director of communications at the Department of Health and Human Services, described Mr. Wolfe's words as a misstatement. According to Marriott, "reunification is always the goal," and the Health and Human Services Agency "is working toward that" for children who had been separated due to Trump's policy. This statement also presented the option that children could be connected to family members other than the parent (Shear, Goodnough, and Haberman 2018).

For guidance, the Justice Department made a request to Judge Dolly M. Gee of the Federal District Court in Los Angeles. She oversees the *Flores* settlement, which prevents immigration officials from detaining children for more than 20 days even if they are with their parents. The judge would decide if families could be detained together past the 20-day limit or not.

On July 8, 2018, the Trump administration suffered a setback when a federal court denied long-term detention of immigrant families. Judge Gee ruled that there was no reason to amend the *Flores* consent decree. The amended decree would also have allowed housing children in facilities that were not licensed by child welfare agencies. This change was not allowed. The judge described the request to modify the decree as "a cynical attempt … to shift responsibility to the Judiciary for over 20 years of congressional inaction and ill-considered executive action that have led to the current stalemate" (Gee 2018).

Peter Schey, president of the Center for Human Rights and Constitutional Law, was the co-lead counsel for the first *Flores* lawsuit in 1985. Regarding Judge Gee's decision, he stated, "The court clearly finds that the attorney general's efforts to strip children of their fundamental rights were completely unfounded and based on an intentional misreading of the 1997 *Flores* Agreement." Schey also emphasized that no part of the *Flores* settlement called for the separation of families. He added, "On the contrary, the settlement has offered detained children the right to humane treatment and reasonably prompt release from custody, unless they are a flight risk or a danger, for some 20 years without incident" (Jordan and Fernandez 2018).

Along with this *Flores* ruling, a second case in San Diego was dismantling the practice of family separation. On June 26, Judge Dana Sabraw of San Diego set a deadline of Tuesday, July 10, 2018, for the youngest children to be returned to their parents. But of the 102 children who were under the age of five, only 54 parents had been identified, located, and vetted. There were challenges in connecting up the children and their parents. According to Sarah B. Fabian, a Justice Department lawyer, nine parents could not be reunited with their children right away because the adults had been deported, and nine others could not be located (Jordan and Fernandez 2018).

John Sandweg, who was the head of U.S. Immigration and Customs Enforcement during the Obama administration, stated that migrant parents who are separated from their children after crossing into the U.S. may end up losing their children permanently (R. Brown 2018). Adult deportations take place quickly, but child deportations do not. The time span between the deportation of a parent and the deportation of the child could be years. Children who stay in the U.S. become wards of the state or end up being adopted. Sandweg pointed out that child separation could create thousands of orphans in the U.S. who eventually become eligible for citizenship here when adopted (Ainsley 2018).

Attorney Dianne Post explained that state courts have terminated migrant parents' rights. Their separated children, who are Central American, Mexican, or who have crossed the border from other countries are then adopted into white families. Post calls this practice "nothing less than child kidnapping" (D. Post, personal communication, October 20, 2019).

The *Convention on the Rights of the Child* (CRC) states that it is a

3. Increasing Outrage 59

child's right to be raised by his or her parents. Further, children's right to their nationality, name, and connections with family cannot be stripped away. Articles 7 and 8 in the CRC read as follows:

> Article 7
> The child shall be registered immediately after birth and shall have the right from birth to a name, the right to acquire a nationality and, as far as possible, the right to know and be cared for by his or her parents.

Typically, the names of Latino children include a first name, a second first name, their father's last name and their mother's last name. If children's names were changed without their family's knowledge or consent, the record of family history that the children carry within their names would be lost.

> Article 8
> States Parties undertake to respect the right of the child to preserve his or her identity, including nationality, name and family relations as recognized by law without unlawful interference [UN General Assembly 1989].

The following recommendation pertaining to family unity was unanimously adopted at the Conference of Plenipotentiaries that drafted the 1951 Refugee Convention:

> The Conference, considering that the unity of the family, the natural and fundamental group unit of the society, is an essential right of the refugee, and that such unity is constantly threatened, and noting with satisfaction that, according to the official commentary of the ad hoc Committee on Statelessness and Related Problems (E/1618, p. 40) the rights granted to a refugee are extended to members of his family, recommends Governments to take the necessary measures for the protection of the refugee's family especially with a view to
>> Ensuring that the unity of the refugee's family is maintained particularly in cases where the head of the family fulfilled necessary conditions for admission to a particular country,
>> The protection of refugees who are minors, in particular unaccompanied children and girls, with special reference to guardianship and adoption [UNHRC 1981].

While the possibility of children being reunited with their parents was a cause for hope, an increase in deportations of incarcerated adults loomed on the horizon, however. In June and July of 2018, after the court order that ended family separation, Open the Government and the Project on Government Oversight (POGO) acquired documents through the Freedom of Information Act (FOIA). Internal DHS emails that described failed efforts to reunite families were included. One email explained that in July, DHS employees were instructed to deport families as fast as possible to make space for incoming families. This email raises the possibility that these quick deportations violated due process protections (Project on Government Oversight 2018).[1]

The text of the email appears below. Copy of the redacted email can be found in the appendix. The signature and other information were redacted. Much of the email was written in acronyms that were used within the department but most likely were unfamiliar to those who do not.

When I worked in public schools, my colleagues and I found that we used many acronyms. Once we became aware of the practice, we modified it. It was important to us that everyone with whom we were communicating, especially parents, understood what we were talking about. Communicating through acronyms is a way of obscuring information. Only the circle of people who are privy to the meaning of the acronyms can understand the message. Furthermore, the power of language can be obscured when the truncated forms become the norm.

Katherine Hawkins of the Project on Government Oversight provided the following explanation of the acronyms in the email:

> ERO: Immigration and Custom's Enforcement's directorate of enforcement and removal operations
> FMUA: family units
> FRCs: family residential centers, immigration detention facilities for parents and children
> SWB: southwest border
> UAC: unaccompanied alien children
> USBP: U.S. border patrol
> TOT: a military term meaning time on target [Project on Government Oversight 2018]

> [heading redacted]
> From: [redacted]
> Sent: Thursday, July 12, 2018 6:38 AM
> To: Redacted
> Subject: FW: NTA/WA for FMUAs
> From: [redacted]
> Sent: Wednesday, July 11, 2018 7:54:34 PM
> To: BP Field Chiefs; Field Deputies
> Subject: NTA/WA for FMUAs
> Chiefs,
>
> We have received a request from ERO for assistance in the reunification effort for UAC and parents that were previously separated. As you know, the U.S. Government has been ordered to reunite all UAC with parents by July 26, 2018. ERO and HHS have developed a plan to reunite FRC's. In order to do so, ERO must create space within FRCs. ERO is in the process of repatriating as many FMUA as possible to make space. Additionally, ERO has made a request for all USBP SWB sectors to [redacted] all FMUAs from July 12 until July 26. These cases will be TOT to ERO for further disposition [remainder of line and first half of following line are redacted).
> [three lines redacted]

3. Increasing Outrage

Please ensure disposition to the appropriate level for execution. If you have any questions, please let me know.

>VR
>[redacted]
>[redacted]
>Acting Chief
>Law Enforcement Operations Directorate
>U.S. Border Patrol Headquarters
>[phone number redacted] Office
>[phone number redacted) Cellular
>[redacted—most likely email address]

See a copy of the redacted email in the appendix of this book.

4

The Colossal Failure of Reunification

4.1 Congressional Actions

A Judiciary Committee hearing on oversight of the administration's immigration enforcement and family reunification efforts was held on July 31, 2018. Officials from U.S. Immigration and Customs Enforcement, the Border Patrol, and Health and Human Services were questioned about the family separation policy and efforts to reunify parents and children.

In his prepared statement, U.S. Sen. Chuck Grassley, Republican from Iowa, and chairman of the Judiciary Committee, raised the possibility that parents who were deported were not given clear or complete information about leaving their children in the United States. They may not have even been given information in a language they could understand. Grassley stated:

> The administration claims that all these parents elected to be deported without their children. But public reports indicate that many of them may not have made an informed choice to leave their children behind. Some of these reports suggest that these parents weren't presented information in a language that they could even understand. I am disturbed by these allegations and I hope our witnesses are prepared to give us thorough answers [Committee on the Judiciary 2018].

At this hearing, Sen. Dick Durbin (IL), the second-ranking Democrat in the Senate, stated that despite Secretary Nielsen's assertion that the Department of Homeland Security did not have a policy of separating families at the border, during her tenure over 2,700 children had been separated. By this date, over 700 had not been reunited with their parents. This number included over 400 children whose parents had apparently been deported and 90 children whose parents could not be found. Durbin pointed out that border agents had labeled the families of these 700 lost children as "deleted family units." Durbin further stated, "The family separation policy is more than a bureaucratic lapse in judgment. It is and was a cruel policy

4. The Colossal Failure of Reunification

inconsistent with the bedrock values of this nation." He then called for Secretary Nielsen, whom he described as "the architect of this humanitarian disaster," to step down (Committee on the Judiciary 2018). Nielsen did so on April 7, 2019.

The concept of "deleted family units" is in direct opposition to the rights of the child as described in Article 9 of the *Convention on the Rights of the Child* (UN General Assembly 1989). This article mandates that children who are separated from their parents must maintain regular relations and direct contact with both parents.

The *Convention on the Rights of the Child*—Article 9, paragraph 3, reads:

> 3. States Parties shall respect the right of the child who is separated from one or both parents to maintain personal relations and direct contact with both parents on a regular basis, except if it is contrary to the child's best interests [UN General Assembly, 1989].

On October 17, 2018, senators Elizabeth Warren (MA) and Ron Wyden (OR) of the Senate Finance Committee sent a letter to Alex M. Azar II, secretary of the U.S. Department of Health and Human Services. The letter indicated that on June 23, 2018, the Department of Health and Human Services and the Department of Homeland Security issued identical fact sheets stating, "The United States government knows the location of all children in its custody and is working to reunite them with their families," and that to do so, "there is a central database which HHS and DHS can access and update." The database purportedly included the information on the location of separated children and their parents (Wyden and Warren 2018).

The letter goes on to explain that three days later, Azar testified before the Senate Finance Committee regarding a computer "portal" in Health and Human Service's Office of Refugee Resettlement (ORR) that could easily locate children. Azar went so far as to say, "There is no reason why any parent would not know where their child is located. I could at the stroke of—at keystrokes, I sat on the ORR portal with just basic keystrokes and within seconds could find any child in our care for any parent available" (Wyden and Warren 2018). Follow-up questions about this portal system were asked by Sen. Wyden at the hearing, and after the hearing, several members of Congress sent letters that questioned the accuracy of Azar's statements.

The letter from senators Warren and Wyden to Azar also included findings of a September 20, 2018, report from the Department of Homeland Security Office of the Inspector General (DHS OIG). The title of the report is "Special Review—Initial Observations Regarding Family Separation Issues Under the Zero-Tolerance Policy." As detailed in the letter, the findings include that "the Administration was not fully prepared to implement the 'zero tolerance' policy, that they 'struggled to deal with its aftermath, and that Administration officials potentially misled or provided inaccurate information regarding how DHS and HHS kept track of separated children'" (Office of the Inspector General, U.S. Department of Homeland Security, 2018).

The senators wrote that the OIG found that no evidence of the database described in the DHS/HHS factsheet existed. OIG also revealed that DHS has acknowledged that no "direct electronic interface" between DHS and HHS tracking systems exists. The closest thing to a "central database" that OIG could find was a "manually compiled spreadsheet maintained by HHS, CBP, and ICE personnel." Among these entities, this spreadsheet is called the "matching table." According to OIG, however, this table was not set up until June 23, 2018, the day the fact sheets were issued and three days prior to Azar's testimony (Office of the Inspector General, U.S. Department of Homeland Security, 2018).

Department of Homeland Security Office of the Inspector General Report

The OIG review of September 2018 also revealed that the government reported that it had either reunified or released 2,167 of the 2,551 children over the age of 5 who were deemed eligible for reunification. The number of children under the age of 5 who had been released was 83 (Office of the Inspector General, U.S. Department of Homeland Security, 2018).

Inconsistent information given to parents led to confusion. Some parents did not realize that their children could be separated from them. Parents had difficulties communicating with their children once they were separated. DHS and HHS had produced a flyer with information about the separation process and information about how parents could locate and talk with their children, but some parents received the flyer after they had been separated from their children, and others never received it. Since the flyer was written in either English or Spanish, it was not accessible to parents who could not read these languages. These parents spoke indigenous dialects and did not understand the language of the flyer even if read it was read to them (Office of the Inspector General, U.S. Department of Homeland Security, 2018).

Another result of the policy noted in the report was that children were detained for extended periods of time in temporary facilities that were designed allegedly for short-term detention. Unaccompanied children are supposed to be held in Customs and Border Protection (CBP) for up to 72 hours. After that, they are to be transferred to the Health and Human

Services (HHS) Office of Refugee Resettlement (ORR). The OIG report documents that this time period was exceeded in many cases. The need for medical care or delays in arranging transportation account for some of these delays. However, necessary information about children that would affect their placements was not provided by CBP. These information gaps may also have led to the delays in transfer (Office of the Inspector General, U.S. Department of Homeland Security, 2018).

The OIG review includes additional observations about some practices of the Border Patrol. The resources required to enforce the zero-tolerance policy limited the pool of resources that could go into interviewing and analyzing the behavior of adults to verify that they were related to, not smuggling, the child they were accompanying. DNA testing to verify that an adult accompanying a child was actually the parent was not being conducted by the Border Patrol (Office of the Inspector General, U.S. Department of Homeland Security, 2018).

Border Patrol agents were also not taking other basic steps to correctly identify preverbal children who were being taken from their parents. For example, issuing wrist bracelets with children's names, fingerprinting children, or including photographs of them in their folders could have augmented the identification process (Office of the Inspector General, U.S. Department of Homeland Security, 2018).

On October 24, 2018, a report from the U.S. Government Accountability Office (GAO) revealed reasons for the chaos and confusion that existed as federal agencies attempted to reunify separated children with their parents after the president signed the executive order to allegedly end the zero-tolerance policy. According to the report, the major problem that caused the disorganization was that the Trump administration did not alert the Department of Homeland Security and the Department of Health and Human Services about the zero-tolerance policy prior to implementing it. These agencies heard of it only when it was announced publicly by Attorney General Sessions. Agency officials stated that they "were unaware of the memo in advance of its public release." Therefore, they did not take steps to prepare for a potential increase in children referred to their shelters (U.S. Government Accountability Office 2018).

4.2 Debunking the Myth That Child Separation Ended

According to Mary Miller Flowers, senior policy analyst for the Young Center, it is a myth that separation of children and their parents ended with the signing of the executive order or the court order to reunite families (Young Center for Immigrant Children's Rights 2019).[1]

From July 2018 to February 2019, at least 200 additional children were separated from their parents (Nowak 2019). By July of 2019, that number reached 900 (R. Gonzales 2019). By the end of 2019, the number had risen to 1,000 (Young Center for Immigrant Children's Rights 2019).

Administration officials cited exceptions to the Judge Sabraw's decision as ways to separate children. Most were minor offences like traffic violations. Kevin McAleenan, then acting Homeland Security secretary, referred to exceptions allowed under the order, while adamantly stating, "CPB generally keeps family units together in short-term holding facilities" (R. Gonzales 2019).

A memo introduced by the ACLU in the *Ms. L. v. ICE* law case in the U.S. District Court of Southern California, however, documents several separations. Examples of exceptions to the order from 2019 are presented below.

The first example was perpetrated by a guard working for the administration who was overseeing infants and toddlers who, as Elijah Cummings pointed out, were "laying around in defecation in some silver paper" (Cummings and Meadows 2018).

- E.R.R. and J., a father and his one-year-old infant daughter, were apprehended by CBP and put in a facility where some of the families with whom they were detained had sick children. J. began to cough and get a fever. E.R.R. immediately informed the guards and sought medical attention for his daughter; J. went to the hospital on two occasions for treatment for a high fever. J.'s health began improving, and E.R.R. personally gave her medicine and Gatorade. See Declaration of Nicolas Palazzo, Ex. D, ¶¶ 3–15.

    One day, while J. was sleeping in E.R.R.'s arms, she wet her diaper. Because J. was still recovering from illness, E.R.R. wanted to let her sleep instead of waking her to change her diaper. A female guard took his daughter out of E.R.R.'s arms, criticized him for not changing the diaper, and called him a bad father. The guard then separated E.R.R. and his infant. The government's own documents show that E.R.R. has no other criminal history.
- A nine-year-old child was separated from her father because of an apparent clerical error. CBP wrote the name of a different immigrant on the father's intake form, despite using the father's correct A-number, then separated the family due to parentage doubts. Enriquez Decl., Ex. C, ¶ 23.
- A four-year-old boy was separated because the father's speech impediment prevented the father from answering CBP's questions. The child advocate reported the father presented a birth certificate,

which includes the father's name, but the family was separated anyway. Enriquez Decl., Ex. C, ¶ 23.
- One three-year-old girl was separated from her mother due to her alleged gang ties and criminal record. The child's advocate determined that this was incorrect—the mother fled El Salvador to escape abuse by a gang member. The mother's son was forced to watch his mother be raped and abused, and while she was in the hospital, a gang member held her son and threatened to kill him if she reported her abuse. Nagda Decl., Ex. E, ¶ 37.e. [American Civil Liberties Union 2019].

In addition to these separations, parents have continued to be deported, and in some cases, their parental rights have been terminated. As noted earlier, their children, especially very young children, have been adopted into white families, stripping away their heritage, and family and cultural ties. The ACLU has sent people to the home countries of these families searching for the parents. They often cannot be found, however, especially if they are indigenous and live in remote mountain areas (D. Post, personal communication).

Miscommunication at the government level also led to a loss of communication between children and parents. In some cases, scheduled telephone calls between parents and children were not able to take place. Some reports indicate that children who were scheduled to meet their parents for reunification had to wait for extended periods of time because their parents were brought to the wrong facilities (U.S. Government Accountability Office 2018).

In part, this chaos also resulted from the DHS's adamant and continuing denial that they did not have an official policy for separating parents and their children. This policy may not have originated with DHS, but Attorney General Sessions clearly viewed DHS as a partner in carrying forth the practices of the zero-tolerance policy.

By August 2018, agencies updated their data "to help notate when children were separated from their parents." DHS also "made changes in their data systems to allow them to better indicate cases in which children were separated from their parents" (U.S. Government Accountability Office 2018). Although these changes apparently took place at DHS, they did not reach ORR. According to the GAO report, ORR officials stated that, as of early September 2018, they were unaware that DHS had made the changes. The report implied that despite the adjustments to help clarify whether children have been separated from their parents, "it is too soon to know the extent to which these changes, if fully implemented, will consistently indicate when children have been separated from their parents, or will help reunify families, if appropriate" (U.S. Government Accountability Office 2018).

4.3 Children and Families Lost in the Process

The chaos continued throughout the fall. In January of 2019, a report from the Health and Human Services (HHS) inspector general's office stated that in 2017, the year prior to the implementation of the policy, "thousands" more children were separated from their parents by the Trump administration. The key takeaway from the report reads:

> The total number of children separated from a parent or guardian by immigration authorities is unknown. Pursuant to a June 2018 Federal District Court order, HHS has thus far identified 2,737 children in its care at that time who were separated from their parents. However, thousands of children may have been separated during an influx that began in 2017, before the accounting required by the Court, and HHS has faced challenges in identifying separated children [Office of the Inspector General, U.S. Department of Health and Human Services 2019].

Initially, approximately 2,300 children were reported to have been separated from their families between the time Sessions announced the zero-tolerance policy in May of 2018 and June 2018, when the President Trump signed the executive order to bring it to an end. This new watchdog report, however, revealed that the practice had actually begun in April of 2017, long before Sessions delivered his statement that allegedly ushered in the zero-tolerance policy. Therefore, the total number of children separated from a parent or guardian by immigration authorities was unknown. This new information also meant that the number of children who would have to be reunited with their families was greatly increased.

On February 7, 2019, Commander Jonathan White of the U.S. Public Health Service Commissioned Corps testified to the House Energy and Commerce Subcommittee on Oversight and Investigations. Supporting earlier reports, he said that to the best of his knowledge, HHS wasn't told about the zero-tolerance policy before it was announced publicly. When asked if HHS would have advised DHS or the Justice Department to implement the zero-tolerance policy, White stated, "Neither I nor any career person in ORR would have ever supported such a policy proposal" (House of Representatives Subcommittee on Oversight, Investigations—Committee on Energy and Commerce 2019).

Ann Maxwell, an inspector at the HHS inspector general's office, also testified at this hearing. She said that while the June 2018 court order directed the Department of Health and Human Services to return 2,700 children to their families, that number was only a "subset" of the total

4. The Colossal Failure of Reunification

number of separated children. Maxwell went on to say, "Exactly how many more children were separated is unknown. This is because there is no integrated data system that reliably tracks children who are separated by the Department of Homeland Security and, then referred to HHS for care" (House of Representatives Subcommittee on Oversight, Investigations—Committee on Energy and Commerce 2019).

Months earlier, Health and Human Services Secretary Alex Azar testified to the Senate Finance Committee about a portal at DHH/ORR that could easily locate children. The portal did not exist, so his statement was not true. He refused to appear before the Energy and Commerce Committee, even though he was personally invited by committee chair Frank Pallone, Jr. (House of Representatives Subcommittee on Oversight, Investigations—Committee on Energy and Commerce 2019).

In May of 2019, a series of emails given to NBC News by the House Judiciary Committee also confirmed that there was no centralized database tracking the separated children and their parents. The emails were exchanged between Thomas Fitzgerald, a data analyst at Health and Human Services, and Matthew Albence, who was then the head of Immigration and Customs Enforcement's enforcement and removal operations. Fitzgerald had a list of 2,219 children who had been separated from their parents (Soboroff 2019).

Fitzgerald did not have coordinating numbers connecting the children and their parents. In an email dated June 23, 2018, Fitzgerald asked Albence for this data. Albence replied by asking Fitzgerald if he was saying that he did not have the numbers. Apparently, to Albence's understanding, they should have already been in the UAC portal. In Fitzgerald's follow-up email, the fractures in the data system began to surface. Fitzgerald said that he was working on figuring out the identification numbers but had only about 60 of the 2,219 numbers that actually linked children and parents. He added that they had a list of parents, but no way to connect them to specific children.

Because of incompetence, lack of preparation, cold-heartedness, or systematic serial abuse of migrant children and their families, many of these children have fallen through the cracks of a disjointed data system. For many months, the fate of these children has been shrouded in denials, contradictions, pretense, and confusion perpetrated by the administration. Because there was no tracking system for reuniting children and their families, records had to be reviewed manually. This process has taken months, and continues.

In addition to the major flaws in the record keeping, other factors slowed the process of reuniting children and their families and increased the number of children staying in detention facilities.

For some children, asylum documents were completed, and they were ready to be turned over to sponsors, but the administration stalled the process. For-profit companies hired by the government reaped $750 or more per day for each of these children, so these companies were not motivated to expedite their release. The backlog of cases resulting from this situation led to severely overcrowded facilities (Merkley 2019).

4.4 Subpoenas Issued

On February 26, 2019, by a vote of 25 to 11, the U.S. Senate Committee on Oversight and Reform authorized Chairman Elijah E. Cummings to issue subpoenas to Attorney General William P. Barr, Secretary of Homeland Security Kirstjen M. Nielsen, and Secretary of Health and Human Services Alex M. Azar for records on the Trump administration child separation policy.

The information had been initially requested seven months earlier, on July 5, 2018, and multiple follow-up requests were issued, but the information was never sent to the committee. Requests pertain to "each individual separated child." The purpose of the letter was to "ensure that we can reunite children who have been separated from their families as expeditiously as possible." Data called for included the age, gender, country of origin, alien identification number, the date and location of separation of a child from his or her parents or accompanying adult, a list of all facilities where a child had been detained, the dates of detainment, plans for any transfer that a child was awaiting, and the date and location of family reunification if it had taken place. Similar identification information was sought about the child's parents or accompanying adult, as well as dates and locations of detainment or arrest; locations, facilities and dates of detainments; the status of asylum cases; and deportation details if applicable. The location of a child's separated siblings was also requested (Cummings and Meadows 2018).

When announcing the subpoenas, Chairman Cummings made the following statement:

> When our own government rips vulnerable children, toddlers, and even infants from the arms of their mothers and fathers with no plan to reunite them, that is government-sponsored child abuse. It is our job to step in and protect those children. Further delay is not an option. [House of Representatives Committee on Oversight and Reform 2019].

By July, the Committee on Oversight and Reform received new information about 2,648 children who had been separated from their parents. The new information was not complete, and it pertained mainly to those

4. The Colossal Failure of Reunification

children separated under the zero-tolerance policy. It did not include the children who had been separated prior to April 2018, children who had been reunited with their parents before June 2018, or the more than 700 children who had been separated since June 2018.

The following information about the children is included in the executive summary of the committee's report.

- At least 18 infants and toddlers under the age of 2 were taken away from their parents at the border and were kept apart from their parents for 20 days up to half a year.
- At least 241 separated children were kept in Border Patrol facilities longer than the 72 hours permitted by law.
- Many separated children were kept in government custody far longer than was previously known—at least 679 were held 46 to 75 days, more than 50 were held for six months to a year, and more than 25 were held for more than one year.
- Even after being reunited with their parents, hundreds of separated children continued to be detained in family detention facilities—far longer than the 20-day limit set under the *Flores* case.
- More than 400 children were moved to multiple CPB facilities, more than 80 children were moved to multiple ORR facilities, and at least five children were moved to multiple ICE facilities—including to one, Port Isabel, after the administration claimed that "no children will be housed at that facility … even for short periods."
- At least ten separated children were sent to the "tent city" in Tornillo, Texas, the notorious emergency influx facility near El Paso, before the CEO of the facility's parent company refused to continue operations as a result of the administration's pressure to expand capacity despite delays in releasing children [Committee on Oversight and Reform 2019].

According to the executive summary of the committee's report, the Trump administration was not candid with the American people about its purpose in separating children. It states that children were separated unnecessarily, and that delays in reunification were ongoing. Furthermore, separation from parents was supposedly necessary for criminal prosecution, but parents were never sent to federal criminal custody, or sent only briefly and then released, because prosecutors refused to prosecute their cases. Other parents were sentenced to time served for the misdemeanor of illegal entry. In some cases, parents were readmitted to the same facilities they left just hours before, but their children had already been removed. These parents were then sent to separate detention facilities and in some cases deported without their children (emphases in executive summary) (Committee on Oversight and Reform 2019).

The report also confirms the separation of hundreds of additional children since the zero-tolerance policy ended in June 2018. These continued unnecessary separations have contributed to the current crisis of children suffering in overcrowded, poorly run government detention facilities at the border. The summary adds that despite the federal court order from a year ago to reunite children with their families or an appropriate sponsor, at least 30 children remain separated from their families.

The executive summary concludes with the following statement:

> The information obtained by the Committee indicates that the Trump Administration's decision to separate thousands of babies, toddlers, and children from their parents and put them in government custody for months or years is causing immense suffering. This staff report provides numerous case studies that illustrate their trauma in stark terms. These child separations were not required by law and were not in the best interest of the children. Instead, the policy of separating children from their parents, appears to be a deliberate, unnecessary, and cruel choice by President Trump and his Administration [Committee on Oversight and Reform 2019].

The UN Global Study on Children Deprived of Liberty of November 2019, authored by Manfred Nowak, provides additional information about the number of detentions in the U.S. The report states that from 2013 to 2015, 278,885 children were detained. In the period of eleven months from October 2018 to August 2019, CBP detained 72,873 unaccompanied children and 457,871 members of "family units." The migrants were apprehended at or near the U.S.–Mexico border. Between 2013 and 2018, the number of unaccompanied children who were apprehended annually varied between ca. 39,000 and ca. 69,000 (Nowak 2019).

As of November 2019, the study team estimates that the U.S. was still holding more than 100,000 children in migration-related detention. Nowak stated that the Trump administration's zero-tolerance policy is "absolutely prohibited" under the *Convention on the Rights of the Child*. He described the situation as "inhumane treatment" of both children and their parents and stated that this act of separating children and parents should not happen again (Nowak 2019).

Article 8 of the *Convention on the Rights of the Child* (UN General Assembly 1989) appeared earlier in this book, but it bears repeating here.

> Article 8
> 1. States Parties undertake to respect the right of the child to preserve his or her identity, including nationality, name and family relations as recognized by law without unlawful interference.

4.5 A Fractured Technology System

In November 2019, the Office of the Inspector General released a report titled "DHS lacked technology to successfully account for separated migrant families." This report revealed additional details about the lack of IT functionality to keep track of separated children and parents across various government agencies. The first problem was that the different government agencies used different IT systems. Border Patrol agents used a system called ENFORCE 3 (e3) to record information about detainees from the time of their apprehension to their prosecution or release. ICE field officers used Enforce Alien Removal Module (EARM) to process detainees. Their Enforcement Integrated Database (EID) also stores EARM, but apparently they did not use it. CBP's Office of Field Operations (OFO) officers used the Secured Integrated Government Mainframe Access (SIGMA) platform to process individuals at legal ports of entry. HHS used the Unaccompanied Alien Children's Portal (UAC Portal) to keep track of children in their custody. These multiple systems resulted in a lack of uniform processing of apprehended migrants and led to widespread errors. The deficiencies were known before the zero-tolerance policy was initiated, but CBP did not address them at that time (Office of Inspector General 2019).

In addition, in April 2018, Border Patrol implemented the use of eleven new codes when separating family members. The codes were confusing because of the eleven, three begin with the words "Fraudulent Claim," seven begin with the words "Family Member," and only one begins differently. As a result, Border Patrol personnel mistakenly entered incorrect codes for family separation or assigned children and adults to the wrong family units (Office of Inspector General, Department of Homeland Security, 2019).

Based on their experience of separating families as of November 2017, DHS knew prior to May 2018 that the departments did not have coordinated IT systems that could account for and share information about all members of a family or extended family unit. Despite this shortcoming in the data management system, DHS went ahead and separated the families anyway (Office of Inspector General, Department of Homeland Security, 2019).

New information, released in the November 2019 report, also discloses that in May of 2018, CBP provided an estimate to the Office of Management and Budget (OMB) projecting that under the zero-tolerance policy, it would separate 26,000 children from their parents between May and September 2018. The number of separations did not rise to that level during that time period because of public outcry against the practice and the court order to halt the practice and reunify the children and their parents (Office of Inspector General, Department of Homeland Security, 2019).

5

Detainment at Border Patrol Stations

5.1 Toxic Stress

Soon after the executive order came down ending family separation, Democratic attorneys general from seventeen states and the District of Columbia filed a lawsuit against the administration in which they argued that separating families violated both the due process and equal protection clauses of the Fifth Amendment, federal laws regarding asylum, and the Administrative Procedure Act (APA) (Gerstein 2018). The following week, the attorneys added an additional filing that requested the government to provide more immediate information and access to those detained under zero tolerance on an expedited schedule. The filing included 900 pages of declarations and personal testimonies from parents, advocates, medical experts, and lawmakers. The stories families told were so anguished that one interpreter "broke down into tears" (Desjardins, Barajas, and Bush 2018).

The *PBS NewsHour* examined all of the testimonies and selected a sample that offered a "window into family separations at the border." On July 5, 2018, Lisa Desjardins shared the accounts. Parents described young children who had been reunited as clinging to them, and fearful of being out of their sight. There were reports that detained children were hungry because there was not enough food. The water was chlorinated and not suitable for drinking. The children returned to their parents in dirty clothes. They had lice. One parent questioned if her child had bathed or brushed their teeth while detained. The children went without shoes or blankets although facilities were freezing cold. The children were called names like "animals" and "donkeys." There was no regular policy for sustaining communication between the children and their parents. One father thought he would "lose his mind" because of the separation. He said that he needed "to see my family and take care of them" (Desjardins, Barajas, and Bush 2018).

Medical experts who gave testimony voiced concerns about detained children suffering toxic stress that can interrupt the function and structure of a child's brain as it develops and changes. This kind of stress can also lead to health problems such as stomach aches, trouble sleeping and lack of appetite in the short term (Houshayer 2018).

Later, this stress can lead to diabetes, cancer, and other illnesses. Engaging in unhealthy behaviors such as drug use and smoking also can result. Depression is another outcome of toxic stress (YourTango Experts 2018). Children released from detention had also been treated for suicidal ideation (Desjardins, Barajas, and Bush 2018). As noted earlier in this book, these conditions are similar to those experienced by earlier generations of children who were separated from their families in the U.S.

Trauma is the residue that settles to the bottom of toxic stress. Its elements combine to create a noxious emotional, psychological, and physiological mixture (Zero to Three 2016). Recently, the Center for Disease Control and Prevention gave its first major comment on the connection between child trauma and adult illness. They acknowledge a strong link between harmful childhood experiences and health in adulthood. Their work was supported by many previous studies (Stobbe 2019).

In November 2019, federal judge John A. Kronstadt ruled that the government must provide mental health services to thousands of migrant parents and their children who have suffered what he termed "severe mental trauma" as a result of Trump's family separation policy. The judge applied the doctrine of "state-created danger" in determining his decision. This ruling was described as "truly groundbreaking" by Erwin Chemerinsky, dean of the University of Berkeley School of Law. Mark Rosenbaum, one of the lawyers who argued the case, stated that a policy cannot deliberately try to injure the family bond. He added that cruelty cannot be an enforcement policy, noting that in this case cruelty was the cornerstone policy (Jordan 2019). Additional information about the proceedings of this case, *JP et al. v. Sessions et al.*, is presented in Chapter 12.

As explained previously, when children are separated from their parents, they are first held in the custody of the Department of Homeland Security and are then turned over to the Office of Refugee Resettlement under the Department of Health and Human Services. Both agencies have documents that lay out specific regulations for the care of persons in their custody. The regulations that exist on paper and the experiences of the families impacted by the zero-tolerance policy lie at opposite ends of the spectrum.

5.2 Border Protection Standards

Under the Homeland Security Act of 2002, only food and water need to be provided to persons held in temporary border facilities. The following standards, however, are from the "U.S. Customs and Border Protection national standards on transport, escort, detention, and search," October 2015. These particular regulations pertain to "at-risk" persons held by CBP. These persons need additional care or oversight. The regulations stipulate that before detainees are placed together in a hold room or holding facility, officers or agents shall assess the information before them to determine if the detainee may be considered an at-risk detainee, or at risk of posing a threat to others. Migrant children are part of the "at-risk" population because of their age. Other criteria that determine that a person is in this category are needing life-sustaining medical treatment, being at high risk for sexual abuse, having mental or physical disabilities, or being a family unit.

Information included here is taken from section 5. General regulations, screening, documentations, detentions, and use of restraints are covered. The entire document is available online (U.S. Customs and Border Protection 2015).

Detainees undergo a screening to determine if they should be categorized as at risk. Some criteria of this screening include the person's age, any physical or mental illness, concerns about the person's safety, sexual self-identification, risk of being sexually abused, and the person's own stated concerns about his or her physical safety. A reasonable effort must be made to afford privacy during this screening.

The first requirement for care of at-risk detainees is that they are treated with "dignity, respect and special concern for their particular vulnerability" (U.S. Customs and Border Protection 2015).

> Detainees who present themselves as juveniles are to be treated as juveniles, until established otherwise. Due to a child's age, developmental level of communication, and home language, extra efforts may be required to ensure that he or she can comprehend officer/agent instructions, questions, and applicable forms. At-risk detainees who are known or reported to have mental and/or physical disabilities must receive reasonable accommodations that are in accordance with safety, security, and all applicable laws and regulations.
>
> If officer/agents have reason to believe that any person or entity may harm a child, they must not release the child to that person or entity. When a child is released to another agency or facility, all personal property (including any U.S.-prescribed medications) and legal papers in the juvenile's possession, must accompany the juvenile.
>
> In addition to the at-risk determination process described above, unaccompanied children will be screened for the following: Credible Fear determination; Human trafficking victimization; and the ability to make an independent decision. A reasonable effort must be made to afford privacy to children during this screening.
>
> Detailed information about each child must accurately recorded in the appropriate electronic system(s) of record as soon as practicable. All custodial actions, notifications, and transports that occur after the at-risk detainee has been received into a CBP facility must be included. The electronic system of record must contain the following:

5. Detainment at Border Patrol Stations

Name of the person detained
Country of birth (COB)
Date of birth (DOB)
Date and time placed into unattended secure area
Date and Time removed from unattended secure area
Reason detained
Apprehending officer's/agent's name
Processing officer's/agent's name
Supervisor's name
Transport, Escort, Detention, and Search
Personal belongings secured, receipted, and/or returned
Screened for trafficking (yes/no)
Telephone use, including the identity and/or relationship of the person contacted
Language services provided and language spoken if other than English or Spanish
Reasonable medical care requested/provided/declined
Detainee receipt of list of legal services providers
Bedding provided/declined
Meals provided/meals refused
Visual and/or verbal checks completed
Showers, if provided
Hospitalizations
Any U.S. medications prescribed
Transporting agency, and mode of transportation
Date/Time departing the station
Time in and Time out of each CBP facility
Required forms provided
Date/Time of notice to Immigration and Customs Enforcement (ICE) Field Office Juvenile Coordinator (FOJC) (if applicable)
Date/Time of notice to ORR (if applicable)
Date/Time of response from ICE FOJC (if applicable)
Date/Time of response from ORR (if applicable)
Date/time of placement in ORR custody (if applicable)
Final disposition

Documentation must be maintained in the appropriate electronic system(s) of record for all detainees placed in CBP hold rooms. If the electronic system is inoperable, paper logs must be used until the electronic system is operational. Any information recorded on paper logs must be entered into the appropriate electronic system(s) of record once the system is available.

Customs and Border Protection (CBP)

At-risk detainees must be placed in the least restrictive setting appropriate to their age and special needs, provided that such setting is consistent with the need to ensure the safety and security of the detainee and that of others. Whenever operationally feasible, at-risk individuals will be expeditiously processed to minimize the length of time in CBP custody.

If a parent or legal guardian and U.S. citizen child must be separated, social services may need to be contacted to take custody of the child. CBP should ensure that parents have the opportunity to arrange for care of their children before contacting a social service agency. In those instances where a parent or legal guardian and a non–U.S.-citizen child must be separated, the non–U.S.-citizen child will be classified as an unaccompanied alien child (UAC) and will be processed accordingly.

Unaccompanied juvenile siblings should not be separated, unless deemed necessary for safety purposes. In circumstances where siblings must be separated due to different immigration dispositions, such separation must be documented in the appropriate electronic system(s) of record.

Unaccompanied children must be held separately from adult detainees. A juvenile may temporarily remain with a non-parental adult family member where: (1) the family relationship has been vetted to the extent feasible, and (2) the CBP supervisor determines that remaining with the nonparental adult family member is appropriate, after considering the totality of the circumstances.

Every effort must be made to transfer unaccompanied children from CBP to ORR custody as soon as possible, but no later than 72 hours after determining that a child is unaccompanied. Requested placement notifications for the child must be conducted and logged in the appropriate electronic system(s) of record. The reasons for any detention longer than 72 hours must be logged in the appropriate electronic system(s) of record.

The following items will be given to juveniles:

- Hygiene Articles, Bedding and Clean Clothing—Juveniles will be given access to basic hygiene articles, and clean bedding. When available, juveniles will be provided clean and dry clothing. Officers/Agents may give access to these provisions to any juvenile at any time.
- Meals and Snacks—Juveniles, Pregnant, and Nursing Detainees: Juveniles and pregnant detainees will be offered a snack upon arrival and a meal at least every six hours thereafter, at regularly scheduled meal times. At least two of those meals will be hot. Juveniles and pregnant or nursing detainees must have regular access to snacks, milk, and juice.
- Age and Capabilities—Appropriate Food: Food must be appropriate for at-risk detainees' age and capabilities (such as formula and baby food).

Access to the following will be given to juveniles:

- Showers: Reasonable efforts will be made to provide showers, soap, and a clean towel to juveniles who are approaching 48 hours in detention.
- Access to Medical Care: Any physical or mental injury or illness observed by or reported to an officer/agent should be reported to a supervisor and appropriate medical care should be provided or sought. Emergency services will be called immediately in the event of a medical emergency. Officers/Agents must notify the shift supervisor of all medical emergencies as soon as possible after contacting emergency services and document the incident in the appropriate electronic system(s) of record.
- Consular and Telephone Access: All unaccompanied children must be advised of their right to consular and telephone access in a language or manner the detainee comprehends.

Hold rooms for unaccompanied children must provide the following:

- Toilets and sinks;

- Professional cleaning and sanitizing at least once per day;
- Drinking fountains or clean drinking water along with clean drinking cups;
- Adequate temperature control and ventilation; and
- Clean bedding.

Use of restraints:
The use of restraints on at-risk detainees must be in a manner that is safe, secure, humane, and professional. It is the responsibility of officers/agents to ensure that the need and level of restraints used is consistent with the operational office's policies and procedures. At no time will restraints be used in a punitive manner or in a manner that causes detainees undue pain.

5.3 Violations of Border Protection Standards

Although the above regulations were to be followed for children detained in Border Patrol Facilities, actual conditions in those facilities were far different. The Border Patrol violated its own policy and procedures. Being cold, hungry, crowded into cages, not being able to take a shower, having to live in dirty clothes and not having a place to sleep were conditions that resonate in descriptions of the lives of migrant children in detention centers on the southern border. The following are conditions of incarceration experienced by children in border patrol facilities in McAllen, Antelope Wells, and Clint, Texas; Lordsburg, New Mexico; and Yuma, Arizona.

Ursula Border Station, Texas

As described above, when Sen. Merkley visited the Ursula holding center in McAllen, Texas, he discovered that children were being held in wire-mesh linked cages approximately 30' × 30' (Merkley 2019a). The cages had uncomfortable benches, mattresses and mylar blankets. Michelle Brané, director of migrant rights at the Woman's Refugee Commission, also visited Ursula. She found that there were no toys or books in the entire facility. She saw an official scold 5-year-olds for playing together in their cage. One child clutched a photocopy of his mother's ID card. A 4-year-old girl curled up in a ball and did not talk. A teenager in the cell was taking care of her. She taught other children how to change the child's diaper. The young girl had been separated from her aunt, who was also in the center. Once an attorney began asking questions, the aunt was located. It turned out that part of the problem was that staff members assumed that the child spoke Spanish, when in fact, she spoke K'iche, an indigenous Guatemalan language (Associated Press 2018a).

Antelope Wells Border Crossing, New Mexico

Antelope Wells is a border crossing point that was being used temporarily as a holding facility for migrant families. The building here appeared to be an unheated garage with cement floors. As mentioned earlier, detainees call these cold cement holding places *las hieralas*, or ice boxes. There was no access to running water, because the water was contaminated. There were not even benches, blankets, or furniture at Antelope Wells (Miroff 2018). There were only two outdoor portable toilets used by about one hundred people (Stanton 2018).

Lordsburg Border Patrol Station, New Mexico

Rep. Joaquin Castro of Texas described the scene at the Lordsburg Border Patrol Station in New Mexico as "a mass of humanity wrapped in foil laying on the floor." Rep. Al Green of Texas stated, "The SPCA would not allow animals to be treated the way human beings are being treated at this facility" (Romo 2018). Green also witnessed "scores of children 'stacked' in holding cells and huddled in foil blankets on concrete floors, alongside toilets lacking privacy screens" (Trib Live: The Washington Post 2018).

Yuma Border Patrol Station, Arizona

A soft-sided tent facility was opened in Yuma, Arizona, at the end of June 2019. Its purpose was to alleviate overcrowded conditions at border facilities. Problems that were not directly related to overcrowding, however, were reported by children detained at Yuma. Reports to case managers for the Department of Health and Human Services cite issues brought about by staff members. Problems included children being denied showers and phone calls, and sleeping on concrete floors or outdoors with only a mylar blanket. Children also reported being hungry because they were not given dinner until 9 p.m. One child recalled sometimes falling asleep before dinner and missing the meal entirely. Advocacy attorney Laura Belous, who works for the Florence Immigrant and Refugee Rights Project, stated that children who slept on mats said that guards would kick the mats to awaken them. Other children reported that food was thrown at them as if they were animals. A sixteen-year-old boy stated that when he and other cellmates complained about the food and water, guards removed their sleeping mats and made them sleep on concrete floors (BlueMeanie 2019).

The *Convention on the Rights of the Child* (CRC) protects children's rights to expression. When children speak up and complain about the quality of the food and water they are given, and as a result are deprived of their sleeping mats and are forced to sleep on hard, cold, concrete floors, their rights of expression are violated.

Article 12, paragraph 1, of the CRC reads:

> States Parties shall assure to the child who is capable of forming his or her own views the right to express those views freely in all matters affecting the child, the views of the child being given due weight in accordance with the age and maturity of the child.

Additionally, the convention prevents negligent treatment.

Article 19, paragraph 1, reads:

> States Parties shall take all appropriate legislative, administrative, social and educational measures to protect the child from all forms of physical or mental violence, injury or abuse, neglect or negligent treatment, maltreatment or exploitation, including sexual abuse, while in the care of parent(s), legal guardian(s) or any other person who has the care of the child [UN General Assembly 1989].

Clint Border Patrol Station, Texas

In July of 2019, the *New York Times* working with the *El Paso Times* published information gained from interviews of lawyers, former detainees and staff members lawmakers and aides who visited the Clint Texas Border Patrol Facility, and parents of children who were held there. Visitors were given controlled tours. They were not allowed to bring in phones or cameras and were barred from touring some areas of the facility (Romero et al. 2019).

At Clint, filthy conditions existed. Children as young as two to three months of age were held in overcrowded conditions and were forced to sleep on the floor under mylar blankets that did not provide sufficient warmth in the extremely cold cells. Lights glared 24/7, making sleep even more difficult. Some children reported sleeping without beds or sleeping outside because of overcrowding. Others said they were hungry, so they could not sleep. Older children were held responsible for taking care of the younger children (Koerner 2019).

Children were not able to clean themselves, so their clothes reeked with stench. They were not given toothbrushes or soap. Babies and toddlers did not have diapers. Children were infected with lice, scabies, chicken pox and shingles. One child demonstrated strong suicidal ideation and had to sleep by the agents so they could monitor her as they processed other migrants. One baby's medication was confiscated and thrown away. The mother begged for the medicine, but Border Patrol agents asked her, "Who told you to come to America anyway?" (Romero et al. 2019).

5.4 Dangerously Unsanitary Conditions

In 2017, similar conditions existed in facilities in the Rio Grande Valley. Toilets were not private. Detainees were unable to shower, brush their teeth, or use soap and a towel. They slept on concrete floors with the lights on. The case went to court, and Judge Dolly Gee ruled that these circumstances violated the 1997 *Flores* settlement, which requires immigrant children to be held in "safe and sanitary" conditions and to maintain "concern for the particular vulnerability of minors" (Flynn 2019).

Despite this previous court ruling and the current revelations of the conditions in the detention facilities, in June of 2019, the Trump administration dug in and argued the language of "safe and sanitary" conditions in court. One government lawyer argued that soap and a toothbrush might not be necessary items under the rules for facilities that detained children for a short time (Dickerson 2019).

A panel of three judges in the U.S. Court of Appeals for the Ninth Circuit found it difficult to believe that government lawyers thought these facilities could be deemed "safe and sanitary" if children weren't provided with basic toiletries and suitable sleeping conditions (Flynn). They ruled on the basis of "common sense" that the children should have the hygiene items (Dickerson 2019). Furthermore, many these items are part of the government's own list of supplies that should be available to child detainees in border detention facilities.

Aaron Hull, the chief patrol agent of the El Paso, Texas, sector disagreed with the descriptions of the conditions inside Clint and other detentions facilities in the area. He argued that the sites were rigorously and humanely managed, even though several migrant children have died in federal custody.

President Trump dismissed the reports as "fake news." In a tweet on July 7, 2019, he wrote, "First of all, people should not be entering our Country illegally, only for us to then have to care for them. We should be allowed to focus on United States Citizens first" (Trump 2019).

The situation at the southern border, however, prompted Michelle Bachelet, United Nations High Commissioner of Human Rights, to issue a scathing rebuke of the conditions forced upon the migrants at the U.S. border. Bachelet was appalled by the treatment of the children. She empathized with their struggle to endure a perilous journey to escape violence and hunger. She pointed out the cruel irony that children who believe they have finally arrived in a safe place discover they are separated from their families and are locked up in places that fail to acknowledge their dignity. The following is the press release for her statement from July 8:

5. Detainment at Border Patrol Stations

GENEVA (8 July 2019)—UN High Commissioner for Human Rights Michelle Bachelet said on Monday she is appalled by the conditions in which migrants and refugees—children and adults—are being held in detention in the United States of America after crossing the southern border. She stressed that children should never be held in immigration detention or separated from their families. She noted that immigration detention is never in the best interests of a child.

The High Commissioner stated that several UN human rights bodies have found that the detention of migrant children may constitute cruel, inhuman or degrading treatment that is prohibited by international law. She said:

"As a paediatrician, but also as a mother and a former head of State, I am deeply shocked that children are forced to sleep on the floor in overcrowded facilities, without access to adequate healthcare or food, and with poor sanitation conditions.

Detaining a child even for short periods under good conditions can have a serious impact on their health and development—consider the damage being done every day by allowing this alarming situation to continue."

Noting the disturbing report by the Department of Homeland Security's Office of Inspector General on the conditions in migrant centres along the southern border, Bachelet urged the authorities to find non-custodial alternatives for migrant and refugee children—and adults.

"Any deprivation of liberty of adult migrants and refugees should be a measure of last resort," she said. If detention does take place, the High Commissioner emphasized, it should be for the shortest period of time, with due process safeguards and in conditions that fully meet all relevant international human rights standards.

"States do have the sovereign prerogative to decide on the conditions of entry and stay of foreign nationals. But clearly, border management measures must comply with the State's human rights obligations and should not be based on narrow policies aimed only at detecting, detaining and expeditiously deporting irregular migrants," she added.

In most of these cases, the migrants and refugees have embarked on perilous journeys with their children in search of protection and dignity and away from violence and hunger. When they finally believe they have arrived in safety, they may find themselves separated from their loved ones and locked in undignified conditions. This should never happen anywhere [Bachelet 2019].

The UN Human Rights Office's presences in Mexico and Central America have documented numerous human rights violations and abuses against migrants and refugees in transit, including the excessive use of force, arbitrary deprivation of liberty, family separation, denial of access to services, refoulement, and arbitrary expulsions.

The High Commissioner recognized the complexity of the situation and the challenges faced by states of origin, transit and destination. She called on them to work together to address the root causes compelling migrants to leave their homes by implementing crosscutting policies that take into account the complex drivers of migration. These include insecurity, sexual and gender-based violence, discrimination, poverty, the adverse impacts of climate change and environmental degradation.

Bachelet also paid tribute to individuals and civil society organizations that have been providing migrants with the most basic of rights, such as the rights to water, food, health, adequate shelter and other such assistance. She added, "The provision of lifesaving assistance is a human rights imperative that must be respected at all times and for all people in need—it is inconceivable that those who seek to provide such support would risk facing criminal charges" (Bachelet 2019).

5.5 From Trauma to Torture

In *Report of the Special Rapporteur on Torture and Other Cruel, Inhuman, or Degrading Treatment or Punishment,* Juan Mendez (2015) wrote that immigration detention frequently subjected children to "overcrowding, inappropriate food, insufficient access to drinking water, unsanitary conditions, lack of adequate medical attention, and irregular access to washing and sanitary facilities and to hygiene products, lack of appropriate accommodation and other basic necessities."

The *United Nations Global Study on Children Deprived of Liberty of 2019,* authored by Manfred Nowak, also cautions, "Immigration detention of children is not only a children's right's violation in itself but it also frequently causes other human rights violations" (Nowak 2019).

The UN complete definition of torture found in Article 1 of *UN Convention against Torture* (UN General Assembly 1984) reads:

> For the purposes of this Convention, the term "torture" means any act by which severe pain or suffering, whether physical or mental, is intentionally inflicted on a person for such purposes as obtaining from him or a third person information or a confession, punishing him for an act he or a third person has committed or is suspected of having committed, or intimidating or coercing him or a third person, or for any reason based on discrimination of any kind, when such pain or suffering is inflicted by or at the instigation of or with the consent or acquiescence of a public official or other person acting in an official capacity. It does not include pain or suffering arising only from, inherent in or incidental to lawful sanctions.

Psychologists and law professors attest that the treatment of migrant children in detention facilities at the border is torture.

Sondra Crosby and George Annas are professors of health law, ethics, and human rights at Boston University. Crosby has evaluated torture victims from throughout the world, including detainees in U.S. detention at Guantanamo Bay. Both she and Annas acknowledge that torture can have lifelong psychological and physical effects. They state, "It is not an exaggeration to say that the current treatment of children in these detention centers is torture" (Crosby and Annas 2019).[1] Crosby and Annas describe the conditions in which migrant children who are separated from their parents exist as cramped, dirty, and squalid. They note that the children sleep under bright lights on cold concrete floors; eat poor-quality food; have no access to soap, showers, or toothbrushes; and only limited access to bathrooms. They compare these conditions to those of the secret CIA facilities, "black sites." Like the child detention facilities, the black sites had undergone formal review and approval of the U.S. Department of Justice (Crosby and Annas 2019).

Jaana Juvonen, professor of developmental psychology, and Jennifer Silvers, assistant professor of developmental neuroscience at UCLA, state that parenting is a crucial ingredient for the survival of our species. Children's brains have evolved to need parenting in the same way that their bodies require food and rest. The need for caretaking is not flexible—research findings clearly support the necessity of keeping families together. They state that evidence from neuroscience suggests that the policy of separating children from their families is not just inhumane, it is also, "by definition, torture." They point out that U.S. federal law adopts the UN definition of torture which includes the words, "any act by which severe pain or suffering, whether physical or mental; is intentionally inflicted on a person for such purposes as ... punishing him or her he or she or a third person ... has committed or is suspected of having committed." They conclude that based on science, the practice of separating children from their caregivers inflicts suffering on children (Juvonen and Silvers 2018).[2]

Physicians for Human Rights studied affidavits from 26 asylum seekers, including nine children. All of the families were separated. The physicians agreed that Trump's family separation policies fit the UN definition of torture. Months after being separated, children and adults suffered from insomnia, nightmares, flashbacks, anxiety. Their ability to carry out daily activities was impaired. The ways in which children were taken from their families were even more horrifying than the separations—while their parents slept, or when their parents were seeing a doctor, or in court (Braine 2020).

In addition to the definition of torture found in the *Convention Against Torture* (UN General Assembly 1984), Article 16 of the convention prohibits inhuman or degrading acts that are not at the level of torture defined by Article 1.

Article 16, paragraph 1, reads:

> Each State Party shall undertake to prevent in any territory under its jurisdiction other acts of cruel, inhuman or degrading treatment or punishment which do not amount to torture as defined in article 1, when such acts are committed by or at the instigation of or with the consent or acquiescence of a public official or other person acting in an official capacity [UN General Assembly 1989].

Article 22 of the *Convention on the Rights of the Child* ensures protection and humanitarian assistance for children who are seeking refugee status whether they are unaccompanied or accompanied by their parents or by another person.

Article 22, paragraph 1, reads:

> States Parties shall take appropriate measures to ensure that a child who is seeking refugee status or who is considered a refugee in accordance with applicable international or domestic law and procedures shall, whether unaccompanied or accompanied by his or her parents or by any other person, receive appropriate protection and humanitarian assistance in the enjoyment of applicable rights set forth in the present Convention and in other international human rights or humanitarian instruments to which the said States are Parties.

Article 37 (a) of the *Convention on the Rights of the Child* specifically states that no child shall be tortured. Section (b) protects children from deprivation of their liberty. Section (c) requires that children shall be treated with humanity, respect, and dignity.

Article 37 reads:

> (a) No child shall be subjected to torture or other cruel, inhuman or degrading treatment or punishment. Neither capital punishment nor life imprisonment without possibility of release shall be imposed for offences committed by persons below eighteen years of age;
>
> (b) No child shall be deprived of his or her liberty unlawfully or arbitrarily. The arrest, detention or imprisonment of a child shall be in conformity with the law and shall be used only as a measure of last resort and for the shortest appropriate period of time;
>
> (c) Every child deprived of liberty shall be treated with humanity and respect for the inherent dignity of the human person, and in a manner, which takes into account the needs of persons of his or her age. In particular, every child deprived of liberty shall be separated from adults unless it is considered in the child's best interest not to do so and shall have the right to maintain contact with his or her family through correspondence and visits, save in exceptional circumstances [UN General Assembly, 1989].

The *International Convention on the Elimination All Forms of Racial Discrimination* (UN General Assembly 1966a), Article 7, reads:

> No one shall be subjected to torture or to cruel, inhuman or degrading treatment or punishment.

Article 10, paragraph 1, reads:

> All persons deprived of their liberty shall be treated with humanity and with respect for the inherent dignity of the human person.

6

Detainment in Office of Refugee Resettlement Facilities

6.1 Facility Regulations

The problem was not that U.S. agencies did not have regulations for the care of detained children. There were reams of regulations. The problem was that the agencies chose not to comply with their own regulations.

Once unaccompanied children are transferred from the Department of Homeland Security (DHS) to the Department of Health and Human Services (HHS), the Office of Refugee Resettlement (ORR) takes over responsibility for children. ORR determines and implements placement decisions and reunifies the children with qualified sponsors and family members who are capable of providing for the child's physical and mental well-being. They provide home assessments for certain categories of unaccompanied alien children at risk and conduct follow-up services for certain categories of children.

Additionally, this office oversees infrastructure and personnel of their funded care provider facilities and supervises on-site monitoring visits for these facilities to ensure compliance with Division of Unaccompanied Children Services (DUCS) national care standards. Duties of ORR include analyzing and reporting statistical information on the child. They also deliver training to federal, state, and local officials who have substantive contact with the children. ORR works with the Department of Justice Executive Office for Immigration Review Cooperation and with the Department of Justice's Executive Office for Immigration Review to provide legal orientation presentations to sponsors of unaccompanied children. Finally, they ensure, to the greatest extent possible, that all unaccompanied children in custody have legal representation or counsel (Resettlement Division of Unaccompanied Children's Services).

The majority of unaccompanied children are cared for through a network of ORR-funded care facilities. Care providers are licensed by their state and must meet ORR requirements to ensure a high level of care. The requirements are extensive and detailed. The ORR guide, "Children entering the United States unaccompanied," includes six sections that address children's needs, including "Placement in ORR care provider facilities"; "Safe and timely release from ORR care"; "Services"; "Preventing, detecting, and responding to sexual abuse and harassment"; "Program management"; and "Resources and services available after release from ORR care" (Office of Refugee Resettlement).

ORR provides three kinds of care:

> Shelter Care—A shelter is a residential care provider facility in which all of the programmatic components are administered on-site, in the least restrictive environment.
>
> Staff Secure Care—A staff secure facility has a higher staff-to-unaccompanied-alien-child ratio, for children who may require close supervision but do not need placement in a secure facility. This ratio is higher than that of a shelter that controls disruptive behavior and prevents escape. Services are tailored to address an unaccompanied alien child's individual needs and to manage the behaviors that necessitated the child's placement in this more restrictive setting. The staff secure atmosphere reflects a more sheltering, home-like setting than secure detention does. Unlike many secure care providers, a staff secure care provider is not equipped internally with multiple locked pods or cell units.
>
> Secure Care—A secure provider is a facility with a physically secure structure and staff able to control violent behavior. ORR uses a secure facility as the most restrictive placement option for an unaccompanied alien child who poses a danger to self or others or has been charged with having committed a criminal offense. A secure facility may be a licensed juvenile detention center or a highly structured therapeutic facility [Office of Refugee Resettlement 2019].

Office of Refugee Resettlement facilities operate under cooperative agreements and contracts. Like CBP sites, they are directed to provide unaccompanied children with nutritional services, medical examinations, and phone calls to parents. Additionally, ORR is directed to provide children with classroom education, health care, socialization and recreation, vocational training, mental health services, family reunification, access to legal services, and case management. Care provider facilities' case management teams use effective screening tools to assess children for mental health and victim trafficking issues.

The following descriptions are derived from directives for services that the policy specifies for unaccompanied children. They are drawn from *Children Entering the United States Unaccompanied*, sections 3, 4, and 5 (Office of Refugee Resettlement 2015).

The number of regulations alone speaks to the level of care expected to be given to children, although in many cases the care fell far short of the standards. These sections describe services related to specific concerns raised in this book. I have included much of the original language in the guide but have made some modifications due to the length of the document.

Safety Planning from Section 3.3.4

Care providers are required to develop a written safety plan that includes policies and procedures for both the children in their care and staff members. Emergency situations must be addressed. These situations include evacuations, medical or mental health emergencies, disease outbreaks, and incidents where children leave the premises without permission. Care providers and foster programs must meet the safety requirements maintained by state and/or local licensing entities. Fire code, local zoning, and building code regulations are specifically cited.

Care provider facilities must meet minimum safety and security related requirements for controlled entry and exit, video monitoring in common living areas, a communication and alarm system for all areas of the residential structure, and video monitoring and the ability to permanently download footage of the exterior of the building and surrounding premises. They must also have a system for counting residents, a written policy that provides that staff regulate resident movement, and a daily log of arrivals, departures, and room assignments.

Academic Educational Services, from Section 3.3.5

Several educational services must be provided for these children. An educational assessment must be administered within 72 hours of admission to determine the child's academic level and needs. Services are then based on the child's academic, literacy, and linguistic levels. Children must receive at least six hours of structured education, Monday through Friday throughout the year. Basic academic subjects, science, social studies, math, reading, writing physical education, and ESL—if applicable—must be taught.

Local education standards are adapted or modified to develop curricula and assessments based on the average amounts of time unaccompanied children stay at the care provider facility. Remedial education and after school tutoring are provided as necessary. Independent studies, special projects, pre–GED classes, and college prep tutorials must be provided as needed for a child's learning advancement. The project officer must approve all academic breaks. Breaks that exceed two weeks are not approved.

Academic reports and notes of a child's progress are updated and included in the child's case file. These documents are sent to another case provider if the child is transferred or they are released to the child upon discharge.

Vocational educational services are also provided. They are described in section 3.3.6 of the document (Office of Refugee Resettlement 2015).

It is important to note that in some facilities, these regulations are being followed, and children are getting decent care (D. Post, personal communication, October 20, 2019).

Services Related to Culture, Language and Religious Observation, from Section 3.3.7

Children entering ORR custody come from a variety of cultures, practices, languages, and beliefs. Care providers must have cultural awareness systems in place to support the cultural identity and needs of each child. They supply this support by allowing unaccompanied children regular contact with safe family members or other support systems by means of telephone calls, letters and visits. They also support children by addressing them by their given names. Providers include cultural practices in daily activities such meals, clothing choices, and hygiene routines. Culture-specific events and holidays are celebrated, and academic education addresses various cultures within the classroom setting.

Recreation and Leisure Time Services, from Section 3.3.8

Care providers must design recreational and leisure-time plans for the children in their care. Weather permitting, these activities are held outdoors. These plans include one hour per day of large muscle activity, and an additional hour per day of other structured leisure time activities—excluding watching television. These activities are separate from the physical education requirement of the educational plan. Sites that do not have sufficient recreation areas are required to take children off-site for this leisure time. Children can go to parks, community recreation areas, or other locations. Providers must provide higher staff-to-child ratios in these areas. Television programs, movies, and video games must be screened for appropriateness before being viewed by unaccompanied children.

6. Detainment in Office of Refugee Resettlement Facilities 91

Clothing and Personal Grooming, from Section 3.3.11

Care providers must provide children with new clothing and personal hygiene items, as well as items for grooming, including hair care. Children are allowed to wear their own clothing if the clothing they bring to the facility is appropriate. Footwear cannot be used as a means to control behavior.

Head scarves may be worn for religious reasons, and the shaving of facial hair may not be required if it violates a youth's cultural norms, religious beliefs, or personal preferences.

Care providers must have standard policies and procedures about gang-related symbols and tattoos. These symbols, tattoos, accessories, or paraphernalia on a child must be either covered or confiscated.

Behavior Management, from Section 3.3.13

Behavior management strategies used by the care provider must meet child welfare best-practice standards. The providers are given written policies and procedures for behavior management that include rules, rewards, and consequences for behavior.

Medical Services, from Section 3.4

ORR provides the following medical services to unaccompanied children:

- Routine medical and dental care
- Emergency health services
- Medical examinations
- Immunizations
- Prescribed medicines and special diets
- Mental health interventions
- Procuring and maintaining medical records
- Emergency health services

Health Care Eligibility and General Standards, from Section 3.4.1

Health care extends from the first day a child is placed in the physical care of ORR to the day the child leaves custody. ORR mandates that licensed medical practitioners acting within their scope of practice provide or supervise all medical evaluation and management. A licensed mental health professional must deliver mental health services. Hospitals providing services to unaccompanied children must be accredited by the Joint Commission or other nationally recognized accrediting body.

Initial Medical Examination, from Section 3.4.2

Each child must have a medical examination within 48 business hours of admission. This exam assesses general health and includes the administration of complete immunizations according to U.S. standards. It also identifies health conditions that warrant further attention and contagious diseases.

Management of Communicable Diseases, from Section 3.4.6

Whenever unaccompanied children are in a child provider facility, providers must monitor them for symptoms of communicable diseases and act accordingly to protect others against possible infection. Other children held in custody and staff members could be susceptible to these illnesses. Facilities must be aware of the list of notifiable diseases in their state, and they must have policies and procedures to identify, report, and control these diseases in accordance with state and local laws and regulations. Each facility is mandated to inform ORR of each suspected or confirmed case and follow ORR medical guidelines on managing cases and contacts. ORR has protocols for diseases for public health concern that have been diagnosed in unaccompanied alien children, including varicella and tuberculosis. The care provider is responsible for training all staff members about its current communicable disease plan.

Trafficking and Services for Victims, from Section 3.3.3

All unaccompanied children must be screened by their care providers to determine if they are potential victims of a severe form of trafficking. An assessment tool is given to providers so they can identify victims of trafficking. There are two different kinds of trafficking recognized by law: labor trafficking and sex trafficking. Labor trafficking pertains to a child who has been recruited, harbored, transported, provided, or obtained through the use of force, fraud, or coercion for the purpose of involuntary servitude, peonage, debt bondage, or slavery. Sex trafficking means the child was recruited, harbored, transported, provided, obtained, patronized, or solicited for a commercial sex act, which is any sex act for which anything of value is given to or received by any person. A child is not a trafficking victim unless there is forced labor or commercial sex.

6. Detainment in Office of Refugee Resettlement Facilities

If a child is suspected to be a trafficking victim, ORR has procedures in place for referral for further assessment. Children identified as severe trafficking victims are eligible for services and benefits, regardless of immigration status.

Care providers who have child victims of trafficking in their care must take additional steps to ensure their safety. These steps include carefully verifying all family and sponsor relationships in order to screen for traffickers; adjusting the child's in-care safety plan as appropriate to allow only supervised phone calls or to revise the child's list of phone/visitation contacts; training staff about how victims are subject to many methods of coercion and control, including strong bonds with an abuser, and not understanding the full reality of abuse; helping unaccompanied children to identify healthy relationships and to understand recruitment and deception tactics used by traffickers; implementing additional safety measures, such as increased staff supervision or in-depth, trauma-informed interviews; creating a safety plan that includes a list of safe persons, phone numbers, places to contact, and a list of unsafe persons and places; and engaging individual children in developing a plan of action to take if they feel threatened or unsafe.

Guiding Principles for the Care of Unaccompanied Children Who Are LGBTQI, from Section 3.5

All children and youth in ORR care are entitled to human rights protections and freedom from discrimination and abuse. It is the responsibility of care providers to make certain that children who are lesbian, gay, bisexual, transgender, or intersex (LGBTQI) are treated fairly and served during their time in ORR custody.

These children must be treated with the same dignity and respect as other unaccompanied children. They must receive recognition of sexual orientation and/or gender identity. LGBTQI children cannot be discriminated against or harassed based on actual or perceived sexual orientation or gender identity. Their care must take place in an inclusive and respectful environment.

Care providers must maintain the privacy and confidentiality of information concerning a child's sexual orientation and gender identity. Correct names and pronouns in accordance with the youth's gender identity must be used. Housing of LGBTQI youth is determined by an assessment of the youth's gender identity and housing preference, health and safety needs, and state and local licensing standards. Care providers must offer an individualized assessment to determine whether additional or alternate restroom accommodations are needed. LGBTQI youth are allowed to dress and express themselves according to their gender identity. If a pat-down is necessary, the youth chooses the gender of the staff member who will conduct the pat-down.

Additional standards that reinforce the principles described above, and more details about protections of LGBTQI are found in the full text of this document.

6.2 Regulations Regarding Sexual Abuse and Harassment

In addition to the services provided by ORR, section 4 of "Children entering the United States unaccompanied" explains definitions, policies and requirements of providers that focus on preventing, detecting, and responding to sexual abuse and harassment. Selected information from that section is presented here.

Sexual Abuse, Adapted from Section 4.1.1

The first section of this document defines explicit sexual abuse acts of a minor by another minor and of a minor by an adult. Acts include child pornography, touching through clothing, direct touching, voyeurism, and rape.

Sexual Harassment, Adapted from Section 4.1.3

The acts are differentiated depending upon whether they are committed by a minor or an adult. The acts include verbal comments, gestures, phone calls, emails, texts, social media messages, pictures, or other electronic communication of a sexual nature. The messages are directed to a child by a staff member, grantee, contractor, or volunteer. Any demeaning messages referring to gender, sexually suggestive or derogatory comments about body or clothing, or obscene language or gestures are included in this definition.

Zero Tolerance, from Section 4.2

ORR states that they have a zero-tolerance policy for all forms of sexual abuse, sexual harassment, and inappropriate sexual behavior at all care provider facilities. ORR also claims to make every effort to prevent, detect, and respond to such conduct.

Prevention of Sexual Abuse Coordinator and Compliance Manager, from 4.3.1

Each facility must employ a "Prevention of Sexual Abuse Compliance Manager" ("PSA Compliance Manager") who is familiar with the Interim Final Rule and related policies. This manager oversees all of the compliance efforts of the program and is the contact person for ORR's PSA coordinator.

Applicant Screening, from 4.3.2

ORR views applicant screening as critical to identifying qualified staff. They state that integrating sexual abuse prevention into the applicant screening and selection process is critical to ensuring the safety of children and youth. When hiring staff, coordinators, or volunteers, facilities must consider sexual abuse prevention when making hiring decisions.

Care providers must take several steps to demonstrate their commitment to preventing sexual abuse. The intention of these steps is to deter some individuals who are at risk of abusing children and youth from applying for employment. The steps include the following:

- Informing each applicant in writing of policies to prevent and report sexual abuse and harassment
- Requiring an applicant to sign a document indicating that they have read and understood the policies
- Sharing a copy of the code of conduct (see below) with each applicant
- Maintaining a copy of these documents in the applicant's personnel file

Employee Background Investigations, from 4.3.3

Background investigations are another critical component of the screening process. Background checks provide additional information about the suitability of an applicant to work with children and youth in ORR care.

ORR has minimum standards for the scope of background checks because state licensing requirements vary from state to state. Before being hired, all staff, contractors, and volunteers must complete background investigations that meet ORR's minimum standards and state licensing requirements.

If state licensing requirements do not require a national criminal history fingerprint check, the care provider facility must complete the fingerprint check using a public or private vendor.

Individuals Who Must Complete Background Checks

If state law or licensing regulations prohibit a care provider facility from conducting background checks before hiring an applicant, the care provider facility must notify ORR's Prevention of Sexual Abuse Coordinator and provide documentation of the state law or licensing requirement.

The following individuals must complete background checks before they are hired and gain access to children or youth:

- Executive and program management staff as well as administrative staff with direct access to children or youth.
- All temporary, part-time, or full-time employees and contractors with direct access to children or youth.
- Anyone who may have unsupervised, direct access to children or youth, including volunteers.
- Immigration advocates and legal service providers under policies established in an agreement between the care provider facility and service provider. ORR must approve the organization's background check policies and procedures before granting it access to any child or youth. Care provider facilities may have additional requirements according to their state licensing requirements.
- Foster parents (transitional and long-term) and all foster parent household members aged 18 and over.

Attorneys of record do not need to complete a background check, but care provider facilities must have policies to confirm the identity and the status of attorneys of record before providing them access to children.

Medical and mental health professionals (e.g., doctors, nurses, nurse practitioners, psychiatrists, licensed clinicians) who provide services on site but are not employed by the care provider facility do not need to complete background investigations. Such professionals must, however, have up-to-date applicable state licensure requirements.

Components of Background Investigations

The scope of background investigations must comply with state licensing requirements and ORR minimum standards, which include:

- An FBI fingerprint check of national and state criminal history repositories.
- A child protective services check with the staff's state(s) of U.S. residence for the last five years.
- Background investigation updates at a minimum of every five years of the staff/contractor/volunteer's start date or last background

6. Detainment in Office of Refugee Resettlement Facilities

investigation update. Care provider facilities may require the updated background investigation more frequently as necessary.

If they are not able to complete all the required background investigation components, care provider facilities must notify ORR's Prevention of Sexual Abuse Coordinator in writing. ORR will work with the care provider facility to ensure that background checks are completed.

Staff Code of Conduct, from Section 4.3.5

The Office of Refugee Regulations is committed to providing a safe environment to all unaccompanied in its care, including protecting them from sexual abuse and sexual harassment. In order to ensure the safety of children, who are under the age of 18, care provider facility staff, contractors, and volunteers must comply with the following code of conduct. This code of conduct does not apply to foster parents, who are subject to state licensing requirements.

1. Staff will not engage in any form of sexual abuse or sexual harassment, as defined at section 4.1 of ORR's UAC policy guide.
2. Staff will not verbally or physically abuse any unaccompanied alien child.
3. Staff will not engage in sexual contact with anyone while on duty or while acting in the official capacity of their position.
4. Staff will not exchange letters, gifts, pictures, phone numbers, email addresses, or social media information with any UAC in ORR care or within three years of the child's discharge. Requests for exceptions must be submitted in writing to and approved by care provider management.
5. Staff may not have contact with any unaccompanied alien children outside of the care provider facility beyond that necessary to carry out job duties while the child is in ORR care or within three years of the child's discharge. Requests for exceptions must be submitted in writing to and approved by care provider management.
6. Staff must confine their relationships with UAC families and sponsors to those activities which fall within the scope of the staff's job duties. Requests for exceptions must be submitted in writing to and approved by care provider management.
7. Staff may not engage in a romantic or sexual relationship with a UAC while the child is in ORR care or within three years of the child's discharge.
8. Staff may not live with a UAC within three years of the child's discharge.

9. Staff must report knowledge, suspicion, or information about sexual abuse, sexual harassment, or inappropriate sexual behavior according to mandatory reporting laws, federal laws and regulations, and ORR policies and procedures.

10. Staff with knowledge or information of a staff member violating this code of conduct must report this knowledge or information to their supervisor.

11. Staff members have a continuing affirmative duty to disclose any misconduct that occurs on or off duty.

Care provider facilities must immediately terminate any staff member who violates this code of conduct. Care provider facilities must suspend any staff member suspected of violating this code of conduct, pending investigation.

Staff Training, from Section 4.3.6

Care provider facilities must provide training to all staff, contractors, and volunteers to ensure that employees understand their obligations under ORR policies. Care provider facilities must tailor trainings to the unique needs, attributes, and gender of the unaccompanied alien children in care at the individual care provider facility.

Care Provider Reporting Requirements, from Section 4.10.2

Care provider staff, volunteers, and contractors must immediately report the following to all appropriate investigating entities as described below:

- Any knowledge, suspicion, or information regarding an incident of sexual abuse, sexual harassment, or inappropriate sexual behavior;
- Retaliation against children, staff, volunteers, or contractors for reporting an incident of sexual abuse, sexual harassment, or inappropriate sexual behavior; and
- Any staff neglect or violation of responsibilities that may have contributed to an incident or retaliation.

Care providers must have written reporting policies and procedures that are approved by ORR.

6.3 *Reporting to Authorities*

In accordance with mandatory reporting laws, state licensing requirements, federal laws and regulations, and ORR policies and procedures, the above must be reported immediately but no later than 4 hours after learning of the allegation to at least one of the following:

- The state licensing agency;
- Child Protective Services (CPS); and/or
- Local law enforcement.

Local Law Enforcement

If the state licensing or CPS agency directly reports an allegation to local law enforcement, the care provider does not need to make a separate report but must confirm and document when such a report has been made. Care providers must report allegations of sexual abuse involving an adult to local law enforcement, regardless of whether state licensing or CPS reports the allegation. It is important to note that even when reports are made, however, cases are not always investigated (D. Post, personal communication, October 20, 2019).

In Arizona, Sheriff Joe Arpaio was sued for inadequately investigating nearly 1,000 child abuse cases. Arpaio had proclaimed that he was "America's toughest sheriff." The abuse took place over a three-year period from 2004 to 2007. The state paid $3.5 million to settle 400 of the sexual abuse cases (*The Guardian* [U.S. edition] 2015). Mismanagement and incompetence in some CPS departments can also lead to staggering backlogs that paralyze investigation systems (D. Post, personal communication, October 20, 2019).

Reporting Sexual Assault Incidents

Care providers must report immediately (no later than 4 hours after learning of the allegation) any knowledge, suspicion, or information regarding an incident of sexual abuse, sexual harassment, or inappropriate sexual behavior. The care provider must report any retaliation or staff neglect or violation of responsibilities that occurs in ORR care via the Sexual Abuse Significant Incident Report (SA/SIR). Allegations of prior sexual abuse and harassment that occurred in the minor's home country, during the journey to the U.S., in the U.S., in DHS custody, or in any other context must be reported to ORR via the Significant Incident Report (SIR) according to ORR's policies and procedures.

Reporting to the Federal Bureau of Investigation (FBI)

Care providers must report immediately (no later than 4 hours after learning of an allegation of sexual abuse as defined in 34 U.S.C. § 20341) to the FBI. Care providers must submit a completed SA/SIR to the FBI, Health and Human Services' Office of the Inspector General (OIG), and to ORR's SA/SIR mailbox. The SA/SIR must include, at a minimum, the following information:

- A summary of the alleged abuse;
- Date of the alleged incident;
- Date of the report;
- Names and contact information for potential witnesses;
- Names and contact information for appropriate contacts at the care provider; and
- Relevant contact information for all other parties receiving the report, including but not limited to:
  ◊ CPS;
  ◊ The state licensing agency; and
  ◊ Local law enforcement.

For any incident that is reported to the FBI, all related SA/SIR addendums should be reported to OIG and to ORR's SA/SIR mailbox. SA/SIR addendums should not be reported to the FBI.

Reporting an Allegation of Sexual Abuse or Harassment That Occurred at Another Care Provider

Upon receiving an allegation that a child was sexually abused or harassed at another care provider, the care provider that received the allegation must report the allegation to CPS and state licensing and to ORR according to the reporting procedures described above.

6.4 Media Visits and Monitoring

Responding to Inquiries from the Media, from Section 5.1.4

ORR polices take into consideration the best interests of the child when responding to requests from the media. They are committed to both transparency and accountability while protecting the privacy and safety of children in their care. ORR allows care provider organizations to respond to any and all inquiries about their own organization. Media requests that are beyond the scope of care providers are addressed by ORR in conjunction with the Administration for Children and Families (ACF).

ORR Policies on Requests to Visit ORR Care Provider Facilities, from 5.2

Interested parties, including advocacy groups, faith-based organizations, researchers, government officials, and other relevant stakeholders who wish to visit a care provider facility must request a visit through ORR. Criteria that evaluate the request for the visit include the validity of the purpose of the visit, protection of the privacy and well-being of children during the visit, sufficient staff to conduct the visit and maintain protection of the children, and sufficient notice of the request (two weeks prior to the visit).

ORR Monitoring Activities, from 5.5.1

ORR monitoring is ongoing and multi-layered. Components assessed include program design, management, services, safety and security, child protection, case management, personnel management, stakeholder relations, and fiscal management. Monitoring activities include desk monitoring, routine site visits, site visits in response to Project Officer (PO) or other requests, monitoring visits (comprehensive week-long visits that take place at least every two years).

Follow-Up and Corrective Actions, from 5.5.2

If a care provider is found to be out of compliance with ORR polices or procedures based on monitoring activities, ORR will communicate the concerns in writing to the program director or appropriate person through a written monitoring or site visit report, with corrective actions and child welfare best practice recommendations. The need for a corrective action occurs when the care provider is in noncompliance with explicit ORR policy and procedures.

6.5 Complaints of Sexual Abuse

Despite extensive regulations, reports of sexual abuse surfaced from border facilities. On February 26, 2019, Rep. Ted Deutch (FL-22) released documents to Axios showing 4,556 complaints to the ORR and 1,303 complaints to the Department of Justice from children who said they were assaulted within the past four years while they were detained by the Office of Refugee Resettlement (Owens, Kight, and Stevens 2019).

Deutsch stated, "These documents detail an environment of systemic sexual abuse by staff on unaccompanied children." He added, "These documents tell us that there is a problem with adults, employees of HHS, abusing children." Cmd. Jonathan White, who oversaw the care of migrant children in ORR custody, responded angrily and stated that the accused adults were not members of the HHS staff (A. Gomez 2019).

In discussing abuse at child detention centers for ProPublica, an investigative nonprofit, Lisa Fortuna, director of child and adolescent psychiatry at Boston Medical Center, says, "If you're a predator, it's a gold mine." She adds, "You have full access, and you have kids that have already had this history of being victimized" (Grabell and Sanders 2018).

Nayeli Chavez-Duenas is a clinical psychologist who wrote shelter guidelines for the National Latina/o Psychological Association. She explains that many migrant children have undergone trauma in their home countries. They have also endured long, arduous journeys, and they are seeking stability. They also do not understand American laws. The combination of these factors makes them highly vulnerable to predators. She states in ProPublica:

> When a perpetrator is trying to pick up a victim they're picking somebody that they think is less likely to report the abuse.... Children and youth that are coming from outside of the country, that have no legal status here, that don't speak English, that don't have access to lawyers or people who can protect them—they already may think that they're not going to be believed [Grabell and Sanders 2018].

Chavez-Duenas also makes the point that the children may also not speak up for fear of hurting their immigration case.

Reports filed by government case managers working with children from the Border Patrol detention center in Yuma, Arizona, revealed that incidents there were not the result of overcrowding, but rather were caused by the actions of the agents. A 15-year-old girl from Honduras reported that an officer groped her during a pat-down in front of other children. He put his hands under her bra and made her pull down her underwear. He laughed and talked with other officers in English during the entire incident. His actions made her feel embarrassed (Soboroff and Ainsley 2019). As of the end of 2019, no information was available about what happened in this case (D. Post, personal communication, December 31, 2019).

Incidents such as this affect the behavior of the victims for a long time, and they influence other women. Deirdre Sparling, a member of Refugee Aid who has opened her Arizona home to migrants needing shelter, explains that migrant women sleep fully clothed. She attributed this practice to the migrants' need to move on constantly, sometimes during the middle of the night. They have to be ready to leave quickly if necessary. Woman and girls also sleep fully clothed of as a means of protecting themselves from sexual attacks. It is not only women who've already been assaulted who do this, all but all female migrants. Even if they have not been sexually assaulted or molested themselves, they have heard the stories from other women. Wearing clothing during the night made it a little more difficult for these attacks to be committed (D. Sparling, personal communication, March 28, 2020).

Women and girls are not the only ones assaulted. According to Maria Cancian, deputy assistant secretary for policy as HHS's Administration for Children and Families from 2015 to 2016, when staff members who have minimal experience are hired quickly, the challenges to maintaining standards can escalate (Grabell and Sanders 2018). As noted earlier, in the hastily constructed tent city in Tornillo, Texas, waived required background checks for staff members. Such action, along with separating children from the protection of their parents, can leave children vulnerable to sexual assault and other harm caused by both adults and minors.

At Southwest Key's Kokopelli facility in Arizona, fingerprints were required for background checks, but Levian Pacheco, hired on May 23, 2016, did not submit his for six months. He passed the background check but was accused of groping three boys. Two of the alleged assaults happened in children's rooms. One occurred in a facility bathroom. Pacheco was arrested in September of 2017. His case was forwarded to the Department of Health and Human Services. Pacheo, who is HIV positive, was then accused of sexually assaulting eight boys from the ages of 15 to 17. Fernando Magaz, another Southwest Key worker, was arrested and fired on charges of kissing and fondling a 14-year-old girl in June 2018 (Haag 2018).

Article 34 of the *Convention on the Rights of the Child* (UN General Assembly 1989) protects children from sexual assault. Article 34 reads in part:

> States Parties undertake to protect the child from all forms of sexual exploitation and sexual abuse. For these purposes, States Parties shall in particular take all appropriate national, bilateral and multilateral measures to prevent:
> (a) The inducement or coercion of a child to engage in any unlawful sexual activity [UN General Assembly, 1989].

6.6 Forced Drugs

In addition to the charges of sexual abuse, there were claims from detained migrant children whose behavior was controlled by antipsychotic drugs. The children were told they were vitamins. In June 2018, Common Dreams reported that a lawsuit revealed that children held at the Shiloh Treatment Center in Manvel, Texas, were forcibly injected with drugs that made them feel "dizzy, lethargic, and even incapacitated." The drugs, given without parental consent, included Clonazepam, Divalproex, Benztropine, and Duloxetine, used to treat seizures, Parkinson's disease, and depression (Conley 2018).

The following month, Judge Dolly Gee found the Shiloh Treatment Center in violation of the *Flores* settlement. She ordered that all of the children involved in the lawsuit be released from Shiloh. The only exceptions were children who posed a risk to themselves or others as determined by a licensed psychologist or psychiatrist (Johnson 2018).

Article 33 of the *Convention on the Rights of the Child* protects children from illicit use of narcotic drugs. Article 33 reads:

> States Parties shall take all appropriate measures, including legislative, administrative, social and educational measures, to protect children from the illicit use of narcotic drugs and psychotropic substances as defined in the relevant international treaties, and to prevent the use of children in the illicit production and trafficking of such substances [UN General Assembly 1989].

7

A Horrifying Reality

7.1 Prisons for Children

Despite the promise of the regulations and intended safeguards, life for children in CBP and ORR detention facilities did not go well. In Arizona, a proposed law would have required all child detention facilities, including federal facilities, to be licensed by the state. The law did not pass. When licensure is not required, highly irregular situations can develop. For example, in Arizona, child-care contractors were alleged to have transported children to an empty office building, where they stayed for two days. The children slept on the floor and ate pizzas that were delivered to them (D. Post, personal communication, October 20, 2019).

Because of the exemption described earlier by Juan Sanchez from Southwest Key, two of the worst facilities, Tornillo in Texas and Homestead in Florida, were not subject to state or local licensing standards. The loophole was created because the facilities were proposed as temporary emergency shelters that were located on federal property (Levinson 2018).

Tornillo, Texas—Tent City

Freelance journalist Alice Driver visited the border for *National Geographic* and the *New York Times*. Driver went to Tornillo in June of 2018. She hoped to visit the detention camp there, but because she is a member of the press, she was not allowed to tour the camp.

Tornillo was made up of tents, or what the government called "soft-sided structures." There was little outside scrutiny of the camp. Visitors were seldom allowed, and workers had to sign nondisclosure agreements (Burke and Mendoza 2018). The government issued photographs of the interiors of the tents, crammed with bunk beds or long plastic tables and dozens of metal chairs. Rep. Will Hurd, R.–Texas, toured Tornillo and reported that the facilities were "safe and well run" (Lach 2018).

That general statement, however, did not provide any details about what was actually taking place in the camps. Those details needed to be uncovered.

In an October 2018 article, Driver characterized the detention of 13,000 migrant children as "America's horrifying reality." She described the plight of thousands of children who had already "fled unimaginable violence" and "crossed entire countries alone" to discover that their right to request asylum in the U.S. meant that they had to "survive a camp that more closely mirrors a place for interned prisoners than for children." To get to this camp, they were roused "in the middle of the night" and put on a bus. They found themselves in a hastily constructed "tent city in a desert wasteland where temperatures hover around 100 degrees" (Driver 2018).

According to a fact sheet distributed by the U.S. Department of Health and Human Services, however, the unaccompanied children at Tornillo received the following: an individual bed, care and supervision, case management, counseling, access to legal services, medical care, three meals a day and snacks, recreation, soccer, basketball, movies, arts and crafts, board games, televised sports events, religious services, an on-site barber, and private showers. Regarding education, the fact sheet states, "Minors in the program receive educational services from teachers under the oversight of an experienced senior public-school administrator using textbooks and workbooks." Medical services they received included medical screenings and "all vaccinations recommended by the Centers for Disease Control."

The Tornillo camp was designed for 450 children, but the government planned to house as many as 3,800 children there, ranging in age from 13 to 17. Eighty percent of the detainees were boys and 20 percent were girls (U.S. Department of Health and Human Services 2018).

Mark Greenberg oversaw the care of migrant children during the Obama administration and helped write the guidelines for emergency shelters. He stated that these guidelines are written so that "to the greatest extent possible" conditions in the emergency shelters corresponded to those in regular shelters. Greenberg added, though, "There are some ways in which that's difficult or impossible to do" (Dickerson 2018).

Driver described children who played soccer at Tornillo in extreme heat. The encampment was surrounded by a chain-link fence. Barbed wire encircled the top. She stated that the children were not provided "schooling, classes of any kind or books" (Driver 2018). ORR regulations require schooling and legal services for detainees, but according to the *New York Times*, "The children are given workbooks that they have no obligation to complete." *The Times* also reported, "Access to legal services is limited" (Dickerson 2018).

The *Convention on the Rights of the Child* (UN General Assembly 1989) protects a child's right to schooling. According to Article 28, children have the right to education. The article reads:

> States Parties recognize the right of the child to education, and with a view to achieving this right progressively and on the basis of equal opportunity,

Article 37, paragraph (d) of this convention protects children's rights to legal assistance. This article reads:

> (d) Every child deprived of his or her liberty shall have the right to prompt access to legal and other appropriate assistance, as well as the right to challenge the legality of the deprivation of his or her liberty before a court or other competent, independent and impartial authority, and to a prompt decision on any such action [UN General Assembly, 1989].

Tornillo held more detainees than all but one of the federal prisons in the U.S., and construction continued. According to the Associated Press, costs for running Tornillo were 50 percent higher than government disclosures showed. Costs for what was supposed to be a temporary 30-day facility could cost taxpayers $430 million (AP News 2018). Costs soared because everything had to be trucked into this remote site, including water, food, and diesel fuel to run generators for cooling and heating. Staff members and detainees needed transportation to and from the site. Sewage had to be trucked out (Associated Press 2018b).

Like the Native Americans in the Carlisle schools 130 years ago, the teens were given identical haircuts and government-issued shirts and pants. They moved about the facility in single-file lines with staff at the front and back. No detainees were allowed to hug each other. The vast majority of these children had not committed any crime. Many had come to the U.S. alone, seeking asylum. They were in the custody of the U.S. Department of Health and Human Services, which must provide care for them under U.S. law (Burke and Mendoza 2018).

In addition to violating other rights, giving all of the children the same haircut and clothes, so that they all looked alike, violated their rights as persons of indigenous origin. Article 30 of the *Convention on the Rights of the Child* (CRC) protects a child's right to enjoy his or her own culture. The article reads:

> In those States in which ethnic, religious or linguistic minorities or persons of indigenous origin exist, a child belonging to such a minority or who is indigenous shall not be denied the right, in community with other members of his or her group, to enjoy his or her own culture, to profess and practice his or her own religion, or to use his or her own language [UN General Assembly 1989].

7.2 Long-Term Toll

The United Nations Global Study on Children Deprived of Liberty of 2019 states that for almost 100 years, observational studies have revealed that when children are separated from their parents or other significant adults their physical, intellectual, social, and emotional development is inhibited (Nowak 2019).

Dr. Ryan Marlow, a Stanford clinical psychologist, expressed concern that children might be able to get by while they are in places like Tornillo, but the longer they spend there, the greater the effect on their "emotional and psychological well-being" (Burke and Mendoza 2018).

Dalila Reynosa-Gonzalez, who participated in protests at Tornillo as a member of the Methodist Immigration advocacy group Justice for Our Neighbors of East Texas, talked about a boy who was released from Tornillo. He told her stories about it being a "stark and lonely place and spoke of isolation, fear, and disorientation" (Burke and Mendoza 2018).

Issues about the background of staff members at Tornillo made the situation even worse. On November 27, 2018, the inspector general sent a memo to the assistant secretary of the Administration for Children and Families, alerting her office to "serious safety and health vulnerabilities" at the Tornillo site. According to the memo, the required FBI fingerprint checks that provide a person's criminal history record across federal, state, and local jurisdictions had been waived for 1,300 staff members. Tornillo was conducting a non-fingerprint background check, but this check is "not as extensive" as the FBI check that ORR requires, and it provides "less comprehensive data." The possibility that a person with a criminal history could have direct access to children is increased when the non-fingerprint check is used. Tornillo also waived checks on child abuse neglect, known as C/AN checks, that determine if "an individual has a record of substantial mistreatment of a child" (Levinson 2018).

Additionally, the clinician-to-child ratio of 1:55 for mental health workers at the site was far higher than the ORR's general requirement of a 1:12 ratio. Tornillo's proposed budget for the last 3.5 months of 2018 raised the ratio even higher, to 1:100. Regarding the concerns about background checks and high clinician to child ratio, the inspector general warned, "Both issues warrant ORR's immediate attention because they pose substantial risks to children receiving care at this facility" (Levinson 2018).

As noted earlier, Tornillo was designed to be a temporary emergency shelter that would hold around 300 children, but the numbers kept climbing, and the length of time children stayed there kept lengthening. By the end of 2018, the number of detainees housed there had risen to 2,700. In January of 2019, the shelter closed and all children were reported to have been either released to sponsors or transferred to other shelters (Mekelburg 2019).

Homestead

Like Tornillo, Homestead Detention Center was designed to be a temporary shelter. It was not subject to state regulations because it was on federal land. Even the *Flores* settlement was not regarded by the administration as applying to children in this shelter, so the length of a child's detention could become indefinite. Since there was no state supervision, the Miami-Dade School System had no knowledge of Homestead's educational programming. School Superintendent Alberto Carvalho questioned the "inequity of the quality of standards of education" that the children received (Kumpf 2019). In April of 2019, Homestead housed 2,300 teenagers and was expanding to hold 3,200. By July there were around 3,000 children housed there (Madan 2019).

On May 31, 2019, attorneys in the U.S. Central District Court of California filed a motion arguing that Homestead must comply with the *Flores* settlement. Interviews with detainees from Homestead were included in that motion. The main complaint was that teenagers had to endure prison-like conditions, adhere to prison-like rules, and remain there too long. Detainees were intimidated by threats that they jeopardized their chances of being released to their families if they broke the rules. Children feared a delay in the processing of their asylum case or deportation if they received a write-up from a staff member. Rules included limiting showers to 5 minutes, meals to fifteen minutes, not lending clothes to anyone, not taking food to their room, and asking permission to use the restroom. Children were monitored as they entered and exited the bathroom. No hugging was allowed—even between siblings. Some children slept in military-like rooms that housed 250 people. When they were ill, children were supposed to be treated at the clinic within an hour, but they reported long delays though they made multiple requests (Kates and Donaghue 2019).

Neha Desai, one of the attorneys interviewing the children, said that the size of the facility alone undermined the basic principles of individual care and attention. She stated, "Many of the kids I interviewed were so fearful and anxious that they were living in this condition of constant toxic stress" (Kates and Donaghue 2019). The conditions had driven some children to cut themselves. Therefore, detainees were not allowed to bring pens or pencils into bathrooms.

Another common practice at Homestead was to arrest children on the morning of their eighteenth birthday. When Nolbiz Orellana, who journeyed to the U.S. seeking asylum from Honduras, turned 18, ICE agents came to Homestead and arrested him. They put him in handcuffs, chained them to his waist, and shackled his legs. They transported him to the Broward Transitional Center, where he was put into a cell with the inmates who were twice his age. Youths like Nolbiz should have been protected by the *Flores* Agreement and the Trafficking Victims Protection Reauthorization Act and its amendments. Instead, from April to August 2018, at least 14 children from Homestead were arrested and taken to a jail cell in Broward on their 18th birthdays (Elfrink 2018).

The nonprofit Americans for Immigrant Justice immediately began filing lawsuits. By the end of August, seven cases were filed. Five of the immigrants were released to relatives or guardians while their cases were processed in court. Aggressive policies against potential sponsors may have prevented them from taking the youths earlier. The other two cases were not settled, so a class-action suit was filed on behalf of the two youths. They were released under a judge's order, but the class-action suit was pursued (Elfrink 2018). (See more details of the class-action suit in Chapter 12.)

Homestead was managed by Comprehensive Health Services, one of the largest government contractors in the country. They provided medical care, mental health, education, and other services. The operations of Homestead totaled 500,000 taxpayer dollars each day. In 2018, Caliburn International Corporation obtained Comprehensive Health Services. Caliburn had planned to sell $100 million of its stock but cancelled its plans due to "market forces." Community pressure to shutter Homestead may have influenced this decision (Kumpf 2019).

In May 2019, former secretary of Homeland Security John Kelly, who was an early proponent of the administration's policy of family separation, became a Caliburn board member. Citizens for Responsibility and Ethics in Washington has sued the federal government for documents that describe Kelly's ties to Caliburn (DNYUZ 2019). Sen. Elizabeth Warren and Rep. Pramila Jayapal (WA-7) also began to investigate Kelly's appointment to the board, a position for which, according to the senators, he would make at least $100,000 per year. On June 6, they wrote a letter to Jim Van Dusen, chief executive officer of Caliburn International, in which they raised questions about ethical issues surrounding Kelly's position on the board (Warren and Jayapal 2019). The text of the letter reads:

June 6, 2019

Dear Mr. Van Dusen:

We are writing to request additional information regarding reports that, earlier this month, General John F. Kelly joined the Board of Directors of Caliburn International Corporation. General Kelly, who served in the Trump Administration as the White House Chief of Staff and prior to that, as Secretary of the Department of Homeland Security (DHS), was at the center of the inhumane and poorly planned immigration policies that put children in cages while separating thousands of families and that benefitted your company. In fact, those policies helped a subsidiary of your company, which operates the "nation's largest facility for unaccompanied migrant children," rake

7. *A Horrifying Reality* 111

in hundreds of millions of dollars in government contracts. General Kelly's role in promoting and helping execute these cruel immigration policies remains a stain on his decades of public service. It is outrageous that he now appears to be cashing in on those same policies, as a board member for the company that benefitted from his actions as a government official.

General Kelly joined the Trump Administration as Secretary of DHS in January 2017, serving for seven months, before becoming White House Chief of Staff in July 2017—a position he held until January 2019. Prior to serving in the Trump Administration, General Kelly was "on the board of advisors of DC Capital Partners, an investment firm that now owns Caliburn." Four months after his departure from the Trump Administration, General Kelly has reportedly joined the Board of Directors of Caliburn International, the parent company of Comprehensive Health Services, Inc. (CHSi), which runs both the Homestead Temporary Shelter for Unaccompanied Children in Florida, which is expanding to hold 3,200 beds for unaccompanied children, as well as three more facilities in Texas. Reports indicate that CHSi could receive more than $340 million in payments in over six months to operate the Homestead site. According to statements you provided to the media, General Kelly will serve on a "board that remains acutely focused on advising on the safety and welfare of unaccompanied minors." Caliburn's compensation policy for board members appears to indicate that General Kelly stands to make at least "an annual cash retainer of $100,000" in this new role. General Kelly's decision to serve in this capacity raises serious questions about ethics and conflicts of interest given the significant role he played in implementing the policies that are enriching your company.

On April 6, 2018, the Trump Administration announced a "zero-tolerance" immigration enforcement policy to prosecute people crossing the border between ports of entry (POEs), including asylum seekers. A month later, the Trump Administration went a step further, saying that the Department of Justice (DOJ) would prosecute parents and separate them from their children. As a result, DHS separated more than 2,300 children from their parents in just six weeks, including children whose families presented at POEs. This policy, which General Kelly advocated for three months into his tenure as Secretary of DHS, was executed in a manner such that we still do not know "the total number of children separated from a parent or guardian by immigration authorities." While the Administration was putting migrant children at increased risk of "severe psychological distress, resulting in anxiety, loss of appetite, sleep disturbances, withdrawal, aggressive behavior and decline in educational achievement," companies like CHSi were receiving hundreds of millions of dollars in federal taxpayer money to run the detention facilities where these children were being held.

By virtue of his positions within the Administration, General Kelly played a significant role in the planning and execution of the federal government's immigration policies over the last two years. Four days after the zero-tolerance policy became public, General Kelly reiterated his confidence that zero-tolerance policy "could be a tough deterrent," and that it was not cruel because "the children will be taken care of—put into foster care or whatever." The "whatever" was presumably a reference to the more than "100 shelters used by the federal government" to take in the "nearly 3,000 children [that] were forcibly separate from their parents," and the "12,500 migrant minors currently in the custody of the U.S. government." This policy, in conjunction with the Trump Administration's other callous immigration strategies, have driven thousands of children in to the care of migrant shelters like yours. Six migrant children have died while in, or soon after being released from, federal custody in the last year—something that has not happened since 2010.

"The number of children in federal custody increased by more than 97% in 2018" while the Trump Administration policies were being implemented, and "the average length of stay for an unaccompanied migrant child in U.S. custody skyrocketed," allowing your company to rake in millions of dollars in taxpayer funds. CHSi, "the only private company operating shelters," especially benefitted from these new policies. It currently runs four shelters for unaccompanied migrant children with plans to open two more, has received $222 million to operate the Homestead facility, and could receive an additional "$341 million in payments between now and November." In fact, as of April 11, 2019, one in six of the 12,500 minors in U.S. custody were located in the Homestead camp. And last month, the Department of Health and Human Services announced, "plans to expand bed capacity at the [CHSi facility in Homestead] from 2,350 to 3,200 beginning in mid–April of 2019 based on need resulting from a current increase in UAC referrals from DHS." In other words, your company has and will continue to significantly profit from the policies General Kelly helped put in place.

It is disheartening that General Kelly, with his decades of public service, used his position to implement such cruel policies and then left the government to profit from them, and we are disappointed that General Kelly has ignored requests that he resign from the Caliburn Board of Directors.

We introduced far-reaching ethics legislation, the Anti-Corruption and Public Integrity Act, which would make it illegal for Caliburn or any DHS contractor to pay General Kelly or any other former senior DHS official a dime for at least four years after they leave office. We intend to keep working to make that plan law so that actions like General Kelly's rapid, cynical, and unethical shift from the government payroll to the contractor's payroll are no longer allowed. In order to help inform this legislation and better understand how General Kelly was appointed to the board of your company, we ask that you provide answers to the following questions no later than June 20, 2019.

With the threat of oncoming hurricanes, Homestead stopped taking in children and moved those who were at the facility to other settings. By August 3, 2019, all children who had been housed at Homestead were either reunified with appropriate sponsors or sent to a state-licensed facility within the Office of Refugee Resettlement network of care providers (Madan 2019).

In September 2019, ORR published modified policies for influx facilities (Office of Refugee Resettlement 2019). These regulations replaced section 1.7 of the prior ORR policy guide. The regulations related to services apply to the contract or grant terms and conditions of ORR's non-state-licensed Influx Care Facilities. Revised criteria included new policies related to placement; operational capacity; admissions and orientation; transfers and discharges; temporary waivers; notifications to Congress; staffing levels and plans; requests to visit the facilities; monitoring of the facility; agreements with federal, state, or local security providers; and services.

The document states that children admitted to these facilities must be age 13 or older. The facilities must provide minimum service in the following categories for each unaccompanied child in their care: proper physical care and maintenance, routine medical and dental care, an individualized needs assessment, appropriate educational services, planned recreation and leisure time activities, at least one individual counseling session per week, group counseling sessions at least twice a week, acculturation services, a comprehensive orientation program, access to religious services of the child's choice whenever possible, a reasonable right to privacy, services designed to identify relatives in the U.S., and legal services information. Educational services will also be provided at the child's level of development and communication skills. These services will take place Monday through Friday and will focus mainly on developing basic academic competencies, and secondarily on English language training (Office of Refugee Resettlement 2019).

Estrella del Norte Shelter

Estrella del Norte in Tucson, Arizona, is run by Southwest Key. According to the *Los Angeles Times*, Antar Davidson was a youth case worker there. The shelter went from housing unaccompanied children to housing those who had been separated from their parents. The caseload expanded, and he realized that the facility was understaffed and unequipped to support children who had undergone the trauma of separation. He witnessed children who were "running away, screaming, throwing furniture, and attempting suicide." Facility records affirm his observations. He also saw the transient facility become more "permanent" and prison-like. He stated, "At that point zero tolerance was in full swing, and you could see the desperation: kids running down the hall, screaming for their moms" (Hennessy-Fiske 2018).

The CEO of Southwest Key announced that the company would reduce the staffing ratio by two-thirds. Since Davidson believed the staff could not already control the children, he knew that the reduction was too drastic. Davidson resigned, stating, "I can no longer in good conscience work with Southwest Key programs." He added, "I am feeling uneasy about the morality of some of the practices" (Hennessy-Fiske 2018).

The *United Nations Global Study on Children Deprived of Liberty of 2019* supports Davidson's statements. The report identifies understaffing as a "serious problem" and cautions that "overwhelmed staff may resort to violent measures to maintain discipline." The report also points out that "burnout" of staff members "results in increasingly negative attitudes toward children and in physical and impulsive responses to confrontation" (Nowak 2019).

7.3 "Tender Age" Shelters

The Trump administration also provided what they called "tender age shelters" for the youngest children. The only other difference between these shelters and the ones for older children was the name. The UN study cited above describes the term "tender age shelters" as a euphemistic and misleading name (Nowak 2019). According to *The Guardian*, "A room built out of chain-link fencing is a cage." "Tender age" suggests that little children are treated with gentleness, or "sheltered." However, they "have in fact been deprived of the shelter of their parents" (Poole 2018).

On June 22, 2018, on the floor of the House, Rep. Ted Lieu of California played an audio clip of the voices of crying children who had been separated from their parents. According to the *Washington Times*, Lieu violated a House rule against playing electronic recording devices in the House chamber. The presiding officer called for Lieu to switch off the clip, but he refused, saying, "I think the American people need to hear this" (Howell 2018).

Jennifer Harbury, a civil rights attorney who has lived and worked along the Texas border for four decades, provided the tape to ProPublica. Harbury stated that she received the recording from a client who "heard the children's weeping and crying and was devastated by it" (Thompson 2018). The client said that there were 10 crying children in the room. They were from the age of 4 to 10, and they had been separated from their parents within the past twenty-four hours. The children called out for their parents, and some gasped for air because they cried so hard (Thompson 2018). According to the *Washington Post*, Rep. Adriano Espaillat (NY-13) described the audio as "heartbreaking." Sen. Catherine Cortez Masto (NV) stated that it was "absolutely gut-wrenching and beyond disturbing." Rep. Pramila Jayapal tweeted that it was "just awful" (Rosenberg 2018).

Dr. Colleen Kraft, then president of the American Academy of Pediatrics, visited a shelter in Texas. The first child she encountered was a young girl who was sobbing and pounding her fists on her mat. She had been removed from her mother the previous night and sent to the shelter. Staff members tried to console her by giving her books and toys. Due to shelter rules like those in Tornillo and Homestead, however, the staff were not allowed to give hugs or pick her up to help her calm down (Merchant 2018).

Young children and babies require various kinds of sensory stimulation for normal development. Hugging is one of the most important. Hugs are essential for the development of a healthy brain and a strong body. A twenty-second hug can lower blood pressure and boost the immune system. It can also increase oxytocin, the hormone that establishes the feelings of bonding and security (Sears 2019). Touch establishes a model that a child will internalize. Eventually, this model can help children regulate their own behavior. When children are frequently deprived of touch, however, they can become hypervigilant and view the world as a dangerous place. This behavior can shape their future relationships and impair their abilities to engage in new experiences (Sripom 2016).

Not everyone was sympathetic to the plight of the children, however. ProPublica reports that on the tape, "the baritone voice of a Border Patrol agent booms above the crying. 'Well, we have an orchestra,'" he jokes. "What's missing is a conductor" (Thompson 2018).

Michael Grimm, candidate for the 11th Congressional District of New York, defended the policy of separating these young crying children from their parents.

> I think it is extremely unfortunate. But what people are forgetting—they just want to listen to those tapes…. I can take you to any nursery … as a mother goes to work and has to leave her child at daycare, your gonna hear those exact same things, okay? [Chapman 2018].

It appears that Grimm did not consider that children who are left at daycare centers would be picked up and taken home by their families at the end of the day. He may be unaware that parents of young children in the U.S. spend months planning for their child's transition to daycare. He did not acknowledge that most children in daycare centers have not survived a grueling journey of thousands of miles to seek asylum in America. Children who attend daycare in the U.S. have not been seized by a foreign government. Apparently, Grimm's statement was not okay with the voters in his district. His election bid was unsuccessful.

The UN global study includes the following evidence from research about the harm caused by early institutionalization (Nowak 2019, 537-538):

- The research sounds a clear alarm against the institutionalization of babies because it "harms early brain development, can result in developmental delays and permanent disability and may have long-lasting effects on their social and emotional behaviour" (Nowak 2019, 537).
- The research draws upon recent neuroscience research that confirms earlier behavioral science research on attachment, indicating that the most profound disruption to the child's healthy brain development is the separation of the children from their parents and other significant adults during childhood (Nowak 2019, 537).
- The research points out, "Medical literature establishes that children experience pain and suffering differently than adults, and

that the long-term damaging effects of mistreatment tend to cause even greater, or irreversible damage in children than in adults" (Nowak 2019, 538), [cf. Paulo Sergio Pinheiro 2006].

The study also explains that even a short deprivation of liberty "can undermine a child's psychological and physical well-being and compromise his or her cognitive development" (Nowak 2019b, 538). It also draws on the work of Dainius Pūras, former Special Rapporteur, that calls for the elimination of institutionalization of children under 5 years of age (Pūras, n.d.).

At the beginning of March 2019, CBS news reported that 16 infants under the age of one were detained at the South Texas Family Residential Center in Dilley, Texas. Soon after that, all of the mothers and infants were released. Mothers were not provided with bottled water, so they had to give their infants formula mixed with potentially unsafe tap water. Murzda reported that even the staff members did not drink the tap water, because it smelled like chlorine (K. Smith 2019).

Every child was sick in some way, according to Katy Murzda, advocacy coordinator at the American Immigration Council's Dilley Pro Bono Project. Many of the infants in the Dilley center lost weight because only one kind of formula was offered. The mothers said that receiving medical services was very difficult while they were at the center (Santas 2019). These delays happened even though ORR regulations list specific medical services that should be provided.

The treatment of young children in these detention centers is a direct violation of the *Convention of the Rights of the Child*. As described in Article 24, children have the right to clean drinking water and health care services.

Article 24 reads:

1. States Parties recognize the right of the child to the enjoyment of the highest attainable standard of health and to facilities for the treatment of illness and rehabilitation of health. States Parties shall strive to ensure that no child is deprived of his or her right of access to such health care services.

2. States Parties shall pursue full implementation of this right and, in particular, shall take appropriate measures:

(a) To diminish infant and child mortality;

(b) To ensure the provision of necessary medical assistance and health care to all children with emphasis on the development of primary health care;

(c) To combat disease and malnutrition, including within the framework of primary health care, though, inter alia, the application of readily available technology and through the provision of adequate nutritious foods and clean drinking-water, taking into consideration the dangers and risks of environmental pollution [UN General Assembly 1989].

8

The Deaths of Children

8.1 Sorrowful Outcomes

As noted at the end of the previous chapter, Article 24 of the *Convention on the Rights of the Child* (UN General Assembly 1989) ensures protection against child mortality and requires state parties to pursue full implementation of this right and to take appropriate measures to diminish children's deaths.

Furthermore, Article 6 recognizes and ensures, as far as possible, every child's inherent right to life itself. Paragraphs 1 and 2 of this article read:

> States Parties recognize that every child has the inherent right to life.
> States Parties shall ensure to the maximum extent possible the survival and development of the child [UN General Assembly 1989].

Writer Alice Driver expressed concern about the safety, wellness, and well-being of immigrant children when she visited the Tornillo shelter in Texas. She stated: "If the United States continues to treat children as prisoners, the question is not if but when they will start to die under such conditions" (Driver 2018). As Driver feared and predicted, the most horrifying results of the treatment of these children have been the deaths of several children.

The first child to die was Mariee Juarez. Mariee was a one-year-old from Guatemala. She had been held in U.S. Immigration and Customs Enforcement custody. Mariee died from complications of respiratory illness after she was released. Her mother filed a lawsuit against the government because she believed her child contracted the illness while she was detained (Acevedo 2019).

The next child to die was Darlyn Cristabel, a ten-year-old child from El Salvador, who had a heart condition. She was caught by Border Patrol agents near Hidalgo, Texas, on March 1, 2018. She complained of chest pains and was sent to the hospital. Two days later, she was transferred to HHS and placed in a shelter in San Antonio. She was considered "medically fragile," and underwent surgery that left her in a coma. In May, she was sent to Phoenix, Arizona, for palliative care. On September 26, she was sent to Omaha, Nebraska, to be closer to her family. She died three days later as a result of fever and respiratory problems (Hennessy-Fiske 2019).

Jakelin Caal, a seven-year-old girl from Guatemala, was the third child to die. She and her father, Nery Gilberto Caal, had travelled from Guatemala to the U.S. on December 6, 2018, along with a group of 161 others. They turned themselves over to the Border Patrol and were taken to the Antelope Wells, New Mexico, port of entry. Her father, who speaks Q'eqchi', a pre–Columbian Mayan language, signed a waiver in English stating that Jakelin had no current health issues (Miroff 2018).

The father and daughter then boarded a bus for the Lordsburg Border Patrol Station in Texas that was 90 minutes away. While traveling, Jakelin began vomiting. Her father alerted officials that she was ill. According to DHS reports, when the bus got to the patrol station, she had stopped breathing and had a temperature of 105.9 degrees. She had to be revived twice by agents who had been informed of her condition by officials on the bus. She was then airlifted to a hospital in El Paso and suffered another cardiac arrest there. On December 8, Jakelin died from sepsis (Taylor 2018).

Over a dozen members of the Congressional Hispanic Caucus called for an independent investigation into Jakelin's death. A delegation of Congress members and representatives-elect toured the Antelope Wells and Lordsburg Border Patrol Stations. Rep. Joaquin Castro of Texas, who chairs the Congressional Hispanic Caucus, said that systemic failures such as the lack of medically trained personnel on the bus deprived Jakelin of adequate care (Castro Press Release 2018). The following are statements from their press conference regarding the visit.

From Congressman Raul Ruiz (CA-36):

> What I found here is that there are some really serious systemic obstacles, and problems, and failures in the system to provide the care that a child so lovingly deserves when they are in our custody.
>
> If it is true that the child had not eaten, and was vomiting for several days, the child does not look normal when they present to the emergency department or anywhere. And a cursory physical exam to determine if the pulse is high or the fever, if she has a fever. Anybody who is dehydrated is not happy, is not excited, they look really sick. At that point, perhaps an aeromedical evacuation could have been called and she could have still been alive.

Assistant Speaker Elect Ben Ray Luján (NM-3):

> No running water, no area to bathe, no water to cook. At Antelope Wells, not just for the undocumented immigrants—these asylum seekers—but also for the agents. We found out that the food provided both at Antelope Wells and here in Lordsburg to the asylum seekers is granola bars, small juice boxes, and frozen burritos. And what I

would describe as inhumane holding cells where we saw children with adults, and overcrowded facilities with a shared toilet. Completely open. At Antelope Wells, two porta potties, not just for the agents, but for the hundreds of undocumented immigrants and for asylum seekers that are coming in as well.

Congressman Al Green (TX-9):

There are two sets of victims in this facility. The women and children who are here being processed, and the officers who are having to process them. They are both victims because to a certain extent these officers are doing what they are told, following rules, regulations and orders, but it has caused them to be put in a position where they are hardening.

To tolerate what I have seen is unthinkable. We as members of Congress have got to do more to make sure that this kind of facility is either shut down or we have got to do more to make it a lot better than it is.

Congresswoman-Elect Veronica Escobar (TX-16):

To see more children, more families, who are put in concrete rooms, in conditions that many of us believe are in inhumane, and that are not reflective of the America that all of us know we can and should be.

It's no longer necessarily simply economic migration that we're seeing. But we're seeing asylum seekers who are running for their lives, who are trying to save the lives of their families. These are not criminals; these are not people trying to do us harm. The families that we have seen today are people just like you and I. People who are looking for a better life. People who are looking for hope, and who unfortunately end up finding almost as much misery when they cross our borders as the misery that they fled.

Congresswoman-Elect Sylvia Garcia (TX-29):

This first, beyond everything, is a human tragedy. Today [December 18, 2018] is International Migrant Day. Think about that. And here we are talking about a young angel, seven-years-old, who died here in the process of just trying to come here for a better life. Think about the father who had to carry her into that small room, Dr. Ruiz—so small I think my closet is probably larger—put on a hard table where now sits two microwaves. Not a bed. And that's where she was determined to be so ill. But also think about the mother who they had to find, and give her word that her daughter has died. The daughter that she thought she was waving goodbye to, to come to a better world here in America. It's a human tragedy, but it's one of our own making.

Despite the outrage, the administration deflected blame for Jakelin's death, placing the fault on her family. White House spokesman Hogan Gidley said: "Does the administration take responsibility for a parent taking a child on a trek through Mexico to get to this country? No" (Miroff 2018). As reported by Salon.com, Homeland Security Secretary Kirstjen Nielsen stated on *Fox and Friends*: "This is just a very sad example of the dangers of this journey. This family chose to cross illegally" (Derysh 2018).

The deaths of the two children while in the custody of the border patrol agency led to stricter procedures guaranteeing better medical care for migrants. One of these new requirements was a health screening for all migrant children. Prior to this time, when families arrived with severe medical needs, the border patrol agents had to assist them. The agency's medical contracts were expanded so nurses and nurse practitioners could serve the families at "high risk" and at high-traffic areas of the border. Additionally, more funds were earmarked for translation services so that migrants who speak in indigenous dialects would be able to communicate and understand written documents.

Within two weeks of the death of Jakelin Caal, another Guatemalan child died in Border Patrol custody. Felipe Alonzo-Gomez and his father were apprehended on December 18, 2018, after they crossed the border near the Paso del Norte bridge that connects Juarez, Mexico, and El Paso, Texas. After a week in custody, Felipe was coughing and his eyes seemed glossy. He was taken to the hospital. His temperature was 103 degrees. He was prescribed antibiotics and ibuprofen and was released from the hospital. He and his father went to a temporary holding facility. He was given medication at 5 p.m. Around 10 p.m. he was nauseated and lethargic, so he was taken back to the hospital. On the way, he vomited and lost consciousness. Felipe died shortly after getting to the hospital. It was Christmas Eve, 2018 (Jordan 2018). Later, the Guatemalan Foreign Ministry reported that Felipe died of Influenza B, complicated by a staph bacterial infection that led to sepsis (CNN Newsource 2019).

8.2 Metering

The Trump administration created the situation that led migrants, including Felipe's father, to cross the border illegally. In 2018, large numbers of families seeking asylum in the U.S. began coming to the border. Asylum seekers were told that they had to enter the U.S. through ports of entry, rather than between ports. At the same time, the administration also began a process called "metering." It had been used by the Obama administration when ports of entry were overloaded, but the Trump administration was the first to use it extensively (Fredrick 2019).

The system involved limiting the number of those seeking asylum who were allowed into the U.S. through the ports of entry each day. Essentially, metering—and the directive that migrants should not enter between ports—became ways of strictly curtailing the number of migrants who gained asylum. Under the metering plan, CBP officers stationed at border crossings required migrants to add their names to a list to wait for their turn to request asylum. The list was maintained by a person on the Mexican side of the border. Each day the officers would inform that person of the number of asylum seekers who could be processed. Wait times at various

8. The Deaths of Children   121

ports of entry ranged from one to three days to six months. At some ports, no names were called for several days in a row (American Immigration Council 2020).

Although DHS claimed that the zero-tolerance policy and metering at ports of entry were different issues, a CBP official reported that the backlogs created by these competing directives likely resulted in additional illegal border crossings (Office of the Inspector General, U.S. Department of Homeland Security, 2018).

Rep. Joaquin Castro spoke out, decrying metering and pressuring the Department of Homeland Security for more humane treatment of migrants since two deaths had taken place within two weeks. His statement reads in part:

> There is a humanitarian crisis at our southern border, and the policies of the Trump Administration are making that crisis more tragic.
>
> Specifically, the Trump Administration's policy of metering, or disallowing certain people from presenting themselves for asylum at the U.S.-Mexico border, at ports of entry, is encouraging and incentivizing desperate people who are fleeing violence, and oppression, to go around to more remote and rural areas of the border, to great danger to themselves, and often to their children.
>
> And I believe that's contributing to more serious injuries, and possibly in these cases, more deaths.
>
> Today's visit reaffirmed the fact that the federal government, under the Trump Administration, still has a long way to go in making sure that migrants are treated humanely. That there is proper medical care—personnel, equipment, staff, supplies, all of it—to treat migrants who encounter medical emergencies [Castro 2019].

The Guatemalan Foreign Ministry issued a statement disclosing that they had requested medical reports to clarify the cause of Felipe's death and that they planned to meet with his father to "hear his version of the facts" (El Ministerio de Relacionas Exteriores de Guatemala 2018).

> El Ministerio de Relaciones Exteriores informa que hoy 25 de diciembre se recibió la alerta por parte de agentes de la Patrulla Fronteriza quienes informaron del lamentable fallecimiento de un menor de origen guatemalteco, de quien se tiene conocimiento que ingresó acompañado de su padre por el Paso, Texas el pasado 18 de diciembre y el 23 de diciembre fueron trasladados a la estación de la Patrulla Fronteriza en Alamogordo, Nuevo México.
>
> El Cónsul de Guatemala en Phoenix está ya en el seguimiento de este hecho y se ha trasladado hasta el lugar donde está a la espera de poder entrevistar al padre del menor, para poder conocer su versión de los hechos.
>
> La causa de la muerte está en investigación y se han solicitado los informes médicos que se practiquen para esclarecer la causa de la muerte del menor.
>
> La Canciller de Guatemala Sandra Jovel ha instruido atender este caso con la mayor diligencia posible, así mismo indicó que el Gobierno de Guatemala dará toda la asistencia y protección consular necesaria al padre, así como se hará cargo del proceso de la repatriación de los restos del menor hacia Guatemala.
>
> El Gobierno de Guatemala a través del Ministerio de Relaciones Exteriores solicitará

una investigación clara y resguardando el debido proceso sobre este caso a las autoridades estadounidenses.

The English translation (translated via https://translate.google.com/):

December 25, 2018
   The Consulate of Guatemala in Phoenix, Arizona reports on the unfortunate death of a lower Guatemalan at the United States border.
   The Ministry of Foreign Affairs reports that today, December 25, an alert was received by border patrol agents who reported the unfortunate death of a minor of Guatemalan origin, who is known to have entered el Paso, Texas, accompanied by his stepfather on December 18. On December 23, they were moved to the border patrol station in Alamogordo, New Mexico.
   The Consul of Guatemala in Phoenix, Arizona, is already following-up on these facts and are waiting to interview the father of the child to get to know his version of the facts.
   The cause of death is being researched and reports have been requested from doctors who practice to clarify the cause of death of the child.
   The Foreign Minister of Guatemala, Sandra Jovel who has instructed this case with the greatest diligence, also indicated that the Government of Guatemala will give every assistance and consular protection needed to the father, as well as being responsible for the process of repatriation of the remains of the minor toward Guatemala.
   The Government of Guatemala, through the Ministry of Foreign Affairs, will request a clear research and safeguarding of due process on this case to the U.S. authorities.

Trump administration officials continued to blame the parents for the deaths of children on the dangerous journey to the U.S. The Department of Homeland Security (DHS), however, requested the Coast Guard and public health services to send medical personnel to the border immediately to help with examinations. An average of 50 people a day were in need of emergency care. Health problems ranged from the flu and infections to tuberculosis and pregnancies (Dinan 2019a).

A year later, the DHS's inspector general released two brief reports that concluded there was "'no misconduct or malfeasance' by DHS personnel" in the deaths of Jakelin and Felipe. Names are not given, but details match the descriptions of the children and the circumstances surrounding their deaths (Ortiz and Levenson 2019). According to her autopsy, Jakelin died of "sequelae of Streptoccal sepsis," a massive infection. Felipe's autopsy report said that he died of "complications of influenza B infection with Staphylococcus aureus bacteria and sepsis" (Moore 2019). At the time the report came out, CBP was resisting recommendations to provide flu vaccines to migrants detained in their facilities (Wallace 2019).

8.3 *Further Tragedy*

After the deaths of Darlyn Cristabel Cordova-Valle, Jakelin Caal Manquin and Felipe Alonzo-Gomez, more children's deaths at the border

8. The Deaths of Children

were reported. To date, information on the following deaths of children has been made public:

Juan de León Gutiérrez, age 16, from Guatemala: Juan crossed the border alone on April 19, 2019. He was sent to Southwest Key's Casa Padre shelter in Brownsville, Texas. Two days later, he was hospitalized after staff saw that he was sick. Nine days after that, he died from an infection in the frontal lobe of his brain (Hennessy-Fiske 2019).

Wilmer Josue Ramirez Vasquez, age two and a half, from Guatemala: Wilmer and his mother had been taken into custody by border agents on April 3, 2019, near the Paso del Norte International Bridge that connects Ciudad Juarez, Mexico, and El Paso, Texas. He was hospitalized for illness on April 6. Apparently, he had pneumonia, and he remained in the hospital for over a month (Flores 2019). He died on May 14, 2019. *The Washington Post* cited a report from the El Paso county medical examiner's office that said that Wilmer died of "multiple intestinal and respiratory diseases" (Moore and Sacchetti 2019).

Carlos Hernandez Vasquez, age 16, from Guatemala: There were two versions of the circumstances surrounding Carlos' death. This first report was released just after he died. Carlos was traveling alone and was apprehended for illegally crossing the border on May 13, 2019. He was taken to a central processing center in McAllen, Texas. Six days later, twice the 72-hour limit required by law, Carlos was diagnosed with the flu and given medicine. He was transferred to the Weslaco Border Patrol Station, reportedly so his illness could be contained. On May 20, 2019, he was found unresponsive (BBC News 2019).

An official cause of death was not immediately announced. The day after his death, however, U.S. Customs and Border Protection (CBP) temporarily closed the McAllen center because a quarantine was imposed by medical personnel "after a 'large number' of detainees were found to have high fevers and symptoms of a flu-related illness" (VOA News 2019).

On December 5, 2019, a revised report about the details of Carlos's death was issued by ProPublica. This report was based on a video of Carlos in a concrete cell in Weslaco, Texas. ProPublica obtained the video through Texas open records laws. The Weslaco police department had done a brief investigation of Carlos's death. ProPublica's report added new information to initial reports. It stated that Carlos was actually seen by a nurse at the processing facility in McAllen who said he should be checked two hours later and sent to the emergency room if his condition worsened. Instead, he was transferred for quarantine at a Border Patrol station in Weslaco. There, he was put into a cell with one other patient at the facility. The cell video shows Carlos "writhing for at least 25 minutes on the floor and on a concrete bench." He then staggers to the toilet and collapses on the floor. For four-and-a-half hours, he remained there in the same position. His cellmate is seen on the video waking up and walking to the toilet where he finds Carlos "lying in a pool of blood on the floor" (Moore, Schmidt, and Jameel 2019).

The video footage differs from the account that was given by the agency the day Carlos died. CBP claimed that an agent had found Carlos "unresponsive" while checking on him. According to the facility's "subject activity log," an agent had checked on Carlos three times during the early morning hours but did not report anything "alarming." Since the video shows that Carlos' "agony was apparent," the only way the officials could have not seen his situation is if they had not checked him or not checked him adequately. The coroner who conducted Carlos's autopsy said she was informed that the agent who was checking on Carlos looked into the cell through a window. On December 6, 2019, Rep. Bennie Thompson (MI-2), chairman of the House Homeland Security Committee, accused the Trump administration of misleading Congress about the circumstances surrounding Carlos' death and urged an immediate completion of an internal investigation (Moore, Schmidt, and Jameel 2019).

Valeria Martinez Ramirez, age 18 months, from El Salvador: Valeria drowned in the Rio Grande along with her father. They were attempting to cross the border at the time of their deaths. A heart-wrenching photograph that ignited extensive public sorrow and anger shows the bodies of Valeria and her father face-down at the river's edge. The specific circumstances of the drowning were unclear and under investigation (Silva 2019).

Juana Anastasia Miranda Aquilar, age 3; Marleny Mereidy Rivera Reyes, age 20 months; and Denilsen Chicas Perez, age 18 months, all from Guatemala: The children died near the Rio Grande in South Texas. The children were traveling with Denilsen's mother, Briseyda Chicas Perez, who also died. Yaquelin Mereidy Reyes Sopon, Marleny's mother, and Neily Yoseli Aguliar Ochoa, Juana's mother, who were also with the children, survived. The mothers and their children had travelled over 1,000 miles from Guatemala to the Mexican border, where they became lost. Those who died succumbed to heat exhaustion and dehydration (McDonnell 2019).

8.4 Medical Needs of Children Who Reach the Border

The grueling journey from Central America to the U.S. border presents grave hazards that endanger the lives of young children. Often, they do not have access to medical services or even water along the way. Many children are in poor health when they arrive at the border. Once they get to the border, they often had to wait weeks or months to enter the United States because of the metering policy that limited the number of immigrants who can request asylum or assistance each day.

The Huffington Post interviewed experts about the health conditions and needs of children in Customs and Border Patrol facilities. Dr. Julie Linton, co-chair of the American Academy of Pediatrics, an immigrant-health special-interest group, advised treating sick children quickly. She cautioned that undiagnosed symptoms can escalate into serious illness. The signs of sepsis, for example, are different in children than in adults. Even small changes like an increased heart rate or rapid breathing can signal this life-threatening illness, and the possibility of mortality increases with each hour of delayed treatment (Chapin 2019).

Dr. Lisa Ayoub-Rodriquez, a member of the same professional group, said that children in these facilities may be dehydrated and their immune systems may be compromised. They are at risk for not being able to fight off illnesses and getting seriously ill. She advocates a safe, restful environment in which to recover. Facilities with floor-to-ceiling cages, lights glaring 24/7, and cold, hard concrete floors where children are forced to sleep with only mylar blankets are places that exacerbate illnesses (Chapin 2019).

Mid-level health professionals often treat children, but experts believe that pediatricians should examine sick children because they know what to look for. Wilmer Josue Ramirez Vasquez's autopsy report showed several parasites that are common in Central America. Bert Johannsen, a pediatrician from El Paso who has treated hundreds of migrant children, said that he factors a child's place of origin into his diagnoses. If a child from El Paso has diarrhea, he considers gastroenteritis. If his patient is from Guatemala, he considers other bacteria, parasites, and cryptosporidium. Parasites are treatable if they are recognized and dealt with quickly (Moore and Sacchetti 2019). Unfortunately, the parasites were not identified early as a cause of Wilmer's illness.

In the *Report of the Special Rapporteur on the Right of Everyone to the Enjoyment of the Highest Attainable Standard of Physical and Mental Health*, Dainius Pūras, former Special Rapporteur, stated:

> The current structures of confinement produce a vast geography of pain that transcends borders, resource settings and political systems. This is intimately linked to the right to health and well-being, not only to those deprived of liberty, but also of communities, families, children and future generations [Pūras n.d.].

For every child who is separated, there is a parent or parents and other family members who are enduring the trauma of that separation as well. Sen. Merkley relates many stories of parents he met who were living in fear, pain and confusion because they did not know the whereabouts of their children or they were worried about their welfare. One father, Marco

Antonio Munoz, became distraught after being told his family would be separated. He was moved to a jail in Starr County, Texas, because he was "disruptive and combative." Later he was put in a padded cell where he is reported to have committed suicide (Merkley 2019). The ACLU reports that several other parents have attempted suicide or committed suicide (ACLU 2019).

After his visit to two border stations in 2018, Rep. Joaquin Castro pointed out that there was a lack of the medical care, equipment, staff, and supplies to care for migrants who faced medical emergencies. Castro added that there was a long way to go before the federal government's treatment of migrants could be considered humane. He also stated that these shortages and inhumane policies impact not only the migrants, but also the border patrol agents as well (Castro Press Conference 2019).

8.5 *The Price Paid by Border Patrol Agents*

Many border patrol agents remain in their jobs although they are required to place young children and their families in horrifying circumstances. Their jobs exact a price. Merkley writes, "The darkness, the evil, of child separation damages the souls of everyone it touches" (Merkley 2019). In 2018, he questioned CBP officials at the McAllen processing center about how they felt about implementing the policy. Only one responded, saying, "We don't make the policies. It's our job to implement them." Merkley noted that the man did not appear to be very happy about it. He sees border patrol workers as a third set of victims of the Trump administration's immigration policies.

One border patrol veteran who was interviewed at the Clint Detention Center said, "It gets to the point where you become a robot." He acknowledged that as part of his daily routine, he follows orders and removes beds from children to make additional space in holding cells. He calls his own actions "heartbreaking" (Merkley 2019).

In an October 2019 article in Quartz, Justin Rohrlich examined the results of the impact of the treatment of migrant children on border patrol agents (Rohrlich 2019).[1] He explained that in recent years, the number of law enforcement suicides in the U.S. has exceeded the number of deaths in the line of duty. He also cited data from Badge of Life, a nonprofit working to prevent police suicide, that shows for each police suicide there are at least 1,000 cases of post-traumatic stress. He pointed out that mental trauma is nearly a daily occurrence for law enforcement officers. This trauma puts them and the people they serve at risk. Rohrlich further revealed information from a government report obtained by Quartz that showed "the rate of suicide at CBP is almost 28% higher than any other law enforcement agency" (U.S. Customs and Border Protection 2019).

From 2007 to September 11, 2019, 115 CBP employees committed suicide. Jenn Budd, former senior Border Patrol agent and immigrants' rights advocate, told Rohrlich that it is the nature of the new tasks required of CBP agents, rather than an increased workload, that is the cause of the escalation of CBP suicides. He believes that agents' mental health is impacted by being forced to work in processing centers where asylum seekers are held for extended periods of time. Budd added that when migrants died while agents were on duty, these agents may have said that the deaths were not their fault, but internally they were still affected (Rohrlich 2019).

Border Patrol also provides little quality information or professional help for those agents seeking assistance. Instead of clinical mental health professionals, CBP uses peer counselors who have minimal training. Even their chaplains are officers who perform both faith-based counseling and law-enforcement duties. They are not full-time clergy who have divinity degrees. Budd also described a culture of silence within CBP that causes people to feel ashamed if they ask for help, making agents reluctant to do so (Rohrlich 2019).

New CBP recruits are given medical examinations, but they are not given personality assessments or psychological screenings. Marla Friedman, police psychologist, told Rohrlich that these evaluations are necessary because they reveal the "mental elasticity" of new recruits, and their views about sustaining their mental health despite the "perceived stigma" of getting care. She added that evaluations would narrow the pool of candidates to those who would engage in mental health screenings and treatment as ways to further their personal and professional growth (Rohrlich 2019).

9

Further Harm

9.1 Institutionalized Abuse

Despite the late Elijah Cummings' pleas for the improvement in the treatment of migrant children in the U.S., the policies and practices of the Trump administration continue to lead to further harm because the abuse of immigrants has become institutionalized.

In an article in the *Washington Post* from December 5, 2019, Lawrence Tribe, Harvard University professor of constitutional law, discusses grounds for Trump's impeachment. He describes Trump as a "serial abuser of power" (Tribe 2019). Tribe sees Trump operating with a pattern of behavior in which he repeats the same offences over and over.

This behavior applies to the situation of the children at the border as well. As each individual situation plays out, the reaction of many people is to seek a solution. But over time, we begin to see a pattern of abuse and realize that the administration has no interest in finding solutions to the plight of the migrants. Their goal is to deter migrants from coming to the United States.

Trump and members of his administration have employed a variety of deceptive tactics as they have carried out their work. As seen in the reunification debacle, they created gnarled labyrinths of ineffective IT systems that led to confusing communication, missing children, heartbroken parents, and the deception of the American people. In the case of zero tolerance, the administration devised secret plans and rolled them out without informing members of the administration who would be responsible for implementation. They told outright lies about implementing a zero-tolerance policy and having a portal that stored vital information about children and their families. Members of Congress and the press were barred from viewing child detention facilities. Tours of child detention centers presented a sanitized version of the conditions in the facilities. Victims were blamed. Deaths of children were spun as the responsibility of parents who were trying to bring their families to the U.S. for a safer and better chance at life. The president himself has referred to the migrants as "animals."

As noted earlier, the president justifies his actions with his words. At rallies, President Trump has characterized immigrants with the following words over 500 times: "predator," "invasion," "alien," "killer," "criminal," and

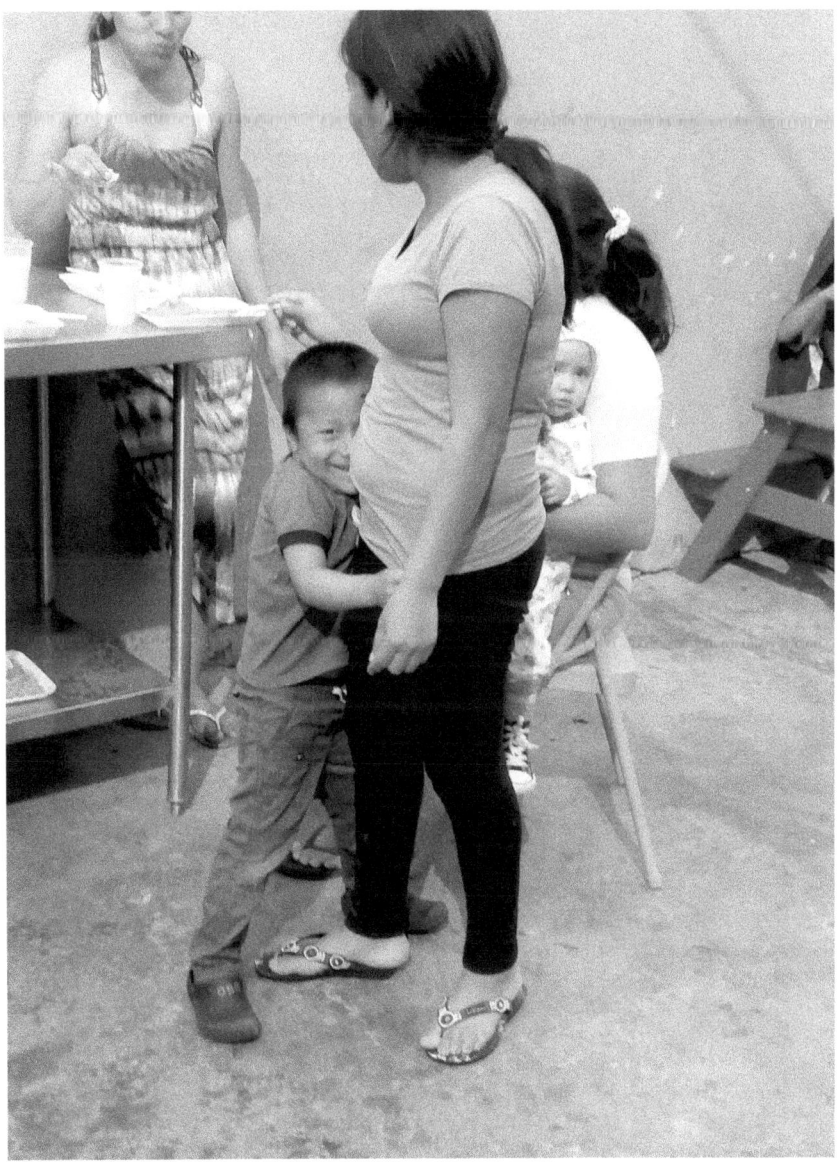

Camera-shy boy with his mother (author's photograph).

Above: Leti, asylum seeker from Guatemala (courtesy Deirdra Sparling). *Right:* Olga and her daughter Leti, asylum seekers from Guatemala (courtesy Deirdra Sparling).

"animal" (Fritze 2019). When listeners hear these words repeatedly from a person in power, they internalize them, pass them on to others, and may act on them in harmful ways.

These photographs of children and a mother who are trying to seek asylum in the U.S. nullify his words.

Young asylum seeker at the Hosanna Shelter (author's photograph).

9.2 Senior Advisor

One tactic that enabled Trump to perpetuate myths about migrants and carry out his policies is keeping high level positions in a state of flux. During the first three years of the Trump administration, there were six people in the role of secretary of Homeland Security in the Trump administration. John F. Kelly, and Kirstjen Nielsen were appointed. Elaine Duke and Kevin McAleenan were acting. In April 2019, Nielsen retired as secretary of Homeland Security, and McAleenan took the position from May until mid–October 2019. Then he resigned. Ken Cuccinelli, acting director of United States Citizenship and Immigration Services (USCIS), oversaw DHS until mid–November, when Chad Wolf became acting secretary. The administration named acting DHS officials who do not go through the confirmation process in the Senate. Therefore, they are beholden to the administration and are forced to follow directives closely in order to keep their jobs.

The main reason for the revolving-door position of secretary of Homeland Security is Trump's senior strategist, Stephen Miller, who is actually the force that controlled the administration's immigration policies, although he did not hold an official position. In the summer of 2019, Miller purged the leadership positions at the Department of Homeland Security. Within seven weeks, he removed or reassigned the head of every immigration-related department. He has influenced the zero-tolerance policy, the administration's inhumane family separation practices, and he was in favor of strictly limiting the number of refugees who gain asylum in the U.S. (Miroff and Dawsey 2019). He has been quoted as saying, "I would be happy if not a single refugee foot ever again touched American soil" (Sims 2019).

In late 2019, the Southern Poverty Law Center (SPLC) published a six-part series about Miller that unearthed 900 email messages he sent to Breitbart News. He sent the emails from March 4, 2015, to June 27, 2016, when he worked for then Sen. Jeff Sessions of Alabama. The emails were leaked to SPLC's Hatewatch by Katie McHugh, a former editor at Breitbart. She was active in the far right and communicated frequently with Miller. McHugh was fired from Breitbart and has rejected the far right (Hayden 2019).[1]

Michael Hayden, SPLC Hatewatch reporter, says that Miller's emails reveal that he consistently depicted immigrants of color as menacing or violent. He lied by omission, frequently writing about crimes committed by Latin American immigrants as part of a pattern of violence, but did not focus on crimes committed by whites. He also made examples of immigrants who committed crimes and ignored those who prospered and did well. Race or immigration were the subject of eighty percent of his emails—none were neutral about any non-white or a foreigner. In an email dated January 5, 2016, with the subject line "off-the-record observation," Miller wrote, "It has never been easier for illegal aliens to commit crimes of violence against America" (Hayden 2019).

Hatewatch reports that Jason L. Riley, a senior fellow at the Manhattan Institute for Policy Research, wrote a *Wall Street Journal* op-ed in which he described numerous studies about the rate of crimes by migrants from the past 100 years. The data show that immigrants, no matter their nationality or legal status, are less likely to commit violent crimes or be incarcerated than members of the native population. The White House tried to discredit Hatewatch's reporting. Nevertheless, Hayden noted that while attempting to do so, the White House did not refute the authenticity of the emails (Hayden 2019).

While Trump uses dehumanizing terms like "animals" to describe immigrants, Miller avoids this language publicly and takes a more cunning approach, disparaging asylum seekers as criminals. Steven Camarota, senior policy adviser for the Washington think tank the Center for Immigration Studies, says that Miller has had a huge role in changing the central point of the immigration debate. Instead of focusing on the plight of immigrants, Miller draws attention to what he espouses to be the best interests of the United States. Miller was aligned with the think tank when he was a congressional aide. He uses "brimstone rhetoric" to keep immigration as a hot issue. He believes immigration is a cultural war that Trump can win. Miller continues to defend the zero-tolerance policy because he sees it as a deterrent that would have been successful if it had continued openly. He also regards the squalid conditions and inhumane detention of immigrants as a deterrent to migration and thinks that publicizing them is not a bad strategy (Miroff and Dawsey 2019).

In a letter to Trump in November 2019, 107 members of Congress called for Miller's ouster. They pressured the president to either call for Miller's resignation or fire him. In the letter, they noted that his emails reveal him as a white nationalist and conspiracy theorist and that he supports "white supremacist ideology and literature, xenophobic conspiracy theories ... [and] white supremacist websites." The representatives point out that because of Miller's role in influencing immigration policy for the Trump administration, "his documented dedication to extremist, anti-immigrant ideology and conspiracy mongering is disqualifying" (Pingree 2019).

The text of the letter reads:

Dear President Trump:

We formally request that you immediately remove White House Senior Advisor Stephen Miller from your administration. A documented white nationalist has no place in any presidential administration, and especially not in such an influential position.

Last week, numerous emails sent by Mr. Miller were made public that clearly establish that he is an avid white nationalist and conspiracy theorist. These emails included material exposing Miller's support of white supremacist ideology and literature, xenophobic conspiracy theories, as well as his promotion of white supremacist websites. According to the Southern Poverty Law Center's Hatewatch blog, which obtained the emails, 80 percent of the more than 900 emails directly referenced race or immigration, and none contained "examples of Miller writing sympathetically or even in neutral tones about any person who is non-white or foreign-born." Given Mr. Miller's role in shaping immigration policy for your administration, his documented dedication to extremist, anti-immigrant ideology and conspiracy-mongering is disqualifying.

Beyond the disturbing emails that Mr. Miller wrote, is the clear conclusion that he brought his dedication to white nationalism with him into your administration and translated this hateful ideology directly into your administration's discriminatory immigration policies. Mr. Miller's documented hatred of Muslim immigrants shaped your Muslim ban, and sheds new light on your administration's intent in writing that ban. Mr. Miller's clear support for halting all immigration is evident in many forms, including your continued support for ending DACA as well as the increasing difficulty of obtaining asylum and visas across all categories. There is a clear line between Miller's advocacy for books like "Camp of the Saints,"—a novel celebrated by neo–Nazis for promoting the view of non-white immigrants as "monsters"—and the Administration's inhumane family separation policy, of which Miller was the primary architect.

Stephen Miller's nativism was cited as a major impetus behind your decision to reject a bipartisan compromise immigration bill that would have protected Dreamers due to his belief that the compromise would not reduce enough documented immigration. Appallingly, Mr. Miller referred to refugees as "foreign-born terrorists" in his emails, a belief which clearly translated to the unprecedented low ceiling on refugee admissions and even lower actual entrants at a time of the worst international refugee crisis in history. These are just a few obvious examples of Mr. Miller's white supremacist influence on your immigration policy, and it seems likely that his perfidious adherence to extremist ideology has shaped your administration in ways that are not yet public. Miller's emails and the sentiments expressed in them are incompatible with public service and render him unfit to shape any policy—immigration or otherwise

We refuse to tolerate white nationalism and xenophobia in the White House or elsewhere in the United States. Mr. Miller must be fired immediately [Pingree 2019].

In addition to the members of Congress, 27 senators, led by Kamala Harris, also sent a letter to president calling for Miller's ouster (Wyrich 2019). Dozens of civil rights organizations followed suit (Karanth 2019), as have a coalition of Jewish organizations (Oster 2019).

9.3 Remain in Mexico—Migrant Protection Protocols (MPP)

In December 2018, metering led to "Migrant Protection Protocols" (MPP) or the Remain in Mexico policy. Under this program, migrants who come at the southern border—either at a port of entry or after crossing between ports of entry—are given notices to appear in immigration court. They are then sent back to wait in Mexico. They are directed to go to a specific port of entry at a specific date and time for their next court hearing (American Immigration Council 2020).

Many places where the asylum seekers have been sent are extremely dangerous. The U.S. State Department lists Tamaulipas as a Level 4 threat risk. According to Human Rights First, this is the same level of risk as in Afghanistan, Iraq, Syria, Somalia, North Korea, and Yemen (Human Rights First 2019).[2] The nearby city of Nuevo Laredo and the Matamoros port of entry are also highly dangerous. Due to the MPPs, as of October 2019, 50,000 migrants and asylum seekers were waiting in Mexico (Human Rights First 2019). This number included 16,000 children, about 500 of whom were babies (Young Center for Immigrant Children's Rights 2019).

The administration slanted the purpose of this policy as bringing "integrity" to the immigration system and as an "effective" alternative to family detention and separation. This is not true. As Human Rights First states, "The Trump administration has refused to implement humane, effective, and fiscally prudent strategies to manage refugee arrivals in ways that uphold U.S. law and treaty commitments" (Human Rights First 2019).

In October 2019, Human Rights First published *Orders from Above: Massive Human Rights Abuses Under the Trump Administration Return to Mexico Policy*. The report was based on interviews with asylum seekers, attorneys, humanitarian volunteers, and government officials in Mexico. It also continued field research, observed MPP court hearings, and gathered information from human rights organizations, legal monitors, and the media. Their report was an update of earlier reports written in March 2019 and August 2019. The following information is from the major findings from the October report:

- The Trump administration is delivering men, women and children seeking refuge from Cuba, El Salvador, Honduras, Nicaragua, Venezuela, and other countries to some of the most dangerous areas of Mexico. DHS continues these dangerous forced returns despite widely reported media, academic, and NGO reports that organized criminal groups and corrupt Mexican law enforcement officials, among others, target asylum seekers for kidnapping, rape, and other violent attacks.
- There are already over 340 public reports of attacks including rape, kidnapping, torture, and other brutality against asylum seekers returned to Mexico under MPP—a sharp increase from August when Human Rights First identified 110 publicly reported attacks

against returned individuals. But these kidnappings and assaults are still likely vastly underreported, as the overwhelming majority of returned individuals have not spoken with journalists or human rights investigators.
- **The MPP fear-screening process is a farce that returns asylum seekers to grave danger.** CBP continues to fail to refer asylum seekers for these deeply flawed fear-screening interviews, which appear to be increasingly cursory and perfunctory. DHS has returned individuals to Mexico under MPP who were previously targeted there, including a transgender woman from El Salvador, who had been kidnapped and raped.
- **In violation of its own policy, DHS returns Mexican nationals and vulnerable individuals, including those with serious medical issues, pregnant women and LBGTQ persons.**
- **Refugees and migrants are stranded in Mexico in often inhumane and horrific conditions.** More than one thousand children, families, and adults are sleeping in the streets of the Matamoros port of entry without adequate access to water or proper sanitation, too afraid to enter the city because of the extreme violence there.
- **MPP is a due process charade** that effectively makes it impossible for the vast majority to be represented by counsel in their immigration court removal proceedings. Nearly 99 percent of all returned asylum seekers were unrepresented through August 2019, according to the latest available data from the immigration courts. Not only does MPP endanger the safety of refugees, but also threatens the safety of American lawyers and volunteers who DHS is essentially pushing to cross into areas of Mexico plagued by kidnappings and deadly violence to attempt to provide some assistance [Human Rights First 2019].

Orders from Above: Massive Human Rights Abuses Under the Trump Administration Return to Mexico Policy includes 30 reports of violent incidents against asylum seekers who have been returned to Mexico. Some asylum seekers were kidnapped by organized crime syndicates in Nuevo Laredo; others have been kidnapped and harmed in different areas of the border region; many have been assaulted; some were previously targeted in Mexico, but were still returned there; and others were "individuals from vulnerable populations [who] may be excluded from the on a case by case basis" (Human Rights First 2019). The following are examples of these victims:

- Asylum seekers are kidnapped by crime syndicates in Nuevo Laredo

A three-year-old boy from Honduras and his parents were kidnapped after DHS returned them to Nuevo Laredo. The boy's parents were separated, and the woman reported hearing the kidnappers beat and electrocute her husband. When she last saw him lying on the ground, beaten and bleeding, he told her, "Love, they're going to kill us." The woman and her three-year-old son were released but she does not know if her husband is alive.

A child and his father were kidnapped the same day DHS returned them to Nuevo Laredo and the kidnappers threatened to take the child's kidneys. They were held with dozens of abducted women and children, and around twenty men. The kidnappers separated the women from the men and beat the men who tried to see what was happening to the women. One man who tried to escape was shot and killed. "One of the kidnappers told me that the kidneys of my [child] were good for removal," the father sobbed, recounting his ordeal to Vice News. "I can't sleep thinking about it. Every night, I dream about everything that has happened to us." After this trauma, the father said his child "has stopped talking altogether."

- Asylum seekers are kidnapped in Ciudad Juarez

A Guatemalan family with two children were kidnapped for ransom by men in Mexican federal police uniforms after DHS returned them to Ciudad Juárez in July. The family told an immigration attorney that the kidnappers tortured some of the migrants held with them, duct-taping plastic bags over their heads to suffocate them. They and others managed to escape when their abductors unexpectedly left. However, the family later saw the same men who had kidnapped them near the shelter where they were hiding.

- Asylum seekers are assaulted and threatened

A teenage Guatemalan asylum seeker was attacked and beaten in the street in Mexicali, according to attorneys from a legal services organization that visited Mexicali in September. On the day prior to Human Rights First's visit to Mexicali in June, forty men attacked residents of a migrant hostel with metal bars and pipes, severely injuring several individuals including a Central American asylum seeker.

- Asylum seekers are expelled from the U.S. even though they had been previously targeted in Mexico

Three children, all under the age of ten, and their mother sought asylum in the United States but were sent by DHS to Matamoros. They were returned to Mexico even though they had previously been abducted in Villahermosa. The family was held by kidnappers for nearly a month and only managed to escape when other migrants held with them helped the family to escape when the woman's youngest daughter became gravely ill. When the mother told CBP about the kidnapping and her fears her family would be harmed if returned to Mexico, the officer told her that "we have orders from above to return all."

- Asylum seekers from vulnerable populations are returned to Mexico in violation of internal MPP policy

A boy with Down syndrome and a deaf, mute woman returned by DHS to Matamoros;

A child who suffers brain seizures and needs medical care his father said he could not secure in Mexico;

9. Further Harm

Multiple pregnant women, including a woman experiencing contractions and another woman who ultimately gave birth in a tent in Matamoros, according to a complaint filed with the DHS OIG by the ACLU of Texas and the ACLU Border Rights Center;

- Asylum seekers are returned to Mexico without screenings

A Honduran asylum seeker and his 9-year-old son were sent to Matamoros without a fear screening even though the man explained to CBP officers that he and his son had been kidnapped and that he was subsequently tortured by Mexican law enforcement officers Tamaulipas who burned him with cigarettes. The man showed Human Rights First researchers several small round scars on his stomach that appeared consistent with his account. **He said a CBP officer threatened to separate him from his son if he persisted in insisting that he feared return to Mexico** [Human Rights First 2019].

On November 22, 2019, the Florence Project, which responds to and serves asylum seekers throughout Arizona, and their partner organizations across the country united to advocate the preservation of the United States asylum system and against the remain in Mexico plan. A new phase of this plan was about to be implemented in the Tucson sector. Earlier in the week, a similar plan had been announced to send asylum seekers to Guatemala instead of allowing their applications to go forward in the U.S. The Florence Project views the plan to move migrants from Tucson to Mexico as "another step to eviscerate the asylum system and strip away the fundamental human rights of migrants" (The Florence Immigrant and Refugee Rights Project, email communication, November 22, 2019).

As of November 18, 2019, the Florence Project reported, "There have been at least 400 publicly reported cases of rape, torture, kidnapping and other violent assaults against asylum seekers and migrants who have been forced to return to Mexico under this illegal policy."

The Florence Project warned that if this plan continues to be implemented, it will "put more lives at risk and prevent asylum seekers from accessing legal resources, justice, and community support." They add that these asylum seekers are purposely being sent away from "a community where they have access to hospitality groups, support, and legal services" (The Florence Immigrant and Refugee Rights Project, email communication, November 22, 2019).

Removing these people from this support system will ensure that asylum seekers who could have received humanitarian and legal assistance at the Arizona border will now be denied both.

The policy was subject to challenges in the Ninth District Circuit Court. On February 28, 2010, the court ruled to halt the policy in Arizona and California, but the decision was stayed the following day. Then on March 11, the U.S. Supreme Court ruled in an 8–1 decision that the policy could continue.

9.4 Deportation Courts

In an article for the *New York Times Review of Books*, titled "Inside the Deportation Courts," attorney Madeleine Schwartz described the proceedings that took place in four Texas courts that she visited in August 2019. Schwartz explained that immigrants engaged in deportation proceedings have no right to appointed counsel. Since it is almost impossible to retain a lawyer in Mexico and difficult to get one in the United States, migrants are left to defend themselves in immigration hearings (Schwartz 2019).

Notices to Appear (NTAs) are four pages long, confusing, written in English and are often mailed to people who live in camps, shelters, or other temporary housing. Therefore, delivering them to the correct recipient can be nearly impossible. Debbie Nathan writes, "Such documents are legally required to list an immigrant's physical address so that an immigration court can send notices as the case progresses." She then describes the plight of a family whose address was listed as "Facebook." Other notices listed the family's address as two Mexican shelters, one in Nuevo Laredo and the other in Matamoros. The family knew nothing about these shelters and had never been to either one (Nathan 2019).

The NTAs give two reasons why immigrants need to appear in person. The first is that the migrant is not an American citizen in immigration court. The second is that he or she is a citizen of another country. If the judge decides that the allegations against the individual are correct, the person can remain in the U.S. if granted asylum, cancelation of removal, or an adjustment in status. The person can also choose to leave the U.S. This is called "voluntary departure," and must be undertaken at the individual's expense. If immigrants miss their hearings, even through no fault of their own, they can be deported without a hearing.

Many of the migrants, if they do figure out when they are supposed to appear for their hearings, are often called to report to court as early as 4:00 in the morning. The courts are often in places that are known to be dangerous, which makes the trip difficult. It is even less likely that they will be able to find counsel who are willing to do that kind of treacherous travel in the early morning hours (Young Center for Immigrant Children's Rights 2019).

Under the remain in Mexico program, instead of coming to a regular court with a judge in person and a lawyer for their hearings, migrants often come to a makeshift tent. The tent has been set up with a video feed. Judges appear on the screen from as far away as New York or Los Angeles. These courts are closed to the public even though immigration courts are supposed to be open. Lawyers and journalists have been blocked from entering these courts (Young Center for Immigrant Children's Rights 2019).

9. Further Harm 139

Additionally, the judges in over 60 U.S. courts who hear the immigration cases have little autonomy when making decisions. Unlike other judges, they are part of the executive branch, and can be reassigned or fired by the attorney general. They can be sanctioned if they do not process cases quickly. Trump hired over 200 new judges. The Associated Press reports that approximately 50 percent of these appointees were lawyers for ICE. The judges were required to meet a quota of 700 cases a year. The Trump administration eliminated their power to close cases and has transferred that power to the attorney general (Schwartz 2019).

In one court that Schwartz visited, six notices had been sent to a nearby shelter, but none of the defendants were in court. Their notices had been "returned to sender." The judge quickly listed their notices to appear as exhibit one, and the notices that were mailed and returned to sender as exhibit two. She then sent a clerk to see if the defendants were in the waiting room. They were not. Then, the judge declared the evidence "clear, unequivocal, and compelling." She then stated into the record that the court would sign an order for their removal. She commented to the government attorney on the speed of their timing—finishing the cases for the day before noon. As quickly as that, the judge had added six cases to her quota of 700 for the year (Schwartz 2019).

Attorney Dianne Post states that there were reports of immigration judges retiring, asking for transfers, taking medical leave, and even quitting rather than follow administration rules of denying asylum to everyone. She argues that we need more of that from everyone—including border patrol agents. "Just don't do it!" If enough people refused to go along with the unfair practices of the administration, they would have to relent (D. Post, personal communication, December 31, 2019).

As the articles of UN conventions show, the actions of the court violate international law. The ICCPR (UN General Assembly 1966a) consists of four parts. It has a total of 52 articles. Three of these articles pertain to due process for children and their families. According to attorney Dianne Post, Article 13 provides right of due process for aliens when they are on the soil of another country. In a court where Schwartz visited, however, asylum seekers did not even receive the notices to attend court, and the notices had been marked "return to sender." The migrants were denied due process, yet the judge considered the notices as part of the "clear, unequivocal, and compelling evidence" on which she based her decision to deport the migrants (Schwartz 2019).

Article 13 reads:

> An alien lawfully in the territory of a State Party to the present Covenant may be expelled there from only in pursuance of a decision reached in accordance with law and shall, except when compelling reasons of national security otherwise require, be

allowed to submit the reasons against his expulsion and to have his case reviewed by, and be represented for the purpose before, the competent authority or a person or persons especially designated by the competent authority.

Articles 14 and 26 provide equal protection for any alien in the courts. Article 14 emphasizes that all persons shall be equal in the courts and entitled to a fair hearing and shall be presumed innocent until proven guilty. The charge against a person must also be explained in a language that the person can understand. According to this article, legal counsel should be assigned to the person, but U.S. immigration courts do not provide legal counsel. Article 26 reinforces the idea that a person will receive equal protection without discrimination on specific grounds, including race, color, language, national origin, birth or other status.

Individual complaints regarding violations of the ICCPR can be made to the UN Human Rights Committee.

Article 14 states in part:

1. All persons shall be equal before the courts and tribunals. In the determination of any criminal charge against him, or of his rights and obligations in a suit at law, everyone shall be entitled to a fair and public hearing by a competent, independent and impartial tribunal established by law…

2. Everyone charged with a criminal offence shall have the right to be presumed innocent until guilty according to law.

3. In the determination of any criminal charge against him, everyone shall be entitled to the following minimum guarantees, in full equality:

    a. To be informed promptly and in detail in a language which he understands of the nature and cause of the charge against him;

    b. To have adequate time and facilities for the preparation of his defence and to communicate with counsel of his own choosing;

    c. To be tried without undue delay;

    d. To be tried in his presence, and to defend himself in person or through legal assistance of his own choosing; to be informed, if he does not have legal assistance, of this right; and to have legal assistance assigned to him, in any case where the interests of justice so require, and without payment by him in any such case if he does not have sufficient means to pay for it;

    e. To examine, or have examined, the witnesses against him and to obtain the attendance and examination of witnesses on his behalf under the same conditions as witnesses against him;

    f. To have the free assistance of an interpreter if he cannot understand or speak the language used in court;

    g. Not to be compelled to testify against himself or to confess guilt.

Article 26 states:

All persons are equal before the law and are entitled without any discrimination to the equal protection of the law. In this respect, the law shall prohibit any discrimination and guarantee to all persons equal and effective protection against discrimination on any ground such as race, colour, sex, language, religion, political or other opinion, national or social origin, property, birth or other status [United Nations 2020].

9.5 Further Cruel Actions

The Transit Ban

The transit ban is another policy, issued in July 2019, that prevented migrants from gaining asylum in the U.S. This policy prohibited anyone who has travelled through a third country from gaining asylum here if they have not first gained asylum in the other country through which they have travelled. The ban was placed on unaccompanied children as well as adults. But under the Trafficking Victims Protection Reauthorization Act (TVPRA), unaccompanied children must be screened and transferred to federal custody once they arrive at our border (Young Center for Immigrant Children's Rights 2019).

Cutting Recreational and Educational Services

In June 2019, English classes, recreational programs, and legal aid were cancelled for children housed in federal migrant shelters nationwide. According to Mark Weber, a spokesman for the Department of Health and Human Services (HHS), the funding stream for any activities that have been determined to be "not directly necessary for the protection of life and safety, including educational services, legal services, and recreation," have been discontinued (Sacchetti 2019a).

Budget constraints brought about by increasing number of unaccompanied minors coming into the shelters was the given reason for the cuts in services. The *Flores* settlement mandates education and recreation for children in federal custody. Education classes should take place Monday through Friday. Basic English language competencies are designated as a priority (A. Flores 2019).

Denying children time for leisure and recreation is a violation of Article 31, paragraph 1 of the *Convention on the Rights of the Child* (UN General Assembly 1989). In addition to the legal protections cited above, denying detained children access to legal assistance is a violation of Article 37, section (d), of the CRC.

Article 31 reads:

> States Parties recognize the right of the child to rest and leisure, to engage in play and recreational activities appropriate to the age of the child and to participate freely in cultural life and the arts.

Article 37, section (d), reads:

> Every child deprived of his or her liberty shall have the right to prompt access to legal and other appropriate assistance, as well as the right to challenge the legality of the deprivation of his or her liberty before a court or other competent, independent and

impartial authority, and to a prompt decision on any such action [UN General Assembly 1989].

Deporting Migrants Receiving Critical Medical Care

August 2019 was a particularly cruel month for migrant children and their families. In stark contrast to previous, longstanding legal practice, federal authorities notified families of critically ill migrant children to leave the U.S. within 33 days. The children had medical deferments that enabled them to receive treatment that might not be available in their own countries (Levin 2019).

Ken Cuccinelli, acting director at U.S. Citizenship and Immigration Services (USCIS), cut the program and sent notices to approximately 400 migrants, informing them that their applications would not be considered, and that they could be deported (Dinan 2019b).

The administration did not announce the termination of the policy and did not provide time for public comment. In September, families and doctors appeared at a hearing before Congress. One boy testified that he had cystic fibrosis and that if he was sent back to Honduras, his home country, he would die. Dr. Fiona Danaher, a pediatrician from Massachusetts, called the policy "unconscionably inhumane" (Sakelaris 2019a).

In September, Kevin McAleenan, then-acting Homeland Security secretary, ordered a complete restart of the program, but emphasized that approval would be subject to close scrutiny. Weeks later, Cuccinelli admitted that he bungled the rollout. He said that given another opportunity to implement the policy, he would implement it prospectively, not retrospectively (Dinan 2019b).

Attempts to Lift Limits on Detention Time

In August, the administration proposed new rules authorizing border agents to detain migrant families for more than 20 days as allowed by the *Flores* settlement. The administration argued again that a detention period of only 20 days was a loophole that encouraged border crossings for families with children (Sakelaris 2019b).

The proposed change did not take place. U.S. District Judge Dolly Gee heard arguments from the Justice Department and advocates who support the *Flores* settlement and issued a permanent injunction blocking the proposed changes. Gee wrote that the proposed regulations "fail to implement and are inconsistent with the relevant and substantive terms of the *Flores* settlement Agreement." She added that the agreement is a binding contract that was never appealed (Sacchetti 2019b).

The Public Charge Rule

In October 2019, George Daniels, a federal judge from New York, blocked a Trump administration rule just before it was about to be implemented. The "public charge" rule would assess immigrants' use of public benefits when they applied for more permanent standing in the United States. Judge Daniels ruled that the Trump administration overstepped its authority in attempting to expand the guidelines for public charge. Applying for more permanent standing usually means someone is applying for a green card. Under Trump's plan, the history of use of public benefits—food stamps, Medicaid, cash assistance, and other programs—would be scrutinized when any immigrant applied to live in the United States. The administration was attempting to strip away financial and other supports for those struggling to come to this country, limiting admittance only to those who could immediately support themselves financially. Acting USCIS director Ken Cuccinelli was a major supporter of the plan.

Article 23 of the *Convention Relating to the Status of Refugees* (UN General Assembly 1951) states that refugees must be given the same public relief as a citizen. This article of the convention would be violated if the "public charge rule" came to fruition (Dianne Post, personal communication, September 27, 2019).

Article 23 reads:

> The contracting states shall accord to refugees lawfully staying in their territory the same treatment with respect to public relief as is accorded to their nationals.

Eliminating Vaccines by Customs for Migrants in Border Protection

The administration denied flu vaccine to people in the custody of Customs and Border Patrol. At least three children in U.S. custody had died of flu since December 2018, but the vaccines were withheld. Children age 5 and under, especially those below age 2, are vulnerable to complications of the flu (Cohen and Bonifield 2019). A statement released by CPB said, "In general, due to the short-term nature of CBP holding and the complexities of operating vaccination programs, neither CBP nor its medical contractors administer vaccinations to those in our custody" (WebMD 2019).

The reason given for not administering the vaccine was that migrants are supposed to stay in CBP custody for under 72 hours. They then move on to the care of Health and Human Services, where they can receive the vaccine. However, many migrants remain in CPB custody well past the 72-hour limit. During this extended time, they can contract and spread the flu.

Sen. Elizabeth Warren and twelve other senators wrote a letter to Kevin McAleenan, acting secretary of the Department of Homeland Security, and Alex Azar, secretary of the Department of Health and Human Services, expressing their concern that vaccines would not be administered through CPB. They were particularly concerned that the vaccines be given to prevent individual illness and community and national outbreaks (Warren, Blumenthal, et al. 2019; original includes questions that required responses by the officials by September 20, 2019, signatures, and citations). The text of the letter reads:

> Dear Acting Secretary McAleenan and Secretary Azar:
>
> We are writing to express our serious concerns over the U.S. Department of Homeland Security's (DHS) recent announcement, through U.S. Customs and Border Protection (CBP), that migrant families currently detained at CBP holding centers will not be vaccinated for the flu ahead of this year's flu season. This dangerous decision not to administer vaccinations for a disease that has already proven fatal to children in CBP's custody is immoral and irresponsible, placing entire communities at risk of the flu and its associated complications. CBP must do more to ensure the health of migrant children and families under its care, and we strongly urge the agency to reconsider its plan not to vaccinate those in its custody.
>
> Children, the elderly, and pregnant women are among those at the highest risk of contracting the flu. According to the Centers for Disease Control and Prevention (CDC), "the best way to prevent seasonal flu is to get vaccinated every year." In addition to reducing the likelihood that vaccinated individuals become infected with the flu, flu vaccines help prevent outbreaks from spreading throughout communities and the nation as a whole. The CDC currently recommends that all individuals above the age of 6 months receive a flu vaccine by the end of October 2019 to protect against the disease for the upcoming flu season. The American Academy of Pediatrics also recommends "routine influenza immunization of all children without medical contraindications, starting at 6 months of age." Furthermore, the U.S. Citizenship and Immigration Services (USCIS) policy manual notes that the CDC requires that immigrants receive flu vaccines.
>
> Since 2018, at least seven children who had been in federal custody—including CBP—have died. Though the flu is a preventable illness, medical professionals have recently reported that at least three children in U.S. custody died, in part, from the flu. CBP's largest detention center, located in McAllen, Texas, also had to temporarily stop processing migrants earlier this year due to a flu outbreak that affected nearly three dozen detainees. Overcrowded conditions in CBP facilities may have contributed to the spread of the flu, which can spread to others "up to about 6 feet away." A recent investigation by the DHS Office of Inspector General, for example, found "serious overcrowding" in CBP's centers, and revealed that children at several facilities "had no access to showers," "limited access to a change of clothes," and had "limited space for medical isolation."
>
> Despite these recent deaths, CBP confirmed late last month that it would not be vaccinating the migrant families it has detained ahead of this year's flu season. A CBP spokeswoman justified this decision by citing, in part, the "short-term nature of CBP holding[s]." The following day however, DHS and the U.S. Department of Health and

Human Services (HHS) announced a new rule to amend the Flores settlement Agreement, which, if implemented, would allow for the long-term, potentially indefinite detention of children and parents in DHS facilities. CBP's decision not to vaccinate those in its custody, especially considering this new potential for prolonged detentions, jeopardizes the health of the children and parents under its watch. Furthermore, this decision "could make wider flu outbreaks more likely," which "could result in additional risk to CBP personnel" and the American public.

CBP's decision not to vaccinate against this preventable harm, which has already proven fatal for children in its custody, is inexcusable. In response to our concerns, we ask that you provide answers to the following questions no later than September 20, 2019.

On December 10, 2019, six protestors, including at least two doctors, were arrested outside the Border Patrol's San Diego Sector headquarters in Chula Vista, California. The previous day, members of Doctors for Camp Closures, Families Belong Together, and Never Again Action advocated setting up a mobile clinic to administer vaccines to migrants. CBP officials turned them away (Giartelli 2019). The press secretary of the Department of Homeland Security stated on Twitter, "Of course Border Patrol isn't going to let a random group of radical political activists show up and start injecting people with drugs" (Wolf [@SpoxDHS] 2019). Those who were arrested had lain on the ground to block access to the facility. Even the Centers for Disease Control and Prevention, however, had been putting pressure on CBP to provide the shots to the migrant children (Mosenbergen 2019).

Cutting off medical care and deporting children with critical illnesses can clearly jeopardize their lives. Refusing to provide children with immunizations and recreational opportunities also violates children's standards of health. The following articles of the *Convention on the Rights of the Child* (CRC) protect these rights:

> Article 24(b). To ensure the provision of necessary medical assistance and health care to all children with emphasis on the development of primary health care;
>
> Article 27, paragraph 1. States Parties recognize the right of every child to a standard of living adequate for the child's physical, mental, spiritual, moral and social development [UN General Assembly 1989].

Allowing ICE to Use Migrant Children's Data to Increase Adult Deportations

In late December 2019, Stephen Miller, the Trump administration's immigration adviser, devised a secret plan to embed immigration agents within ORR, which is overseen by HHS. According to the *Washington Post*, six current and former officials of the Trump administration reported that plan's purpose was to gather information about migrant children's parents and relatives and use it as evidence to deport them. The plan went around laws that attempt to keep the refugee program off limits for deportation enforcement. If the adults were not granted custody, the administration determined that they were no longer "potential sponsors." Once dropped from the refugee program, they could be arrested. ICE officials claim they focus on persons with criminal records, but even a minor offense, such as a traffic violation, can fall within this category. Mark Weber, spokesman for HHS, told the *Washington Post* that there were no ICE personnel stationed at the agency, and "no plans for ICE personnel to be placed at HHS." (Miroff 2019).

10

Families in Mexico

10.1 *Refugee Aid*

The events described in this section of the book took place between June 2018 and mid–June 2020. On March 20, the Trump administration closed the Mexican border, restricting all nonessential travel to the United States, purportedly due to fears of spreading the novel coronavirus.

By the spring of 2019, 168,000 migrants had traveled through the border communities of the southwest United States. Faith-based groups, municipalities, and nonprofits provided shelter and care. The following is a profile of Refugee Aid, a nonprofit. Descriptions of the work of two other humanitarian initiatives.

Summer 2018–Winter 2019

In the summer of 2018, approximately 200 asylum seekers arrived in Phoenix, Arizona, each day. Many families were dropped off by ICE at churches or the bus station parking lot. The situation was turning into a public safety hazard for both the immigrants and the city. One family even walked along the side of a heavily traveled highway from the bus station to the airport, carrying their toddler son.

Refugee Aid is a group that I came to know. Arizona resident Mary Jo Forman Miller is a retired attorney. She saw that families had traveled 2,000 miles and were coming from Border Patrol stations where they slept on concrete floors with only a mylar blanket for warmth, and they had little food and water. A magnet on her refrigerator reads, "If you're not OUTRAGED then you're not PAYING ATTENTION." Mary Jo knew that she had to do something, so she and a small group of friends started the grassroots organization Refugee Aid to advocate on behalf of refugee children and families. Ultimately, her group provided a hands-on safety net for families as they made their journey to sponsors in the United States. The group is not politically affiliated. The essence of their work is that all people should be treated humanely.

Olga, Leti, and family at the Phoenix airport (courtesy Deirdra Sparling).

During the winter and spring of 2019, Refugee Aid volunteers met immigrant families when they were dropped by ICE at a dirty ditch next to the Greyhound bus station in Phoenix. Greyhound officials refused to allow the immigrant families on their property unless they had a bus ticket. They were only permitted in the bus station if their tickets had a departure time less than two hours away. Refugee Aid volunteers offered immigrant families towels to sit on in the dirt of the ditch, served them a meal, and either took them to the airport to make sure they boarded the correct plane or brought them to a safe place to stay until they traveled on to meet their sponsors. Many Refugee Aid volunteers hosted families in their own homes, supplying hot showers, food, and a place to sleep (M.J. Forman Miller, personal communication, June 28, 2020).

Refugee Aid also collected non-perishable food, gently used clothing, shoes, lip balm, and items for children who were traveling. They supplied books, small stuffed animals, coloring books, and crayons. The volunteers also helped prepare and serve meals at sanctuary churches. Martha Iskyan and her husband Howard solicited donations of all kinds. Once a week they met with other volunteers and sorted through the clothing, put the items in bags, labeled them in English and Spanish, and distributed donated food to local churches (M. Iskyan, personal communication, May 18, 2020).

One volunteer, who wished to remain anonymous, invited asylum seekers to stay in her home and wrote the following article about their stay.

Trust.
One of the things that influenced me most to take refugees into my home was the idea of trust. It is the same reason that I feel comfortable participating in home exchanges. I just like the idea of trusting people, and I didn't believe the rhetoric about how bad the people seeking asylum were.
So, starting in May of last year, my husband and I began taking refugees from Central America into our home. These families had nowhere to spend the night after being dropped off by ICE at the Greyhound station in Phoenix. Without a ticket in hand and without the means of purchasing one, they were left to the streets. Luckily Refugee Aid and other volunteer organizations rose to the need and provided assistance in arranging transportation to their sponsors (note: the sponsors paid for that transportation). Of course, arranging transportation can take time, so while those arrangements were being made, volunteers provided food, a backpack with toiletries and a change of clothes. Even with that help, they still were left stranded on a small strip of land between the Greyhound station and the road while they waited for their bus or plane to depart.
That's where volunteers like us arrived to pick them up and take them into our homes. Hosting them involved providing showers and a chance to have their clothes washed; a comfortable bed; meals as well as food to take with them on their journey to their sponsors; entertainment to help them escape for a bit from the strain of the trip— but mostly a safe haven where they could rest and relax a bit.
There is much I don't know about the people who stayed with us. Neither my husband nor I speak Spanish, so communication was limited to what could be done via the Google Translate application. What I do know is that we mostly hosted fathers traveling with pre-teen or teenage sons. They carried only the clothes on their backs and usually had little or no money. All of them carried the weight of their situation with them but had a deep faith that sustained them. They were sad to leave the rest of their family behind and none of them would have made the journey if they had a better alternative.
We provided them with a respite and safe haven for the brief time they spent with us. They expressed their gratitude and prayed that God would bless us for what we had done for them. In the end, I do not know what difference we made in their lives and what has become of them, but I do know that they made a difference in our lives, blessing us with their presence. Indeed, their prayer for us came true [Anonymous, personal communication, June 28, 2020].

Gloria S. is a volunteer for Refugee Aid. She helped out at a variety of churches and became friends with volunteers who assisted the seekers. Since she worked closely with the families, and saw the stress that was part of daily life of for the migrant children, she and the other volunteers tried to alleviate that stress. Gloria tells the following stories:

> One day, as I carried a container of brightly colored lip balm into a shelter, I felt a tug on my shirt. Looking down, I saw a young migrant girl who pointed to her blistered, bitten, swollen lips. I quickly handed her some lip balm. This girl was one of many detained children I had seen who were so anxious that they bit their lips raw.
>
> My friend, Marta, is a long-time volunteer. She is Honduran-American and a military veteran. Marta is a dynamo. She actually bought a bus to help transport seekers from the bus station to churches, places to stay, etc. Marta worked all day, every day with the seekers. At any given time, she had as many as 30 people staying with her. When all the beds in her large home were taken, the migrants laid on the floor. Marta's house has at least four bathrooms, but I believe that she also added a porta potty. Outside showers were needed, so Marta's husband set up portable ones. They are such thoughtful and generous people!
>
> Nueva Esperanza was one of the first Churches here to help take seekers. There were about 15 Latino churches that helped starting in October 2018. El Buen Pastor was my favorite Latino Church because I enjoyed the volunteers so much. Another church that helped was Helping with All My Heart. Many of the generous Latino churches were extremely poor themselves. The head of Arizona ICE had contacted one of the church officials in 2018 to ask if the Latino churches would help with the asylum seekers. ICE knew many Latino parishioners were first- or second-generation Americans and therefore would be more willing to help newcomers who were going through what they went through.
>
> Most of the churches had huge kettles and a gas burner tripod to set them on so they could cook a big kettle of chicken soup. They threw whole chicken legs into 10 gallons of water and let them boil, then added veggies, hominy, and other ingredients. El Buen

Marta bought a bus to transport seekers (courtesy Gloria S.).

Pastor had the huge tortilla warmer. The volunteers at this church made homemade tortillas. What a chore! It took hours, but the volunteers wanted the immigrants to be happy and felt all the work was worth it.

All asylum seeker arrivals prayed as soon as they came to the churches. Then they had a meal. Mostly all of them would be crying because they were so thankful to be with us. As soon as they had eaten, some people started showering, and others got medical attention from a group called 100 Angels that did medical care for the asylum seekers in this area. Others went to the clothing room for new clothes. **It was such a cool system!** Then all of the seekers sat in shady areas with bottles of Pedialyte

El Buen Pastor Church (courtesy Gloria S.).

Left: Latino church cooking—soup pot. *Right:* Latino church cooking—tortilla pan (courtesy Gloria S.).

Helping with All My Heart lunch tables for asylum seekers (courtesy Gloria S.).

and chatted while the kids played with the toys or colored. As soon as the first travel arrangements were made, we would fill a backpack with food, snacks, water and a couple small travel toys for the kids and away we went to the airport. Each person had a backpack of their belongings as well as the "family" backpack with the food.

There's an overpass walkway at the airport that I led families across. I taught them

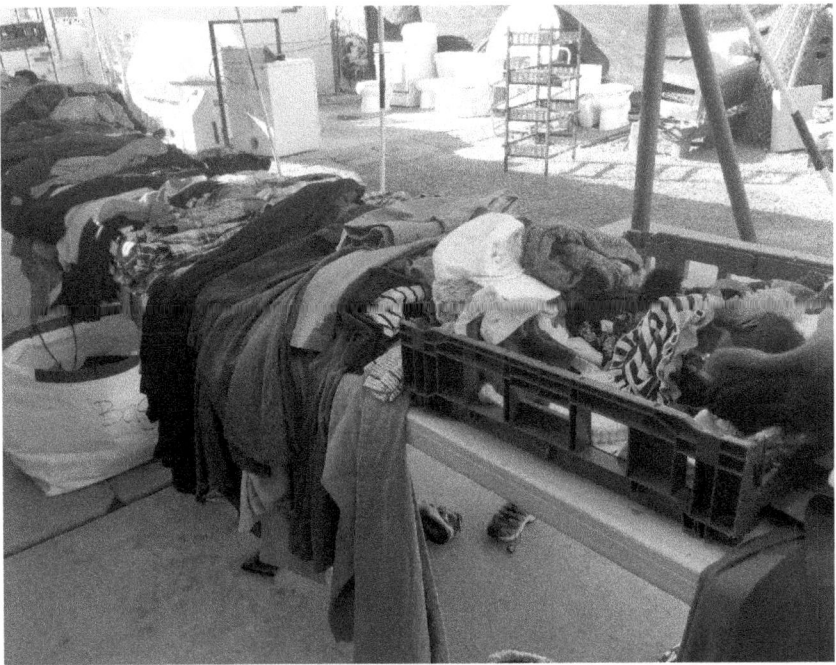

Helping with All My Heart clothing for asylum seekers (courtesy Gloria S.).

things as we walked. There were pictures embedded into the terrazzo floor. I would say the name of the colors, animals, and other objects in English. I knew learning English could protect them from deportation. By the time we got to the other side of the walkway, the children were telling me what the colors and objects were!

The families marveled at the airport. No one had ever been on an elevator, escalator, or seen modern lavatories, or water fountains. I showed them how to use all of them so they wouldn't feel awkward. They were always so anxious to learn and thankful for what they learned. Most of the people that we helped were Guatemalan, and they are so tiny. I made one boy hold his father's hand as we crossed a street because I thought he was 4 years old. They laughed, and then a volunteer told me he was 9 years old [Gloria S., personal communication, June 30, 2020].

A late-night volunteer shift was created so that families arriving from distant cities during the night would be met at the bus station. The families were offered food and blankets and jackets to take as they continued their long journey. If their departure was delayed, they were offered a place to stay for the night. Late-night shift began at 10 p.m. and ran until 2 a.m., when the last bus pulled in. The Refugee Aid volunteer driver remained for the entire four hours so no one would be left behind.

Craig Campbell was one of the volunteers on the late-night shift. Two nights a week, he went to the bus station with bags of food for the migrants

The pretty floor of the overpass inside the Phoenix airport (courtesy Gloria S.).

who were waiting to begin their long bus journey to be with family and friends. On other days, he brought families to churches or shelters that provided asylum seekers with beds and a safe place to sleep until they moved on to their next destination. Craig said that once the families entered the shelter, they settled in and spoke softly to each other. He loved to hear the families quietly visiting in a variety of Spanish dialects that were whispering throughout the room. Then, calm would settle in and the families would drift off to sleep. Craig regards these last minutes of his shift as the most peaceful and rewarding of all (C. Campbell, personal communication, March 31, 2020).

Since large numbers of migrants kept coming into Phoenix, a former elementary school was converted into the Phoenix Welcome Center. The International Rescue Committee (IRC) opened the center. It offered sleeping cots, and rooms for up to 10 people. The center was stocked with clothing, toys, and toiletries. Just a few months after the community set up this safe haven in Phoenix, the government diverted the asylum seekers to Mexico to wait for their court dates (Ortega 2019).

Winter 2019–Spring 2020

In late winter 2019, a change took place when the U.S. government implemented the remain in Mexico Policy. The numbers of asylum seekers coming to Phoenix dwindled to a trickle as families awaiting asylum were no longer allowed to come into the United States. Instead, they languished in often squalid conditions in Mexico. Refugee Aid learned that the families crossing in the Yuma sector of Arizona, who formerly had been taken to Phoenix by ICE, were now being transported to Calexico, California, and expelled into the Mexican city of Mexicali.

Article 31 of the *Convention Relating to the Status of Refugees* (1951) states that a person cannot be given a penalty for coming into a country when they present themselves without delay and show good cause for their presence.

Article 31 reads:

> 4. The Contracting state shall not impose penalties, on account of their illegal entry or presence, on refugees who, coming directly from a territory where their life or freedom was threatened in the sense of Article 1, enter or are present in their territory without authorization, provided they present themselves without delay to the authorities and show good cause for their illegal entry or presence.
> 5. The Contracting States shall not apply to the movements of such refugees restrictions other than those which are necessary and such restrictions shall only be applied until their status in the country is regularized or they obtain admission into another country. The Contracting States shall allow such refugees a reasonable period and all necessary facilities to obtain admission to another country.

Attorney Dianne Post noted that when she interviewed refugees at the Yuma, California, facility every child, except one, had come across the border and then immediately presented him or herself to the border patrol to begin the legal process (Dianne Post, personal communication, September 27, 2019).

Refugee Aid was not deterred. They continued to collect goods, stored them and delivered them to shelters in the border city of Mexicali, with the assistance of their Mexican partner, Caritas. Each week, Refugee Aid volunteers drove from Phoenix to Calexico, California, the sister city of Mexicali, and unloaded shelter supplies and food at Calexico storage units rented by Refugee Aid. The round-trip drive from Phoenix to Calexico takes eight hours. Reyna Martinez, the director of Caritas/Catholic Charities in Mexicali, transported goods to shelters in Mexicali at times when the port of entry could be quickly crossed and coordinated the distributions (M.J. Forman Miller, personal communication, June 28, 2020).

In the winter of 2020, I visited Mexicali with Refugee Aid members and Reyna and her husband. Martha Iskyan was the leader and main translator for the group. We found that the workers in Mexicali also honor the dignity and humanity of the families. Once the clothing arrived at the Caritas Center, each item was carefully folded. The center's director has several large file cabinets in her office. Typically, drawers like this would be used to store file folders. These drawers, however, contain organized stacks of pants and hats. Crates of carefully folded shirts surrounded the director's desk, ready for those who need them. Outside, two bougainvillea bushes in full bloom beautified the entrance to the courtyard that led to a medical clinic, an outdoor recreation area, a children's playground, six outdoor stations for washing clothes, and an open-air eating area. Migrants came here for breakfast, clothing, food supplies, medical services, and to wash their clothes.

File drawer of clean clothes for asylum seekers (author photo).

Sinks for washing clothes (author's photograph).

10.2 The Hosanna Shelter

Walking into the Hosanna shelter reminded me of walking into an old warehouse. The entrance was a corrugated metal door. When raised, it led to an open-air courtyard with a dingy cement floor and walls with chipped red and white paint. A large man wearing a gray tee-shirt, black straw fedora, and a warm smile was cooking pancakes on a grill in the courtyard. Each pancake was a half-inch thick and nearly the size of a dinner

Pancakes for breakfast (author's photograph).

Hosanna Shelter, laundry drying on the clotheslines (author's photograph).

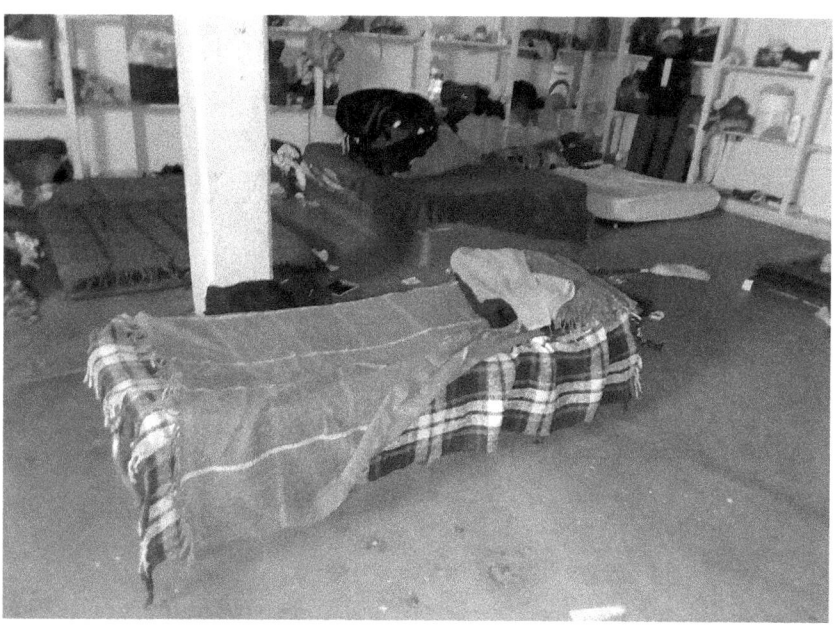

Sleeping area in the Hosanna Shelter (author's photograph).

Child's bed at the Hosanna Shelter (author's photograph).

Guatemalan and Honduran asylum seekers, fellow travelers, and best friends (author's photograph).

plate. Nearby, a young man in a black shirt, sweatpants, and aqua crocs played with a baby in a stroller. Two other men were close by. One was sitting behind a walker, and the other—younger—was standing next him. Nearby, a father and daughter sat on a long seat that—in its former life—had been part of a minivan. To their left, two other men brushed their teeth at the community sink. At the far end of the courtyard, several clotheslines held sweatpants, shirts, and a Disney Princess towel that had been washed in the sink. There were two toilets in the shelter—enclosed by high metal doors. One had a seat, the other did not.

A doorway beyond the courtyard led to the sleeping area for the 70 people who were housed in the shelter. Cracked sheetrock covered some walls. There was no sheetrock on others. Mattresses surrounded by shoes and backpacks were scattered on the cement floor. Shelves along the back and side wall held families' possessions. But the shelves did not provide sufficient space. One woman's suitcase was placed next to a mattress. She had been at the shelter for many months. She kept her personal items in the suitcase. It was ready for the moment when she would move along.

In another part of the room, mattresses were neatly lined up. One mattress was covered with a striped blanket and brightly colored pillows where several teddy bears sat in a row. This area was occupied by several women and their children. A toddler darted among the adults, who huddled together for a photo. Two women posed for another. They told me they were friends. One was from Honduras, the other Guatemala. The solidarity between them was so apparent, that I thought they were sisters.

10.3 La Posada

In Spanish, the word "posada" means a hotel or an inn. It is also the name of a Mexican ritual, just before Christmas, that is a re-enactment of Mary and Joseph's search for a place to stay in Bethlehem. Altagracia Tamayo Madueño is the president of La Posada, a shelter in Mexicali that houses 300 people. She described those who were living there as stuck between countries. They did not want return to their home countries in Central America, and under the "Remain in Mexico" rule they could not enter the United States. At this time, they were trying to stay in Mexico. She was trying to help them do that.

Although the facility was crowded, the families themselves and those who ran their shelter used their ingenuity to make their temporary homes comfortable. La Posada was a former pink motel converted to accommodate migrant families who were waiting for asylum hearings in the United States.

Families having breakfast at La Posada (author's photograph).

Each family shared one room. They had been at the shelter for many months. Some had several court hearings, but had not yet been granted asylum. Military-style cots were provided for sleeping. These cots were hard and uncomfortable because they were designed for short-term rest rather that extended periods of sleep. Altagracia and the families who lived there addressed the problem by lining up two or three cots side-by-side and placing mattresses of various sizes on top to create comfortable beds. Several family members all slept in one of the beds.

Altagracia welcomed anyone who came to La Posada and wanted to give anything. She believes that even if someone wanted to come in and preach, that is fine because it all comes from God. The shelter was organized, and the residents took turns doing tasks like cooking and cleaning. The kitchen was enclosed and spacious. It was well stocked with huge pots, flat copper pans, and bags of onions, bread, and potatoes.

Two young mothers were Altagracia's assistants. They told the kitchen

Reyna Martinez, Father Sam, and Altagracia Tamayo Madueño, president of La Posada (author's photograph).

helpers what to cook and oversaw the activities of the children. Altagracia was concerned that the families were treated with dignity. There was a large gate to the shelter, but she did not want the adults or children to feel like they were in prison. Children ran and played about the large courtyard. A small dog scampered among them. A dusty gray cat stationed itself under an open staircase and observed the day's activities. The children especially enjoyed child-sized picnic tables that Refugee Aid sent them. A group of boys set up a portable pool game on one table while families gathered to eat at full-sized tables. Some children watched *Paw Patrol* cartoons inside in a room with a large-screen television and comfortable couches.

There was also a portable classroom set up on one side of the courtyard. A large banner with the acronym for the *United Nations High Commission on Refugees* and the words "Save the Children" covered one outside wall. The banner announced that this was an Espacio Amigable, or friendly space, and that Save the Children works with girls, boys and adolescents and shares in actions of Child Protection and Education in Emergencies.

Kitchen at La Posada (author's photograph).

During the past six months, 400 volunteers from the Autonomous University of Baja California, in Mexicali, came to the shelter and volunteered at the school. A schedule on the wall displayed the time for classes that children of various ages would attend. There were two shelves of books, a box of children's musical instruments, a set of blocks, and a globe. The poster

UNHCR School at La Posada (author's photograph).

that recorded the children's beliefs about migrants was displayed on one wall. A chart of agreements for coexisting elicited from the children was on another wall. The chart reminds the children to do the following:

- Speak with respect
- Be positive
- Listen to the teachers
- Listen to your companions
- Raise your hand
- Eat outside of the classroom
- Wear shoes
- If anyone bother me, I tell the teachers

The guidelines for behavior reflected the children's respect for each other, adults, and their classroom. It dispels the myths that these children are not reverent. The chart also reflected the respect and dignity that Altagracia advocates for La Posada and that everyone in Refugee Aid showed for the migrant children and their families.

While the Trump administration tightened the vice and caused immeasurable harm to immigrant families, others worked to honor their dignity. These people, like Eleanor Roosevelt, were on "not a tour of

Agreements for coexisting (author's photograph).

inspection," but could not "feel contentment when others were hungry" (Stevenson 1962). Their actions go beyond good deeds or kindness. They protect and reclaim human rights. As Eleanor Roosevelt wrote:

> Where, after all, do universal human rights begin? In small places, close to home—so close and so small that they cannot be seen on any maps of the world…. Unless these rights have meaning there, they have little meaning anywhere [Roosevelt, 1958b].

Many of these rights are those put forth in the *Convention on the Rights of the Child* (UN General Assembly 1989). They include opportunities to be in a safe space, eat decent food, drink pure water, wash up and have clean clothing, attend a religious service, learn in a classroom, play and enjoy recreation.

The following are some of the small places where the human rights of migrant families were honored and reclaimed: in shelters in Phoenix and Mexico; at homes of members of Refugee Aid where families stay the night; in storage units that hold juice, quilts, shirts, pants, shoes, and snacks in Calexico; on blankets at the dirt pit by the Phoenix bus station where meals are served; in Craig Campbell's car and Marta's bus; in Marta's husband's portable showers; in the classroom at La Posada; along "the walkway with the pretty pictures" at the Phoenix airport where Gloria helped children learn English; on the small picnic tables and in the La Posada; by the bougainvillea bushes at the medical center at Caritas in Mexicali.

11

Refugees in the Time of Covid-19

11.1 The First Wave

On March 20, 2020, with the world in the throes of the coronavirus, the U.S. president and the secretary of state went beyond the "Remain in Mexico" policy and closed most traffic across the southern border between Mexico and the United States, imposing yet another devastating hardship on immigrant families.

Since the dawn of his administration, President Trump has promoted three goals to restrict immigration. He wanted to build a wall separating the land between the United States and Mexico, terminate the *Flores* settlement, which defined protections for migrants, and remove unaccompanied migrant children from our country.

The earlier actions on the part of the Trump administration that are described in Chapter 10 created the first wave, a tsunami for immigrant children and families. The scientists who study tsunamis, however, tell us that the waves that follow the initial wave of a tsunami can be larger and even more devastating than the first.

11.2 The Second Wave

Over the last few months, people in the U.S. have experienced indescribable heartaches and hardships as a result the pandemic. By late summer, over 166,000 Americans had died. Doctors, nurses, and other health care workers found themselves engulfed by the power of virus. They saved the lives of thousands of people. They also comforted those whose lives slipped away. They held the hands of people who were dying when it was not safe for family members to come into the hospital. Countless Americans lost their jobs. Others had to risk riding on public transportation to get to jobs where they interacted with the public and served people—both sick and well. For many people, working from home became a way of life. Schools were shuttered, so parents had to take on the task of overseeing children's schoolwork. Americans were isolated, obliged to wear masks, directed to wash their hands endlessly, and resorted to ordering take-out instead of dining out in restaurants.

The impact of the coronavirus is the second wave of the tsunami for immigrants. As I witnessed the heartache caused by the virus on the American side of the border, my thoughts constantly turned to the families in the shelters in Mexicali. Many of the ways in which these families made their living spaces workable might work against them now. The mattress that covered the rows of cots to create a sleeping space for several family members could become a source of transmission of the fatal virus. The floor of the Hosanna shelter would not be a comfortable place for people who were sick. The single sink where 70 people brushed their teeth, washed their hands, and laundered their clothes could quickly become a breeding ground for the virus. Video rooms and small tents where groups of children learned and played together would not afford adequate space for social distancing. The two toilets shared by 70 people could never be sanitized enough to be safe at during a pandemic. How would these families survive?

Mary Jo Forman Miller writes:

> In the spring of 2020, when COVID-19 struck, Refugee Aid began buying bulk food for the shelters they were supporting in Mexicali. Humanitarian Aid was listed as an exception to the border closure so the food did reach the shelters. In addition, Refugee Aid began distributing food to the local Hispanic churches in Phoenix who had assisted asylum seeking families in the spring of 2019. The churches distributed food to members of their underserved communities who were frightened about approaching local food banks, that routinely requested to see their ID and address.

She added simply, "We persevere" (M.J. Forman Miller, personal communication, June 28, 2020).

The Young Center for Immigrant Children's Rights has an office in Harlingen, Texas, across the bridge from Matamoros, Mexico. There are hundreds of tents in Matamoros that make up outdoor migrant camps that have neither water nor electricity. Young Center Director Maria Woltjen visited the camps in January 2020. She describes mothers holding children while they make food over open charcoal fires that pollute the air and make breathing difficult. In the camp at Matamoros alone, there are more than 2,500 families. The camps are dangerous places. Violence reported against asylum seekers includes rape, kidnapping, and torture. At night, members of cartels come into the camps looking for teenage girls. With the outbreak of Covid-19, Woltjen has even greater concerns, because the people in the camps have no way of social distancing and they use communal restrooms.

11. Refugees in the Time of Covid-19

Respiratory health that was already at risk from the fires is an even greater concern with the presence of the virus (Young Center Staff 2020).

The Kino Border Initiative is a faith-based, Roman Catholic and bi-national organization in Nogales, Arizona, and in Nogales, Sonora, Mexico, that assists migrants. The initiative has redesigned ways in which it is providing services during the pandemic. Fr. Sean Carroll, S.J., executive director, reports that they have moved to one meal service per day and provide some food for people to take with them for the afternoon. They have prepared care packages for children and have given these to families during the meal services. Additionally, they offer virtual legal consultations three days a week in collaboration with the Florence Project, and they do some advocacy on issues such as expedited returns of migrants to Mexico from the U.S. (Ignatian Solidarity Network; Kino Border Initiative 2020;[1] Father Sean Carroll, S.J., personal communication, April 21, 2020).

One asylum seeker, whom I will call Antonio, told his story to Joanna Williams, director of education and advocacy at the Kino Border Initiative. Antonio travelled with his 13-year-old daughter from his home in Honduras through Guatemala and Mexico and tried to seek asylum in the U.S. on February 17, 2020. Antonio was then sent to Nogales, Mexico, to wait for the court date for his asylum hearing in El Paso, Texas, on April 29, 2020. Antonio and his daughter lived in a shelter that was open for 14 hours each night from 6 p.m. to 8 a.m. They awoke at 7:00 in the morning and organized their belongings. At 8:00 a.m., they were given food and left for the day. They took their morning meal to a field, ate, stayed for a while, and then walked the city together. Sometimes they went to a park, but the police would come by and move them along. They had nowhere to go. At 6 p.m., they returned to the shelter, went to sleep at 10 p.m. and started the same routine over again the next day (Ignatian Solidarity Network; Kino Border Initiative 2020).

Court dates were cancelled because the border was closed, but Antonio still had to travel 350 miles from Nogales, Mexico, to Juarez to receive a paper that confirmed the date of his new hearing. The bus trip took 10 hours. The bus was crowded with people who may have been infected with or carried the coronavirus. The trip cost 1,200 pesos, about 40 U.S. dollars. The fee was difficult for Antonio to pay because he was not working. The streets of Nogales were not safe, and he could not go to work because he had no one to care for his daughter. There was no workplace that would allow her to come along with him. Antonio could not leave her alone on the streets. Due to the pandemic, Antonio expected that his court date would be delayed for at least another two to three months.

Despite the hardships, Antonio still believes that it is worth the effort to try to gain asylum in the United States. His hope is to give his family a better life. He wants his kids to have a better future and to be able to find work (Ignatian Solidarity Network; Kino Border Initiative 2020).

As difficult as life was for Antonio and his daughter, at least they were able to stay in a shelter in Nogales. Other immigrant families who arrived in Mexico during late March, 2020, were turned out of shelters because of fears of spreading the virus. They received food at the Kino Center but spent their time walking the streets. They were fearful of people who might rob or kidnap them. The families walked in groups as much as possible to protect each other. Many of the children were toddlers who could not walk long distances or teenagers who were vulnerable to assault. Some young children contracted chicken pox. The parents were waiting for court dates in the U.S. that would not take place for weeks, and these dates were subject to change. Families did not have work or money, so they were not sure how they would pay for the travel to the courts. Still, these migrants were thankful to God for what they did have. Like so many other families, they had faith that God will help them get through this trying time.

11.3 *The Third Wave*

Sadly, the virus itself was not end of the tsunami. The third wave was the Trump administration's escalation of its initiatives against migrants. According to the *Boston Globe* (Boston Globe Editorial 2020), since the beginning the coronavirus, the Trump administration implemented more than 40 changes in immigration policies. Shielded by this health crisis, Trump, Stephen Miller, and other administration officials have effectively ceased all immigration to our country.

For many weeks in the spring of 2020, the stories of the plight of migrant families became submerged by news of the pandemic. Trump called the coronavirus the invisible enemy. Along with his attempts to build a physical border, he constructed a barrier of regulations that served as an invisible wall to bar migrant children and their families from the U.S.

The new crackdown on migrants began on March 18, 2020, when Trump put out a tweet in which he declared through an executive order that he would suspend all immigration to the U.S. to prevent the spread of the infection from abroad. There was a flaw in his logic, however, because at this time, the number of Covid-19 cases in the U.S. was higher than in any other place in the world, and by early summer, the European Union banned Americans from entry into their countries because of fear that they would spread the disease (Henderson 2020).

All processing of refugee resettlement claims for asylum in the U.S.

11. Refugees in the Time of Covid-19

stopped on March 18. The new rules were not codified into law by Congress. They came down as executive orders, emergency rules, and regulatory changes.

On March 20, 2020, the director of the CDC, Dr. Robert Redfield, issued an order that turned back and expelled asylum seekers at U.S. southern land borders without any legal process whatsoever. The order was later known as the Title 42 rule. The announcement of the order read:

> The Centers for Disease Control and Prevention (CDC), a component of the Department of Health and Human Services (HHS), announces the issuance of an Order under Section 362 and 365 of the Public Health Service Act that suspends the introduction of certain persons from countries where an outbreak of a communicable disease exists [Centers for Disease Control and Prevention 2020a].

On March 21, the border between Canada and the U.S. was closed as well. Intertwining the closing of the Mexican border with the closing of the Canadian border provided the administration with an opportunity to couch its motives within the pandemic and hide them in plain sight. The president and his political advisor Stephen Miller had been trying to restrict the number of asylum seekers crossing the southern border throughout this administration. As noted earlier, Stephen Miller has been quoted as saying that he would be "happy if not a single refugee foot ever again touched American soil" (Sims 2019).

On April 20, 2020, the CDC order was extended for an additional 30 days. This order combined with the Migrant Protection Protocols (MPP) spelled disaster for migrant families.

> On April 20, 2020, CDC announced an extension of an Order issued March 20, 2020, under Sections 362 and 365 of the Public Health Service Act, and associated implementing regulations, that suspends the introduction of certain persons from countries where an outbreak of a communicable disease exists. The Order shall continue in operation for an additional 30 days [Centers for Disease Control and Prevention 2020b].

The border closing was presented by the administration as a temporary pause on immigration. A secret tape obtained by both the *Washington Post* and the *New York Times* in April 2020, however, revealed new information. Miller told a group of conservative allies on a conference call, "President Trump's decision to suspend family-based immigrant because of the coronavirus is the beginning of a broader strategy to reduce the flow of foreigners into the United States" (Shear and Haberman 2020).

In May, like boiling a frog to death in a slowly heating pot of water, the administration extended the order once again. This time the announcement included the directive that it "shall remain [in] effect until the CDC Director determines that the danger of further introduction of Covid-19 into the United States from covered aliens has ceased to be a serious danger to the public health, and the Order is no longer necessary to protect the public health." The full text of the announcement of the extension reads:

> The Centers for Disease Control and Prevention (CDC) announces the amendment and extension of an Order issued on March 20, 2020 and extended on April 20, 2020 under Sections 362 and 365 of the Public Health Service Act, and associated implementing regulations, that temporarily suspends the introduction of certain aliens based on the Director's determination that introduction of aliens, regardless of their country of origin, migrating through Canada and Mexico into the United States creates a serious danger of the introduction of COVID-19 into the United States, and the danger is so increased by the introduction of such aliens that a temporary suspension is necessary to protect the public health. This amendment and extension goes into effect at 12:00 a.m. Eastern Daylight Time (EDT) on May 21, 2020 and shall remain in effect until the CDC Director determines that the danger of further introduction of COVID-19 into the United States from covered aliens has ceased to be a serious danger to the public health, and the Order is no longer necessary to protect the public health. CDC shall review the latest information regarding the status of the COVID-19 pandemic and associated public health risks every thirty days to ensure that the Order remains necessary to protect the public health [Centers for Disease Control and Prevention 2020b].

The Trump administration's move to seal off the border was not a new idea. The difference was that this time, the coronavirus provided Trump and Miller with the rationale to halt immigration that they have been searching for since Trump took office. In the past, Miller tried to use other healthcare issues as a means of stopping migration, beginning with a mumps outbreak took place at child detention facilities in six states. When child illness spread through Border Patrol facilities and children died, the cry went up again. Upon investigation, however, it was discovered that negligence on the part of the Border Patrol and inadequate access to prompt and proper treatment caused the illnesses to escalate. In 2019, over a dozen U.S. senators sent a letter to Kevin McAleenan, acting secretary of Homeland Security, pleading for children in Border Patrol custody to be given vaccines to prevent a flu outbreak. The government withheld the vaccine, but if the outbreak had occurred, the children would have the shouldered the blame.

According to the *Washington Post*, "U.S. border authorities say the measures are in place to help federal agents, health-care workers and the public by preventing potentially infected migrants from crossing into the United States, while minimizing the population of detainees in U.S. immigration jails" (Miroff, Dawsey, and Armus 2020).

By March 2020, there were 65,000 asylum seekers waiting in Mexico. Fifty-seven percent of the people waiting for asylum hearings in Mexico had been there for six months or more. Court hearings were suspended due to the coronavirus and were not scheduled to resume until June 22, 2020 (Human Rights First 2020a).[2]

At the same time, violence escalated there because the virus curtailed regular activities of the cartels. By May 2020, the number of attacks on migrants rose to 1,114. These attacks included kidnappings, rapes, and assaults. Human Rights First has published the following key findings regarding the CDC order in *Pandemic as Pretext: Trump Administration Exploits Covid-19, Expels Asylum Seekers and Children to Escalating Danger* (Human Rights First 2020a):

- The Trump administration is wielding the CDC order to block and expel thousands of asylum seekers and unaccompanied children, turning them back to escalating violence in Mexico and other highly dangerous places where their lives and safety are at risk.
- Using the CDC order, DHS is likely expelling or blocking from seeking protection at least 4,000 men, women, and children a month.
- Under the CDC order, the administration has expelled 1,000 unaccompanied children.
- While Trump administration officials used debunked public health claims made in the CDC order as a fresh opportunity to turn away asylum seekers and unaccompanied children, many CBP officers and Border Patrol agents fail to consistently observe even the most basic health precautions at border posts, like wearing masks and maintaining safe distancing.
- Asylum seekers turned back to Mexico under MPP continue to face life-threatening danger.
- Violence in Mexico—and the dangers of kidnappings and harm facing asylum seekers forced back there—are on the rise.
- Despite restrictions on movement in Mexico due to Covid-19, reported kidnappings rose in March 2020. The number of murders in the first months of 2020 also increased compared to early 2019, a year when the country suffered its highest homicide rate in more than two decades.
- Asylum seekers forced back into Mexico under MPP and the CDC order face brutal conditions made worse by the Covid-19 pandemic, many lacking safe shelter, adequate medical care, and sufficient food.
- Despite claims by some DHS officials, including Acting CBP Commissioner Mark Morgan, that asylum and MMP fear screening interviews are available on a "case-by-case" basis, the administration is rejecting requests without consideration.

- Nearly 11,000 asylum seekers will wait in danger in Mexico for even longer now due to the Covid-19 closure of immigration courts.
- The Department of Homeland Security and the Executive Office for Immigration Review's (EOIR) recently announced a rescheduling policy for the nearly 11,000 cancelled MPP hearings will only cause additional chaos [Human Rights First 2020a].

In the weeks following March 18, 2020, 10,000 migrants were expelled from the U.S. by border authorities. Their processing for deportation took an average of only 90 minutes each. This purge left U.S. border facilities nearly empty (Miroff, Dawsey, and Armus 2020). At least 1,000 of those expelled have been unaccompanied children. Their rights were ravaged. They had no access to legal process and were not given the opportunity to be reunited with family members in the U.S.

Prior to the CDC order, the children had been protected under U.S. law, the *Flores* settlement, and the William Wilberforce Trafficking Victims Protection Reauthorization Act of 2008. As discussed earlier in this book, they are also protected under the *Convention Relating to the Status of Refugees* and the *Convention on the Rights of the Child* (UN General Assembly 1989). Under the CDC order, however, the administration has sent over 2,000 unaccompanied children back to Mexico or deported them to their home countries.

Border patrol agents who have not been trained in eliciting or evaluating the testimony of children made the decisions about the fate of the children. Maria Woltjen, executive director and founder of the Young Center for Immigrant Children's Rights, states, "This order, first issued in March, flouts the federal anti-trafficking law that requires the government to place unaccompanied children into protective custody and allow them to go before an asylum officer or judge" (Woltjen 2020).

Atty. Dianne Post notes that Article 16 of the *Convention Relating to the Status of Refugees* requires access to courts which is being denied by the rule of allowing border patrol agents who have no training to make asylum decisions (D. Post, personal communication, September 27, 2019). Article 16 reads:

> 1. A refugee shall have free access to the courts of law on the territory of all Contracting States.
>
> 2. A refugee shall enjoy in the Contracting State in which he has his habitual residence the same treatment as a national in matters pertaining to access to the courts, including legal assistance and exemption from caution judicatum solvi.
>
> 3. A refugee shall be accorded in the matters referred to in

paragraph 2 in countries other than that in which he has his habitual residence the treatment granted to a national of the country of his habitual residence.

Human Rights First reported several indicators that show that administration policies were clearly preventing migrants from entering the U.S. During February–March 2020, the number of asylum seekers processed at ports of entry dropped from by 2,500. In April, it dropped by another 5,700. The percentage of new credible fear interviews fell by 86 percent from February to April 2020 (Human Rights First 2020a).

In April, Border Patrol agents stopped processing inadmissible individual requests for protection at ports of entry. The metering lists contained 14,000 names of people who had been waiting in Mexico. The processing of requests for protection for these people ceased as well. By May 2020, the managers of metering lists no longer added any names to the lists (Human Rights First 2020a).

Also, referrals of unaccompanied children to Office of Refugee Resettlement (ORR) care were also greatly reduced. In April 2020, only 58 children were referred to ORR as compared to 2,200 just two months prior. In related actions, the administration pushed for extended detainment in Customs and Border Patrol (CBP) custody rather than transfer to ORR custody. This change violated the *Flores* settlement, which requires children to be transferred to ORR within 20 days. If children entered ORR custody, they would be eligible for placement with their U.S. sponsors. If they remain in CBP custody, expulsion can take place more rapidly (Human Rights First 2020a).

Jennifer Nagda, policy director at the Young Center for Immigrant Children's Rights, argued, however, that ORR had the capacity to process these children in their centers (Yucatan Times 2020). Health precautions such as safe distancing, wearing masks, and using hand sanitizer could have been employed to maintain the children's safety.

The administration also expressed interest in resurrecting the practice of fingerprinting sponsors who came forward to take children into their care. Sponsors were frightened that they could be deported if they subjected themselves to being fingerprinted. Again, it is ironic that guards who did not have background checks and fingerprint screenings were hired to work with children in shelters on federal land, like Tornillo A child's own family members, however, would have to be fingerprinted in order to be allowed to take the child.

The following stories of migrants who were turned away from the U.S. under the CDC order and are trying to survive in Mexico were reported by Human Rights First in *Pandemic as Pretext*:

- A Honduran woman seeking asylum and her three-year-old child and five-day-old baby were expelled to extremely dangerous Reynosa, Mexico, under the CDC order by Border Patrol agents in early April 2020. The baby had been born in a U.S. hospital after the woman crossed the border in late March to seek protection. After being expelled to Mexico, the mother and her very young children were turned away by a shelter that was not receiving new arrivals.
- A Salvadoran family that had fled threats by a gang leader to "rent" their nine-year-old daughter were expelled to Mexico under the CDC order, according to an ACLU of Texas staffer who spoke with the family. Salvadoran gangs exert extraordinary control over territory in the country, even now enforcing their own Covid-19 quarantine measures.
- A Honduran woman and her daughter were expelled under the CDC order despite requesting asylum and were driven to the Guatemalan border by Mexican authorities who tried to force them into Guatemala. The family, who crossed the U.S. border on March 22, 2020, were expelled by Border Patrol agents to Reynosa, where Mexican migration officers detained the family, denied them an opportunity to seek asylum, and drove them to the Guatemalan border and twice attempted to force them to cross even though the border was closed [Human Rights First 2020a].

Articles 32 and 33 of the *Convention Relating to the Status of Refugees* (1951) address situations in which refugees are expelled from a country where they are seeking asylum.

Article 32 prohibits returning the refugee to their place of origin unless that person is a threat to national security or public order. If a person is to be returned, there must first be due process of law with legal representation in the presence of a competent authority within a reasonable time. The Trump administration's immediate returns with no process of law, the refusal of legal representations, and the insistence on using unqualified border patrol agents to make legal decisions all violate this provision of the convention (D. Post, personal communication, September 27, 2019).

Article 32 reads:

>1. The Contracting States shall not expel a refugee lawfully in their territory save on grounds of national security or public order.
>2. The expulsion of such a refugee shall be only in pursuance of a decision reached in accordance with due process of law. Except where compelling reasons of national security otherwise require, the refugee shall be allowed to submit evidence to clear himself, and to appeal to

and be represented for the purpose before competent authority or a person or persons specifically designated by the competent authority.

3. The Contracting States shall allow such a refugee a reasonable period within which to seek legal admission into another country. The Contracting States shall reserve the right to apply during that period such internal measures as they may deem necessary.

Article 33 is stronger that Article 32. It prohibits such returns when a person is put into danger (D. Post, personal communication, September 27, 2019).

1. No contracting state shall expel or return ("refouler") a refugee in any manner whatsoever to the frontiers of territories where his life or freedom would be threatened on account of his race, religion, nationality, membership of a particular social group or political opinion.

2. The present provision may not, however, be claimed by a refugee whom there are reasonable grounds for regarding as a danger to the security of the country in which he is, or who, having been convicted by a final judgment of a particularly serious crime, constitutes a danger to the community of that country.

Article 3 of the *Convention Against Torture and Other Cruel, Inhuman or Degrading Treatment or Punishment* also prohibits "refoulment."

1. No State Party shall expel, return ("refouler") or extradite a person to another State where there are substantial grounds for believing that he would be in danger of being subjected to torture.

2. For the purposes of determining whether there are such grounds, the competent authorities shall take into account all relevant considerations including, where applicable, the existence in the State concerned of a consistent pattern of gross, flagrant or mass violations of human rights.

On June 10, 2020, the Trump administration proposed another set of regulations that would have widespread negative effects on immigration. According to the National Immigration Forum, the changes would impact "everyone seeking protection from the U.S. government" (Zak 2020a).

They also redefine the kinds of persecution that "constitute grounds for receiving protection." A new interpretation of the *Convention Against Torture* excuses pain or suffering committed by a "rogue government official" (Zak 2020a). An asylum seeker could not use that official's actions to claim protection. Therefore, credible fear screenings would be far more difficult to pass.

Asylum can be restricted for anyone who has ever failed to pay taxes or owes back taxes, as well as those with any criminal convictions, even if they have been reversed or expunged. The grounds for determining that an asylum application is "frivolous" have also been broadened, and under the new regulations, asylum officers as well as judges can make this determination. One regulation, which is not new, denies protective status unless asylum seekers have applied for asylum in at least one other country they traveled through on the way to the U.S. The reforms decrease the possibilities of asylum seekers going before an immigration judge (Zak 2020b).

Individuals who make it through the first stage of the asylum process will go to "asylum-only" court proceedings. These new and narrow proceedings would eliminate any other form of relief and would offer only asylum. Judges could also deny asylum without a hearing. This practice eliminates the current rule that asylum applicants must be permitted to testify about their case. A judge could decide that an individual has not put enough evidence in the application itself and deny the person their hearing (Reichlin-Melnick 2020).

In Chapter 9, Madeleine Schwartz described applicants who do not speak English struggling to help each other fill out lengthy and confusing court forms without an interpreter. The problem is not that people cannot supply the information needed for their case, but that the forms and process for completing them are set up to prevent them from doing so (Reichlin-Melnick 2020; see copy of "Notice to Appear" in the appendix).

Article 38 of the *Convention Relating to the Status of Refugees* mandates that violations of this treaty are adjudicated at the International Court of Justice, where one nation brings a complaint against another. Individuals cannot bring private claims. Individual complaints can be made to the UN High Commissioner for Refugees, who supervises but cannot enforce the treaty (D. Post, personal communication, September 27, 2019).

12

Seeking Relief Through the Courts

12.1 Law Cases, 2017–2020

Along with humanitarian efforts, the U.S. legal community has been working tirelessly to defend the rights of migrant families. As noted earlier, the American Civil Liberties Union (ACLU) sent teams to Central America to try to find parents in remote areas who had been deported and separated from their children (D. Post, personal communication, November 9, 2019). The children remained somewhere in the U.S. The following are descriptions of lawsuits filed to reunite family members, terminate practices that harm migrants, uphold existing laws, or protect the rights of asylum seekers in other ways. These descriptions provide only a window into the cases, not the entire picture. Decisions have been determined for some of the cases, but many are still pending, and may continue for months or years. The pandemic has caused delays in some court proceedings. This section begins with a guide to legal terms that appear within these law cases.

12.2 Guide to Legal Terms

- **Administrative Procedure Act (APA):** 1946 law that governs the process by which federal agencies develop and issue regulations. It includes requirements for publishing notices of proposed and final rulemaking in the Federal Register and provides opportunities for the public to comment on notices of proposed rulemaking (EPA n.d.).
- **Animus:** "…whether the act of a man, when in appearance criminal, be so or not, depends upon the intention with which it was done" (Bouvier 1856).

- **Class:** a group whose members are represented in a class action (*Merriam-Webster.com*, s.v. "class").
- **Certiorari:** an extraordinary writ issued by a superior court (as the Supreme Court) to call up the records of a particular case from an inferior judicial body (as a Court of Appeals) (*Merriam-Webster.com*, s.v. "certiorari").
- **Chill:** to discourage especially through of penalty: have a chilling effect on (*Merriam-Webster.com*, s.v. "chill").
- **Compensatory damages:** Money awarded to a victim to compensate for injury or damages (*Merriam-Webster.com*, s.v. "compensatory damages").
- **Conspiracy:** agreement between two or more people to commit an act prohibited by law or to commit a lawful act by means prohibited by law (*Merriam-Webster.com*, s.v. "conspiracy").
- **Credible fear:** a concept in United States asylum law whereby a person who demonstrates that he or she has a **credible fear** of returning to his or her home country cannot be subject to deportation from the United States until the person's asylum case is processed (Wikipedia.org, s.v. "credible fear").
- **Declaratory judgment:** a judgment declaring a right or establishing the legal status or interpretation of a law or instrument (*Merriam-Webster.com*, s.v. "judgment").
- **Defendant:** a person or group against whom a crime or civil action is brought: someone who is being sued or accused of committing a crime (*Merriam-Webster.com*, s.v. "Defendant").
- **Discovery:** the usually pretrial disclosure of pertinent facts or documents by one or both parties to a legal action or proceeding (*Merriam-Webster.com*, s.v. "Discovery").
- **Due process:** a course of formal proceedings (such as legal proceedings) carried out regularly and in accordance with established rules and principles (*Merriam-Webster.com*, s.v. "due process").
- **Enjoin:** to prohibit by a judicial order: put an injunction on (*Merriam-Webster.com*, s.v. "enjoin").
- **Injunction:** a writ granted by a court of equity whereby one is required to do or to refrain from doing a specified act (*Merriam-Webster.com*, s.v. "injunction").
- **Litigate:** to carry on a legal contest by judicial process (*Merriam-Webster.com*, s.v. "litigate").
- **Motion to dismiss:** to put out of judicial consideration: refuse to hear or hear further in court (*Merriam-Webster.com*, s.v. "dismiss").
- **Per curiam decision (or opinion):** ruling issued by an appellate

court of multiple judges in which the decision rendered is made by the court (or at least, the majority of the court) acting collectively (and typically though not necessarily unanimously) (Wikipedia.org, s.v. "per curiam decision").
- **Plaintiff:** a person who brings legal action (*Merriam-Webster.com*, s.v. "plaintiff").
- **Punitive damages:** a way of punishing the defendant in a civil lawsuit, and are based on the theory that the interests of society and the individual harmed can be met by imposing additional damages on the defendant (legal-dictionary.thefreedictionary.com/, s.v. "punitive").
- **Rehabilitation Act:** prohibits discrimination on the basis of disability in programs conducted by federal agencies, in programs receiving federal financial assistance, in federal employment, and in the employment of federal contractors (U.S. Department of Justice 2020).
- **Severed: a.** to try (criminal offenses or defendants) separately in order to avoid prejudice **b.** to split (a criminal trial) into multiple trials in order to avoid prejudice **c.** to try (civil claims or issues pleaded in the same case) separately (*Merriam-Webster.com*, s.v. "sever").
- **Stay:** to temporarily suspend or prevent by judicial or executive order (*Merriam-Webster.com*, s.v. "stay").
- **Temporary restraining order (TRO): 1.** an order of brief duration that is issued ex parte to protect the plaintiff's rights from immediate and irreparable injury by preserving a situation or preventing an act until a hearing for a preliminary injunction can be held **2.** a protective order issued ex parte for a brief period prior to a hearing on a restraining order attended by both parties and intended to provide immediate protection from violence or threatened violence (*Merriam-Webster.com*, s.v. "order").
- **Ultra vires:** beyond the scope or in excess of legal power or authority (*Merriam-Webster.com*, s.v. "ultra vires").
- **Venue: a.** the place from which a jury is drawn, in which a trial is held. **b.** The place or county in which takes place the alleged events from which a legal action arises (*Merriam-Webster.com*, s.v. "venue").
- **Writ of habeas corpus:** any of several common law writs issued to bring a party to a court or judge (*Merriam-Webster.com*, s.v. "habeas corpus").

12.3 Supreme Court Cases

On the last days of June 2020, the Supreme Court of the United States announced the following decisions that impacted the future of asylum seekers:

Deferred Action for Childhood Arrivals (DACA)

On June 18, 2020, in a 5–4 decision, in the case *Department of Homeland Security et al. v. Regents of the University of California et al.*, the Supreme Court upheld temporary legal status for immigrants brought to the U.S. as children. This status, known as DACA, had been unlawfully ended by the Trump administration. Chief Justice John G. Roberts wrote the decision and said that the administration's move to end DACA was "arbitrary and capricious." The reason for the termination had not been properly explained by the Department of Homeland Security in 2017. Therefore, the status remained temporarily in place. The decision was not about DACA itself, but about the failure to comply with the procedural requirement that the government provide a reasonable explanation for terminating the program. As a result of the Supreme Court's decision, 640,000 students and workers can continue to attend college, obtain driver's licenses, and become employed in the U.S. New applicants are also allowed to apply for the temporary legal status (Ulloa 2020). The DACA decision does not directly impact many of those who are seeking asylum at the southern border, but any positive outcome for migrants in the summer of 2020 is worth noting.

Rights to Habeas Corpus and Due Process

A week following the DACA ruling, the Supreme Court announced a 7–2 decision that affects asylum seekers directly. The court ruled that recent asylum seekers whose claims are denied initially have no constitutional rights to due process or habeas corpus. Under the Illegal Immigrant Reform and Responsibility Act (IIRAIRA) of 1996, if a person had a "credible fear" of being persecuted upon returning to his or her home country, he or she could seek relief from a court. If grounds for "credible fear" were not found, the person could be deported immediately. The new decision denies asylum seekers the opportunity to appear before a judge in order to challenge the legality of deportation before the asylum seeker is removed from the U.S. (Totenberg 2020).

The decision was made in the case of Vijayakumar Thuraissigiam, an immigrant from Sri Lanka (*Department of Homeland Security v.*

Thuraissigiam, U.S. Supreme Court No. 19-161, June 25, 2020). He requested asylum from U.S. Customs and Border Protection because he had been kidnapped, arrested, beaten, and tortured by government agents in his home country. He fled to Mexico and then to the U.S., where he had a 13-minute hearing conducted by an executive branch officer, not a traditional judge (Totenberg 2020).

The official made the judgment that there was no "credible fear," so Thuraissigiam was slated to be deported. He contested this decision in district court, but the judge declared that the law did not entitle him to a review.

The Ninth Circuit disagreed, ruling that asylum seekers have the right to petition for habeas corpus in federal court to challenge removal (Barnes and Miroff 2020). According to CNN, "The court cited the Suspension Clause of the Constitution that prohibits the government from depriving someone of their liberty without the opportunity for a court to review the legality of the government's action" (de Vogue and Alvarez 2020).

Supreme Court did not agree, however. Justice Samuel Alito who wrote the decision for the majority stated, "If courts must review credible-fear claims that in the eyes of immigration officials and an immigration judge do not meet the low bar for such claims, expedited removal would augment the burdens on that system" (*Department of Homeland Security et al. v. Thuraisigium* 2020).

Justice Sonia Sotomayor wrote the dissent. Elena Kagan was the other judge who joined with her. Justice Sotomayor wrote, "Today's decision handcuffs the judiciary's ability to perform its constitutional duty to safeguard liberty and dismantles a critical component of the separation of power" (*Department of Homeland Security et al. v. Thuraisigium* 2020).

The *Flores* settlement has been discussed many times throughout this book. It is the agreement that resulted from *Janet Reno, Attorney General of the United States, et al.* (case no. CV85-4544-RJK, C.D. Cal. 1996). This court settlement has been in place for over two decades. It places limits on the time and conditions under which children can be incarcerated in immigrant detention. The Trump administration has tried many times to either impede or terminate the *Flores* settlement in court. The following are cases that focus on the *Flores* settlement.

12.4 Law Cases Regarding the Flores Settlement

Law Case: CV85-4544, *Flores v. U.S*, et al.

Case No.: 2:18-cv-05741-DMG-PLA
Case No.: 2:19-cv-07390-DMG-AGR

Date filed: 5/31/2019 and 9/13/2019
Lawyers: Center for Human Rights and Constitutional Law
Jurisdiction: Central District of California, Western Division
Purpose of the Law Case: To contest proposed termination of the *Flores* settlement
Description: This case was terminated on October 11, 2018. Since then, however, two motions have been filed. The first was a motion to enforce the settlement that claimed that prolonged confinement in secure, unlicensed facility is a breach of the settlement. On September 18, 2019, that motion was held in abeyance on the Homestead shelter since it is now closed. The second motion was in opposition to the defendant's Notice of Termination of the *Flores* settlement, followed by a Motion in the Alternative to Terminate the *Flores* settlement.

On August 30, 2019, the government filed a motion to terminate the *Flores* settlement.

On September 27, 2019, there was a hearing on opposition to the termination notice.

In this hearing, Judge Dolly Gee ruled for the plaintiff and granted a permanent injunction regarding the new regulations keeping *Flores* in full effect. The original settlement allowed the government to publish administrative rules fully complying with *Flores*. At that point the case would terminate. The administration said these rules did comply with *Flores*; Judge Gee said they did not. Her ruling prohibits indefinite detention. Though detainees have to be in a licensed facility, most states don't license facilities that hold families. *Flores* requires a non-secure facility, but Karnes Federal Residential Center is more like a prison. Therefore, the least restrictive placement rule is violated. The rules are inconsistent with the settlement and therefore cannot stand. The *Flores* settlement is a binding contract, a decree, and hence a judgment. It cannot be thrown out because you don't like it and a new sheriff has come to town.

Much litigation has continued under the case (personal communication, D. Post, July 27, 2020).

Flores v. Barr (U.S. Court of Appeals for the Second Circuit 17-3646 NAC [2nd. Cir. October 7, 2019])

This was an emergency motion to release children from custody in ICE family detention centers due to the risks of the spread of Covid-19.

In the spring of 2020, family detention centers in the U.S. held 366 families with children aged 1–17. The Karnes Center and the South Texas Family Residential Center (Dilley) are in Texas, and the Berks Family Residential Center is in Pennsylvania. The centers come under the control of

12. Seeking Relief Through the Courts

the Department of Homeland Security. ICE managed the Karnes and Berks facilities. Dilley was managed by CoreCivic, a private prison operative (Frazee 2019). The health of the residents of the centers was in peril because of the Covid-19 pandemic.

On March 26, 2020, plaintiffs filed an emergency motion seeking prompt release due to Covid-19 risks. The following actions took place:

- On March 27, 2020, the court issued an order to the federal agencies to "make continuous efforts" to release the children from custody because of the risk posed to them by Covid-19 and to provide an accounting of their efforts to release those in custody by April 6.
- On April 24 the court issued an order requiring defendants to release children without unnecessary delay to eligible sponsors.
- On May 22, following interim reports from defendants, the court expressed concern with defendants' compliance and ordered enhanced monitoring and further status reports. The defendants appealed the orders to the Ninth Circuit on June 23 [Civil Rights Litigation Clearinghouse 2020a].[1]

On June 26, 2020, Judge Dolly Gee issued a short, seven-page order in which she blasted the government. Those who were assigned to do investigations and file reports had done so, and ICE and ORR had reduced the numbers in detention to 124 for ICE and 528 for ORR. However, the judge pointed out that as of June 25, 2020, eleven people had tested positive for Covid at Karnes and four employees at Dilley. In addition, many mistakes or omissions were found in the reports from ORR and ICE. The fingerprint waiver process took too long, and there were wrong conclusions about some minors because the officials were confused about the identity of individuals.

But the reports of the independent monitor and the medical doctor doomed ICE and ORR; they reported that the CDC guidelines were not being followed. The documents had errors. Information about which families were in litigation was incorrect. They claimed every child did not have a sponsor, although they did. They were still not in compliance with three orders from the previous round. The judge said ICE and ORR could respond by July 2, but it was clear such response would be a waste of time.

Because ICE and ORR were not following CDC guidance regarding masking and social distancing, they were ordered to release every minor who had been there more than 20 days to a sponsor or with their parents with all deliberate speed—a phrase fraught with meaning.

They also had to urgently implement the CDC protocols "rather than hiding behind unevenly implemented written protocols." In other words, ICE and ORR were simply pointing to the fact that they have such protocols, not that they follow them. Judge Gee ordered them to social distance, do enhanced testing, and enforce wearing masks.

Reports dates were established: July 1 was set for the juvenile coordinators annual report and July 24 for interim reports covering the April and May topics. They were also to give sworn testimony in detail for each child not moved. The judge emphasized that it should be sworn under penalty of perjury (D. Post, personal communication, July 27, 2020).

Judge Gee described the centers as "on fire" because of Covid. She ordered that the children in all three centers be released by July 17, 2020. The children were to be sent "to 'non-congregate settings' that include 'suitable sponsors' and even to their parents, who could also be released if conditions warrant it" (D. Romero 2020). Since the *Flores* settlement applies only to children and not parents, releasing only the children without their parents raised an uproar about the possibly of expanding family separation.

The judge ordered ICE and ORR to give specific reasons for not releasing three named children and stated clearly that no children who aged-out were to be sent to adult facilities. Joint status reports were due on July 8 and July 31 and the doctor and independent monitor were to continue their work. The next hearing was August 7 (D. Post, personal communication, July 27, 2020).

As the deadline approached, the administration and the plaintiffs requested an extension of ten days until July 27, 2020. The order for ICE to remove children with their parents was extended until that date.

On July 27, the judge refused to give the government more time and ordered that the children be released without family separation (D. Post, personal communication, July 27, 2020).

Law Case: *CA and 19 other states v. Homeland Sec. et al.* (Other States: MA, CT, DE, DC, IL, ME, MD, MI, MN, NV, NJ, NM, NY, OR, PA, RI, VT, VA, WA)

Case No.: 2:19-cv-07390-DMG (AGRx)
Date filed: 8/26/19
Attorneys: California Department of Justice
Jurisdiction: California, Central District Court
Purpose of the Law Case: To challenge to a rule that attempts to set aside the *Flores* Agreement. Compliant for Declaratory and Injunctive Relief are sought.

Description: *The Apprehension, Processing, Care, and Custody of Alien Minors and Unaccompanied Alien Children*, 84 Fed. Reg. 44,392 (August 23, 2019). This new rule breaches the *Flores* settlement's terms by stripping children in migration custody of protections ensuring their placement in the least restrictive setting consistent with their best interests and their prompt release from federal custody whenever possible. Instead, the rule permits and calls for the prolonged and indefinite detention of immigrant children in detention facilities.

The rule also replaces state regulation of facilities with federal auditors.

Long-term detention harms children, and then they are released into communities, and states have to provide their care. It violates critical protections for immigrants stated in *Flores*. It threatens children's safety and well-being by intruding into the core state functioning of licensing care facilities for children. It will cause irreparable harm for immigrant children, their parents, and the states that will welcome them upon their release from federal custody.

The rule is *ultra vires*; that is, beyond one's legal power, arbitrary and capricious, a violation of states' rights, an abuse of discretion, a violation of the Administrative Procedure Act, an excess of statutory authority. Further, deterrence is an impermissible reason for civil detention (personal communication, D. Post, October 20, 2019).

12.5 Law Cases Regarding the Separation of Migrant Children from Their Families

The following cases result from children being separated from their families.

Law Case: *Ms. L v. ICE*

Case: 3:18-cv-00428-DMS-MDD
Jurisdiction: U.S. District Court, Southern District of California
Date Filed: 2/26/2018
Judge: Dana Sabraw
Related cases: No. 18-1626; NO. 7/27/18 (*MMM v. Sessions*)
Attorneys:
- ACLU Immigrant Rights Project
- ACLU National (All Projects)
- Juvenile Law Center

Purpose of the Law Case: To reunite a Congolese migrant mother and her 7-year-old daughter who were separated by ICE after enduring a harrowing journey through several countries

Description: Ms. L. and her daughter were detained by ICE as they entered the United States at the port of entry in San Ysidro, California, where they were legally seeking asylum. They were together for three days but were then placed in different rooms. Ms. L. was taken to a detention center in San Diego, while her daughter was taken to Chicago. During the next three months, they were able to communicate by telephone only a few times. Ms. L. was so worried about her child that she could hardly eat or sleep. They were separated for nearly five months. The government claimed that the child was separated because the mother did not have papers to confirm that she was the parent. Her lawyer pointed out that it is common for those who flee a country quickly to arrive in the U.S. without papers. The separation could have been avoided if a DNA test had been administered. After the test was given, mother and daughter were reunited.

A motion to dismiss under Administrative Procedure Act (APA) and Asylum Statute was granted, but a motion to dismiss under due process was denied.

In March 2018, a motion for a national class action suit based on due process claims was granted.

On June 26, 2018, the court declared that the family separation policy violated the Constitution, and the separations could only happen in cases where the parent was genuinely unfit or a danger to the child. The family separations were described as "brutal" and "offensive" by the court. Furthermore, they "shocked the conscience" and violated the due process clause of the Fifth Amendment to the Constitution.

At the time of this ruling, the government claimed that there were 2,700 children who remained in HHS custody who had been separated from their parents. As noted in Chapter 4, the court ordered the children to be reunified with their parents in two stages. Children under the age of five, approximately 100, were to be reunified within 14 days. The remaining children were to be returned to their parents within 30 days. HHS did not meet either deadline (Gelernt 2019). As noted earlier in this book, the reunification process was confounded by the lack of a centralized database that kept track of the families.

Additionally, about 400 parents had been deported to their home countries without their children. They were misled or coerced to surrender their own rights to asylum. They were also led to believe that their children would be on the plane with them, but when their flight took off, the children were not there. The government tried to claim that these parents should not even be part of the case, and that the ACLU should use their resources to find them. As noted earlier by attorney Post, the ACLU sent teams to remote areas of Central America to try to locate these parents.

The idea that the government had no responsibility to help reunite these deported parents and their children was rejected outright by Judge Sabraw. On July 27, 2018, he stated, "The government is at fault for losing

12. Seeking Relief Through the Courts

several hundred parents in the process." On August 2, he reiterated: "The reality is that for every parent who is not located, there will be a permanently orphaned child. And that is 100 percent the responsibility of the administration" (Gelernt 2019).

Despite the judge's words, the government did not take responsibility for locating these parents. That work was left up to the ACLU, and it took an order from the judge to force the government to provide even basic information. Although the ACLU was trying to track families by phone, the government would not release phone numbers to them (Gelernt 2019).

The HHS OIG report described in Chapter 4 revealed the possibility that thousands more families had been separated. Therefore, it is likely that even more parents were deported without their children.

Reunification of plaintiffs in two related cases, *Ms. Q* and *Mr. C.*, was ordered on September 19, 2018 (see case descriptions below). This order was followed by a motion for a settlement that was given preliminary approval, followed by the filing of an emergency motion for implementation. This motion was granted and, therefore, the defendant was ordered to begin the asylum process for those class members in detention.

By February 28, 2019, the defendants had to provide a list of persons subject to removal and tell ICE they could not remove them without providing notice of the settlement and their determination if they want to join.

By September 30, 2019, the defendants had to provide all governing documents memorializing standardized procedures, guidelines and guidance for separating parents and children at the border (D. Post, personal communication, October 20, 2019).

Initially, Alex Azar, secretary of HHS, stated "There was no reason why any parent would not know where their child is located" (Karlin-Smith 2018). By February of 2019, however, HHS took the position that it did not have the resources and effort to do the manual file review needed to identify the thousands of children who might have been separated; and HHS stated that it might be better for the children just to leave them in their current placement. HHS sent the court a declaration in which Commander Jonathan White wrote that taking children from their sponsors to be reunited with their own parents would cause "grave child welfare concerns" and "would destabilize the permanency of their existing home environment" (Gelernt 2019; White 2019). These words echo back eerily to a similar sentiment from the late nineteenth century, the time of the separation of Native American children who were permanently housed at the Carlisle Indian Industrial School.

The next status hearing was held on October 18, 2019. On March 6, 2020, an expanded ruling in the case ordered President Trump to return *all* children going back to 2017 (D. Post, personal communication, March 14, 2020).

Law Case: *DCJV v. ICE et al.*

Case No.: 1:18-cv-09115
Jurisdiction: U.S. Court, Southern District of NY
Date filed: 10/4/2018
Attorneys: Center for Constitutional Rights, Seton Hall, Morgan Lewis and Bockius
Purpose of the Law Case: To petition for a writ of habeas corpus and other declaratory and injunctive relief to release a 2-year-old boy from Honduras.

Description: This is the case of a father who was separated from his son because he had a misdemeanor conviction on his record from eight years before. The lawsuit alleged several violations of the Constitution and laws of the United States, prior court rulings, and international law. A central premise of the case was that "the 'zero-tolerance' policy constitutes cruel, inhumane and degrading treatment." This child was being held in a foreign country and due to his age had "little or no ability to communicate with anyone." The risk of psychological damage was "particularly acute and lasting" (Azmy, Kadidal, Wells Dixon, and Schwartz 2018a). Since he had been confined in the U.S. for a major part of his life, he might be unable to reestablish familial bonds unless the court provides relief.

On October 15, 2018, the court found that continued separation would cause irreparable harm to both the child and his father. The child was ordered to be returned to his father immediately. As of December 27, 2018, the case was stayed due to lack of government funding (D. Post, personal communication, October 20, 2019).

Law Case: *Ms. Q and J v. ICE*

Case No.: 1:18-cv-02409-TJK
Related to: Case No. 18-cv-1458
Jurisdiction: U.S. District Court, District of Columbia
Date filed: 10/24/2018
Attorneys: National Immigrant Justice Center, Center for Constitutional Rights, Gibson, Dunn
Purpose of the Law Case: To seek Injunctive and Declaratory Relief
Citation: Civil Action No. 18-2409 (PLE) (D.D.C. November 21, 2019)

Description: This is the case of a Ms. Q. and her four-year-old child, J., who were separated for seven months after they arrived in the United States from El Salvador. They took a perilous journey to this country. They were brought to a processing center "known as the 'ice box,'" because the temperature was so cold. Their cell was filthy and overcrowded. Later, they were put in a wire cage that resembled a dog kennel. Immigration officials would not provide J. with clean clothes or medical care when he became sick and began throwing up. The officers threatened to deport Ms. Q. and J. to El Salvador. She feared that she would be killed if she returned there.

As in the case of *D.J.V.C. v. ICE*, a central premise of this case is that the "Trump Administration's 'zero tolerance' and family separation policy constitutes torture, and cruel, inhuman and degrading treatment." As a result of the separation from his mother, J. suffered "psychological regressions, and developmental delays, including major speech difficulties and constant crying" (Azmy, Kadidal, Wells Dixon, and Schwartz 2018b).

The child has been returned to his mother, but the suit continues for damages. On December 4, 2018, a motion for a preliminary injunction was granted. On April 12, 2019, the government filed a motion to dismiss the suit as mute.

On July 9, 2019, there was an Order to Show Cause hearing (D. Post, personal communication, July 27, 2020).

Law Case: *J.S.R. v. Sessions*

Case No.: 3:18-cv-01106-VAB
Jurisdiction: Connecticut District Court
Date filed: July 13, 2018
Judge: Victor A. Bolden
Attorneys: Legal Aid of CT, Jerome Frank Legal Services at Yale Law School
Related case: *V.F.B. V. Sessions*
Consolidated with: Case No. 3:18-cv-1110 on July 9, 2018
Purpose of the Law Case: To seek a ruling and order on a motion for a preliminary injunction and relief directed towards the effects of the constitutional violation suffered by these minor children, namely trauma or more precisely, Post-Traumatic Stress Disorder (PTSD).

Description: This case was filed in the U.S. District Court for the District of Connecticut by two children from Central America who had been separated from their parents and were not in communication with them several weeks at a time. The children suffered severe mental and emotional trauma. They argued that they had suffered irreparable harm due to the separation. On July 5, 2018, they each filed motions for a temporary restraining order and preliminary injunction (Civil Rights Litigation Clearinghouse 2020b).[2]

Since J.S.R. and V.F.B. sought immediate reunification with their respective parents, the motion for preliminary injunction was denied. The relief was being addressed in a concurrent lawsuit by the U.S. District Court for the Southern District of California.

On July 11, 2018, Judge Victor A. Bolden in Connecticut ruled that the plaintiffs' constitutional rights had been violated. He agreed that ordering reunification with their parents would simply duplicate the relief ordered in the California case. He pointed out that the purpose of the relief in the California case was to alleviate the constitutional wrong suffered by the parents. This case was different. Its purpose was to remedy the harm suffered by children. The judge released the children to their parents without requiring them to wear ankle monitors.

On August 29, 2018, both parties filed for dismissal. The case is now closed (D. Post, personal communication, October 20, 2019).

Law Case: *Ramirez v. ICE*

Case No.: 1:18-cv-00508-RC
Jurisdiction: United States District Court, Washington, D.C.
Date filed: March 5, 2018
Judge: Rudolph Contreras
Attorneys: Kirkland and Ellis, National Immigrant Justice Center
Consolidated with: *V.F.B. v. Sessions*, case no. 3:18-cv-1110, on July 9, 2018
Purpose of the Law Case: A preliminary injunction was sought to prevent ICE from jailing unaccompanied minors on their 18th birthday.

Description: On April 18, 2018, the court granted preliminary injunction prohibiting ICE from taking unaccompanied minors to jails on their 18th birthday and detaining them there, rather than in the least restrictive placement.

On May 7, 2018, the Department of Homeland Security filed a motion to dismiss the case. On August 30, 2018, the court denied the motion to dismiss, and granted a motion that certified a class of 18-year-olds transferred to ICE detention on their 18th birthdays.

Within months of the class certification, the percentage of transfers of 18-year-olds to adult detention centers dropped from 83 percent to 35 percent (LexisNexis 2020).

On December 31, 2018, the government sought to delay the case during a government shutdown. The court said that in seeking several delays to date, the government had at times seemed to forget what this case

12. Seeking Relief Through the Courts

was about: the allegedly unnecessary and illegal detention of young adults in restrictive detention facilities. The delay was not granted.

On April 18, 2019, ICE moved to decertify the class. Later, ICE revealed that it failed to track approximately 1,500 age-outs from April 2016 to May 2019. In July 2019, on that basis, the motion to decertify was denied.

The trial began in December 2019 (D. Post, personal communication, July 27, 2020). Extensive discovery was conducted by the plaintiffs' attorneys, including taking and defending 31 depositions and obtaining nearly 130,000 documents from the government. Their analysis of evidence and an expert's analysis of the data show that the most likely determining factor as to whether an 18-year-old was detained or released was the field office in the area where the detainee resided. Miami, El Paso, Houston, Los Angeles, Phoenix, and New York had detention rates that were statistically greater than average (National Immigrant Justice Center 2018).

Amendments to the Trafficking Victims Protection Reauthorization Act (TVPRA) require the government to consider placement in the least restrictive setting available, and to provide meaningful alternatives to detention. On July 2, 2020, "a federal court ruled that U.S. Immigration and Customs Enforcement officers failed to consider these less restrictive settings before transferring unaccompanied migrant youth to ICE detention on their 18th birthdays violated U.S. immigration laws." Part of the decision stipulated that the court would also issue an order directing ICE how to go about remedying the violations (LexisNexis 2020).

12.6 Law Cases Regarding Stress and Trauma Suffered by Children and Parents

The following cases were filed on behalf of children and parents who suffered stress and trauma as a result of family separation.

Law Case: *Ms. J.P. et al. v. Sessions et al.*

Case no.: 2:18-cv-06081-JAK-SK
Jurisdiction: Central District of CA
Date filed: July 12, 2018
Referring judge: John A. Kronstadt
Presiding judge: Steve Kim
Attorneys: Sidley Austin, Public Counsel, Immigrant Advocacy Center
Purpose of the Law Case: This lawsuit sought declaratory and injunctive relief for infliction of emotional trauma from separation without showing of parental unfitness. It addressed the need for

screening and trauma-informed and family-centered mental health care.

Description: Three mothers, each with one daughter, fled violence in their home countries of Guatemala, Honduras, and El Salvador. The mothers and daughters were separated upon arrival in the United States. Two of the women were mocked by detention officers, and the third was held in a "cell that resembled a dog kennel." They did not know the whereabouts of their daughters for up to two weeks. They filed this class action suit on July 12, 2018 (Civil Rights Litigation Clearinghouse 2020c).[3]

On September 18, 2018, the defendants filed a motion to dismiss the case. On January 30, 2019, the case was referred for settlement talks with a different judge. Throughout February, March, and April 2019, no settlement was reached. Motions proceeded on discovery and response. The case was sent back to Judge Kronstadt.

On November 5, 2019, he granted the plaintiffs class certification, and a preliminary injunction and denied the defendants' motion to dismiss (Civil Rights Litigation Clearinghouse 2020c).

Judge Kronstadt applied the doctrine of "state-created danger," which holds the government responsible for creating harm, and therefore is responsible for providing the solution.

The defendants had to make available initial mental health screening, diagnosis, and treatment, if requested. On November 27, 2019, the defendants appealed to the Ninth Circuit but voluntarily withdrew the appeal on February 21, 2020. On March 11, HHS and DHS made the services available to the class members. The case is ongoing (D. Post, personal communication, July 27, 2020).

Law Case: *A.I.I.L. et al. v. Sessions*

Case no.: 4:19-cv-00481-JAS, page 1 of 78
Date filed: October 3, 2019
Jurisdiction: United States District Court, Tucson, Arizona
Attorneys: ACLU, Tucson; ACLU Immigrants Project; Paul, Reiss, Rifkind, Wharton, and Garrison, New York
Purpose of the Law Case: This was a class-action lawsuit seeking compensatory and punitive damages for horrific treatment of children and families who were attempting to seek asylum in the U.S.

Description: This lawsuit resulted because of the horrific treatment of Guatemalan and Honduran migrants, including dangerousness at the border, trauma caused by family separation—in some cases for over a year—inadequate health services or no treatment, lack of information, deliberate intention to inflict pain, and punitive conditions. Southwest Key facilities are named in the lawsuit. The actions are nothing short of kidnapping and torture. One official actually said the child "belongs to Trump." The suit revealed the history of separation programs, including parents who were deported without their children and the continuation of separating families despite a court order to stop and public outcry. Migrants were targeted due to race, ethnicity, and national origin. The suit alleged conspiracy and open animus. It was a class action for children's and parents' claims of violation of Fifth Amendment rights of due process for family separation, failure to provide adequate health care, and punitive treatment. It included violation of Fifth Amendment rights to procedural due process for failure to give notice or opportunity to be heard, and failure of equal protection. Also included were Fourth Amendment violations of unlawful search and seizure and conspiracy to interfere with civil rights that are protected under 42 USC 1895(3). The plaintiffs sought compensatory and punitive damages and the establishment of a health treatment fund (D. Post, personal communication, July 27, 2020).

On February 14, 2020, the defendants filed a motion to dismiss for failure to state a claim and for lack of jurisdiction. On March 20, the plaintiffs successfully sought a delay in filing their reply, due to the Covid-19 crisis. The case is ongoing (D. Post, personal communication, July 27, 2020).

12.7 Law Cases That Resulted from Trump Administration Policies

Various policies of the Trump administration that caused harm to migrants are the focus of the following lawsuits.

Law Case: *Al Otro Lado, Inc., et al. v. John F. Kelly, et al., Nielson*

Case No.: 17-cv-02366-BAS-KSC
Date filed: November 22, 2017
Attorneys: American Immigration Council, Mayor Brown Latham and Watkins, and the Southern Poverty Law Center, Center for Constitutional Rights, Shepherd, Mueller, Richter, and Hampton
Jurisdiction: U.S. District Court, Southern District of California (San Diego)
Purpose of the Law Case: Preliminary Injunction

Description: Al Otro Lado, Inc., a nonprofit legal service, alleged that Customs and Border Patrol and the Department of Homeland Security were systematically violating U.S. and international law by denying individuals even the opportunity to apply for asylum. Instead, the government was consistently turning away individuals facing persecution, forcing them to return to countries where they face grave violence and risk of death. On November 2, 2017, the case was sent to private mediation. Two motions to dismiss the case, one in August 2018, and the second a year later, were denied. As of September 9, 2019, motions for production of discovery were granted and a hearing was scheduled for the following month.

On November 19, 2019, the Asylum Ban that was implemented on July 16, 2019, was declared not retroactive for those who arrived earlier than that date and were told to go to Mexico to wait. The court granted the plaintiff's motion for a preliminary injunction. The court determined that the U.S. government positioned asylum seekers in a Catch 22 because Mexico requires them to apply for asylum within 30 days, but they did not have the information they needed to apply. This action was determined to be improper application of this Asylum Ban. The lawsuit asked the U.S. government to follow its own law. As a result, class certification was granted to 26,000 asylum seekers.

On December 4, 2019, the defendants appealed the order granting the preliminary injunction in the Ninth Circuit and filed an emergency motion to stay the court's order of November 19. On December 6, the plaintiffs filed a motion for a temporary restraining order to prohibit the defendants from the following new rule: "Implementing Bilateral and Multilateral Asylum Cooperation Agreement Under the Immigration and Nationality Act" ("ACA Rule"). This new act allows the attorney general to remove a non-citizen, otherwise eligible, to a third country that has entered into a bilateral or multilateral agreement with the U.S. It also establishes screening that determines if a person could be tortured or persecuted if removed to a third country. On December 20, 2019, the defendants filed an emergency motion for temporary stay of the district court order enjoining the defendants from applying this Asylum Ban while the appeal before the Ninth Circuit court was pending. On January 6, 2020, the judge denied the plaintiffs' motion for the temporary restraining order. The case continues (D. Post, personal communication, July 27, 2020).

Law Case: *Make the Road New York, African Services Committee, Catholic Diocese et al. v. Citizenship and Immigration Services*

Case No.: 1:19-cv-07993-GBD
Date filed: September 9, 2019, Motion for Preliminary Injunction
Related case: 1:19-cv-07777 GBD

12. Seeking Relief Through the Courts 197

Parties to the case: Dozens of organizations, especially ones that support people with disabilities
Jurisdiction: Southern District of NY
Attorneys: Paul, Weiss, Rivkand, Wharton, and Garrison; Center for Constitutional Rights; Legal Aid
Purpose: To seek declaratory and injunctive relief

Description: Persons who are designated as Public Charge are people who are totally unable to care for themselves. One hundred years of legal decisions say that the simple receipt of benefits is not a public charge. Congress rejected proposals to deem anyone receiving means-tested benefits a public charge. A 1999 ruling provided guidance and confirmed this settled determination. The Trump administration's rule is a violation of the Administrative Procedure Act (APA). The administration has no authority to impose this rule because it is arbitrary, capricious, and vague. They did not listen to public comment or expert opinion, and they implemented it on a retroactive basis. It violates equal protection and has disparate impact.

On or about October 1, 2019, five federal district courts granted nationwide injunctions against this rule. The courts are in New York, California, Maryland, Illinois, and Washington.

The U.S. District Court District of New York, New York state, New York city, Connecticut, and a Vermont case granted an injunction as a violation of APA. The action taken was determined to be in excess of authority. It violates the longstanding definition of public charge since 1882 that means life-long dependency. It is not in accordance with law and is arbitrary, capricious and an abuse of discretion. There is no reasoned explanation. This rule is about receipt of benefits, not lifelong inability to work. Plaintiffs have standing because the rule will shift costs, cause more health problems, and cause economic injury. It was scheduled to go into effect on October 15, 2019. Congress has not changed definition since 1882 and so has no intent to do so. The rule also violates the Rehabilitation Act because it discriminates against people who are disabled. The harm caused is irreparable to states and people. The balance tips toward the plaintiffs. The injunction must be nationwide for uniformity especially since nine lawsuits have been filed representing 24 different jurisdictions.

California, New York and Washington courts also granted injunctions on October 11, 2019. The government sought to stop the injunctions, but that motion was denied. An expedited briefing schedule was issued on January 8, 2020. The case number is now given as 19–3595.

On January 27, 2020, the Supreme Court by a vote of 5–4 allowed the rule to go into effect pending litigation. The decision focused on what they considered to be improper rulings that included the entire U.S. or districts not in their jurisdictions. These are universal injunctions. They are trying to rein in courts that are not following the administration's agenda.

On February 21, 2020, the Supreme Court again voted by a 5–4 margin to allow the rule to go into effect. Justice Sonia Sotomayor issued a scathing dissent of this decision.

Oral arguments on the case were set for March 2, 2020.

On April 13, 2020, attorneys filed a motion to eliminate the rule during the Covid crisis (D. Post, personal communication, July 27, 2020).

Law Case: *Innovation Law Lab et al. v. Nielson et al.*

Date filed: February 14, 2019
Attorneys: ACLU, Immigrants' Rights, and Southern Poverty Law Center
Judge: Richard Seeborg
Jurisdiction: U.S. District Court, Northern District of California
Purpose: To seek declaratory and injunctive relief because the Remain in Mexico policy violates Administrative Procedure Act (APA), Immigration and Nationality Act (INA 1965), and customary international law on refoulement.

Description: On April 8, 2019, the District Court granted an injunction, determining that the Remain in Mexico policy violates the Immigration and Nationality Act and does not provide safeguards to protect from danger. That the plaintiffs were not "from" Mexico was not the winning argument. Nevertheless, they were entitled to the expedited removal procedure or regular removal process under the statute and were not receiving it. Counsel for the plaintiffs argued that the policy did not comply with Administrative Procedure Act (APA) and that the government had created another species of removal that was not authorized. They also argued that the U.S. was bound by the Refugee Convention regarding refoulement. This convention protects a person from being returned to a place if they have credible fear for their safety if sent there. The policy ignored these issues, and people were injured. On April 8, 2019, a nationwide injunction was issued by Judge Richard Seeborg.

The defendants appealed the order to the Ninth Circuit and requested a stay of the preliminary injunction pending the appeal. On May 7, 2019, the Ninth Circuit granted a stay of the injunction. There was a per curiam decision that was issued in the name of the court by judges Scanlaine, Fletcher, Watford (D. Post, personal communication, October 20, 2019).

The panel found that the defendants were likely to prevail on the merits of the plaintiffs' INA and APA claims. It stated that the plaintiff asylum seekers were properly subjected to the contiguous-territory provision

12. Seeking Relief Through the Courts

of the INA, and that the MPP were exempt from the notice-and-comment requirement because they are general statements of policy (Civil Rights Litigation Clearinghouse 2020d).[4]

They also argued that in this case, the U.S. government was injured by a large number of people. In their view, people who remain in Mexico would be treated humanely by Mexico and given work permits. The policy was seen as being efficient, and the judges did not want to interfere with diplomacy.

Judge Watford on concurrence agreed that the agency did not do enough to meet refoulement law. He recommends that the Department of Homeland Security ask the question of fear, and not wait for the asylum seekers to mention it. He thought plaintiffs would win on that, but it was not enough for him. In his opinion, the issue could be solved with an order to ask the question.

Judge Fletcher concurred in result but disagreed on reasoning. He said Immigrant Nationality Act did not give authority for Migrant Protocol Program (MPP). He said none of the government arguments were persuasive. He did not say why he concurred in the result.

On November 7, 2019, a briefing began for the merits hearing.

On February 28, 2019, the Ninth Circuit agreed with district court and lifted the stay on the injunction. They found that the plaintiffs would probably win on merits because applicants who have fraudulent or no papers did not have a return clause in that part of the law; it was "other aliens," e.g., criminals and terrorists, who did. Additionally, it was a violation of the refoulement law because they were putting the plaintiffs in danger.

On February 29, 2020, the government went to Supreme Court for emergency stay, which the court granted.

On March 4, 2020, the Ninth Circuit ruled that they were correct in their ruling on merits. They were also correct in scope of injunction, but because it was controversial, they would limit to Ninth Circuit states only, i.e., California and Arizona. In anticipation of an upcoming Supreme Court decision, the stay was set to begin on March 12, 2020.

On March 11, 2020, the U.S. Supreme Court issued an order halting the Ninth Circuit's injunction of the MMP. As a result, the MMP remained in effect across the nation.

On April 10, 2020, the government filed a petition for certiorari with the Supreme Court (Civil Rights Litigation Clearinghouse 2020d).

The case is ongoing (D. Post, personal communication, July 27, 2020).

Law Case: *East Bay Sanctuary v. Barr*

Case no.: 4:2019cv04073
Date: July 16, 2019

Attorneys: Southern Poverty Law Center
Judge: Jon A. Tigar
Jurisdiction: U.S. District Court, Northern District of CA
Counsel: Center for Constitutional Rights, ACLU Immigrants' Rights Project, ACLU of Northern California, Southern Poverty Law Center
Purpose: This case seeks declaratory and injunctive relief and a temporary restraining order.
Citation: *East Bay Sanctuary v. Barr* 934 F. 3rd 1026 (9th Cir. 2019)

Description: This case challenged the Trump administration asylum ban of July 16, 2019. This rule barred noncitizens from asylum in the U.S. if they traveled to the U.S.–Mexico border through a third country, unless they first applied for asylum in the third country. There are six different cases. The cases were assigned to Judge Tigar.

This case put a halt to the administrative order to remain in Mexico that was initially limited to Arizona and California and then expanded nationwide. It was overturned by the Supreme Court.

A motion to stay was filed on September 12, 2019.

A temporary restraining order was granted on November 19, 2019 (Dianne Post, personal communication).

The counsel for this case documented Homeland Security's "pattern, practice, and policy of turning away asylum seekers from official ports of entry at the U.S.-Mexico border." They viewed the new rule regarding asylum in a third country as the latest step in "a systemic, government-wide decision to unlawfully deter asylum seekers from seeking safe haven at our borders and to vilify immigrants of color" (Azmy, Schwartz, and Guisado 2019).

On July 6, 2020, the Ninth Circuit Court of Appeals ruled that the transit ban violates laws of Congress and is arbitrary. The Supreme Court has currently placed a stay on the injunction (D. Post, personal communication, July 27, 2020).

Related Decision

On June 30, 2020, Federal Judge Timothy Kelly of the U.S. District Court for the District of Columbia struck down a Trump administration policy that prevents most Central American and other migrants from requesting asylum at the southern border. The case was brought by Human Rights First, Capital Area Immigrants' Rights Coalition, Refugee and Immigrant Center for Education and Legal Services (RAICES), for nine individual asylum seekers (Human Rights First 2020b).

The judge ruled that the administration "unlawfully promulgated" the rule and did not show that it was in the public interest to "stealthily implement the change" and bypass the Administrative Procedure Act. The policy required asylum seekers who had already begun to travel to the U.S. to seek asylum in other countries, even though they had no advance notice that they needed to do so. The government apparently feared that providing advance notice of the rule would create a surge of migrants who would try to the avoid the consequences of the rule by seeking asylum prior to its implementation (Hsu 2020).

In response to the decision, Hardy Vieux, senior vice president for legal at Human Rights First, stated:

> Judge Kelly's ruling is proof that the administration cannot do an end-run around the seekers demonized by this administration. We do not follow the rule of one capricious man, who treats the law as something on which to trample, on his way to a photo op. We are gratified that the judiciary once again affirms that for the last 244 years we have been, and will continue to be, a country ruled by law, not men [Human Rights First 2020b].

Last year, U.S. District Judge Jon Tiger of San Francisco, issued a preliminary injunction that halted the rule. He stated that there was "a 'mountain' of evidence that demonstrated that migrants would not be able to safely seek asylum in Mexico" (Hsu 2020).

Following that judgment, in September 2019, the Supreme Court issued an unsigned order that permitted the Trump administration to continue to implement the rule (D. Post, personal communication, July 27, 2020).

Law Case: *Maria M. Kiakombua et al. v. Customs and Border Protection (CBP)*

Case No.: 1:19-cv-01872-KBJ
Date filed: June 25, 2019
Attorneys: International Refugee Assistance Project, Refugee and Immigrant Center for Education and Legal Services
Jurisdiction: District of Columbia District Court
Purpose: Declaratory and injunctive relief

Description: The intention of this lawsuit was to eliminate a lesson plan that was issued to CBP officers as of April 30, 2019, to screen out asylum seekers. The lesson plan violates the Immigration and Nationality Act (INA), the Refugee Act, the *Convention Against Torture* (CAT), the Administrative Procedure Act (APA), and the Constitution. The Refugee Act of 1980 declares that it is "the historic policy of the United States to respond to the urgent needs of persons subject to persecution in their homelands." The lesson plan, however, instructs the officers in a manner that is contrary to the governing statues and regulations, and unlawfully narrows access to immigration and federal court systems. Among other things, the lesson plan improperly raises the asylum seekers' evidentiary burden, shifts to asylum seekers burdens actually borne by the government, and converts what is supposed to be a non-adversarial threshold screening into a biased and adversarial hearing through which asylum officers are to apply erroneous legal standards to decide ultimate issues that are supposed to await adjudication by the immigration courts (D. Post, personal communication, July 27, 2020).

On August 19, 2019, the defendants moved for summary judgment. They argued that the case should be dismissed because it was not a legal issue over which the court could exercise judicial authority. They claimed there was no evidence that enjoining the lesson plan would remedy the plaintiffs' injuries and that it was not subject to judicial review under the APA. They argued that it had no effect on the credible fear law and viewed it as a minor update to account for developments in case law (Civil Rights Litigation Clearinghouse 2020e).[5]

On September 5, 2019, the plaintiffs filed for summary judgment. They argued that the lesson plan was inconsistent with the statutory and regulatory design of the credible fear process and was in violation of APA (Civil Rights Litigation Clearinghouse 2020e).

On March 5, 2020, the judge issued an order staying the case pending the resolution of appeal in *Grace v. Barr*, a case that raised questions regarding the meaning of several terms that that are also relevant in the Kiakombua case. The case is stayed and ongoing (Civil Rights Litigation Clearinghouse 2020e).

Law Case: *Make the Road et al. v. McAleenan et al.*

Case No.: 19-cv-2369
Date filed: 8/6/2019
Attorneys: American Immigration Counsel, ACLU, Simpson Thatcher and Bartlett
Jurisdiction: U.S. District Court, District of Columbia
Purpose: Declaratory and injunctive relief

Description: A preliminary injunction was sought against expedited removal, a process set forth in a notice dated July 23, 2019, to remove non-citizens encountered anywhere in the U.S. up to two years after their arrival. The suit claims that the process bypassed the Administrative

Procedure Act (APA), was arbitrary and capricious, and allowed an immigration officer to act as a judicial officer. Counsel for the plaintiffs also argue that expedited removal process violated the following: the credible fear determination, due process, the Immigration and Nationality Act (INA), APA, and the suspension clause, i.e., suspending habeas corpus by expedited removal.

On September 27, 2019, minutes before the rule was to take effect, the court granted an injunction nationwide to stop the policy. Consequently, defendants and their agents were prohibited from applying the expanded expedited removal policy set forth in the agency's notice of July 23, 2019, to anyone to whom it would apply, while this action proceeds, until further order of the court. The government appealed (D. Post, personal communication, October 20, 2019).

In June 2020, the D.C. Circuit reversed the decision to grant the preliminary injunction. The appeals court ruled that the district court's injunction drew upon "administrative-law requirements that don't apply to an expansion of expedited removal." Therefore, the case will go back to the district court where it can be continued based on other claims against the rule. The case is ongoing (ACLU of DC 2020).

Law Case: *Padilla v. ICE*

Case No.: 2:18-cv-00928-MJP, document 149 filed July 2, 2019
Date filed: June 25, 2018
Related case no.: 2.18-cv-00939
Attorneys: ACLU, Northwest Immigrant Rights Project and American Immigration Council, Foster Pepper
Jurisdiction: U.S. District Court, Western District Seattle, WA
Presiding judge: Judge Sabraw, presiding over both cases
Purpose: Preliminary injunction and class certification

Description: In this class action suit, the attorneys alleged that the federal government was illegally detaining immigrants without giving them a fair chance of being released on bond. The government was accused of violating the Constitution by requiring immigrants at bond hearings to prove, in order to be released, that they were not a danger and a flight risk. The case cites violations of the due process clause, the Immigration and Nationality Act (INA), and the Administrative Procedure Act (APA). In December 2018, the APA claims were dismissed, but the other claims were not.

On July 2, 2019, the court blocked the rule that denied bond hearings. The court ordered that a bond hearing would be conducted within seven days of a hearing request by a class member of the lawsuit. If a class member's time exceeded the seven-day limit, that person would be released. The court also placed the burden of proof in those bond hearings on the defendant, the Department of Homeland Security, to demonstrate why a class member should not be released on bond, parole, or other conditions. Further, the bond hearing was to be recorded, and the recording or verbatim transcript of the hearing would be produced upon appeal. Finally, a written decision with particularized determinations of the individualized findings would be produced at the conclusion of the bond hearing.

The court modified the injunction to find that the statutory prohibition of the Immigration and Nationality Act against releasing on bond persons found to have a credible fear of persecution if returned to their country and awaiting asylum application violates the U.S. Constitution. The Bond Hearing Class is constitutionally entitled to a bond hearing (under the conditions enumerated above) pending resolution of their asylum applications.

Oral arguments were heard by a Ninth Circuit panel on October 19, 2019.

On December 11, 2019, the court dismissed APA claims. The defendant's other motions to dismiss were denied.

On March 6, 2019, the plaintiffs' motion for class certification was granted.

On April 5, 2019, the plaintiffs' motion for a preliminary injunction was granted.

On May 20, 2019, enforcement of the injunction was stayed until July 1, 2019.

On July 12, 2019, an order of USCA 19-035565 stayed the orders of the district court (D. Post, personal communication, July 27, 2020).

On July 22, 2019, the government filed an appeal.

Following the oral arguments to the Ninth Circuit panel in October 2019, on March 27, 2020, the panel issued an opinion and an order affirming in part the district court's preliminary injunction, although they directed the district court to "reconsider some of the technical aspects of its order." The case is currently ongoing (Civil Rights Litigation Clearinghouse 2020f).[6]

Law Case: *L.L.M. v. Cuccinelli*

Case No.: Civil Action No. 19-2676 (RDM)
Jurisdiction: District Court, District of Columbia

Description: In a decision on March 1, 2020, Ken Cuccinelli was determined to be improperly appointed as acting director of the United

12. Seeking Relief Through the Courts

States Citizens and Immigration Services (USCIS). Such an appointment needs the advice and consent of the Senate, but Cuccinelli's appointment did not get that advice and consent. His appointment also did not follow the vacant seats act. Cuccinelli immediately began following the dictates of Individual #1. Therefore, the asylum directives he implemented are invalid (D. Post, personal communication, July 27, 2020).

13

Seeking Relief Through Congress

13.1 Legislation

While the law community fought to protect migrants in court, members of the House of Representatives and the Senate sponsored legislation. The bills focused on many issues that have been considered in this book, including protecting health and safety, ending cruel treatment, keeping families together, establishing humane standards of detention, and honoring the dignity of migrants in other ways. At the time of this writing, some of these proposed laws have been passed by the House of Representatives and have been passed on to the Senate. Others are still pending in the House. The status of a bill can change at any time, depending upon actions taken in the House or Senate. The following are the descriptions of the bills. Generally, they are listed in chronological order according to the date they were introduced. Companion bills that were introduced in both the House and the Senate are presented together regardless of the date of introduction.

H.R. 532, Alternatives to Detention Act, and Companion Bill S. 1894, Alternatives to Detention Act of 2019

H.R. 532, Alternatives to Detention Act: This bill was introduced into the House of Representatives by Rep. Anthony Brown (MD-04), on January 14, 2019. It has 49 co-sponsors. The purpose of the bill is to require the secretary of the Department of Homeland Security to use alternatives to detention (ADT) for certain vulnerable populations and for other purposes. Vulnerable populations include asylum seekers, victims of torture or trafficking; persons with special religious, cultural, or spiritual considerations; pregnant or nursing mothers; persons who are under 21 years of age or older than 60 years of age; persons who identify as gay, lesbian, bisexual, transgender, or intersex; victims or witnesses of a crime;

persons who have a mental disorder or physical disability; and persons who have been determined by an immigration judge or the secretary of Homeland Security to be experiencing severe trauma or to be survivors of torture or gender-based violence, based on information obtained during intake, from the individual's attorney or legal services provider, or through credible self-reporting.

S. 1894, **Alternatives to Detention Act of 2019:** This is the companion bill to H.R. 532. It was introduced into the Senate on June 19, 2019, by Sen. Catherine Cortez Masto (NV). It has four co-sponsors, senators Edward Markey (MA), Kristen Gillibrand (NY), Richard Blumenthal (CT), and Jeff Merkley (OR). This bill has the same purpose as H.R. 532. According to a press release from Sen. Gillibrand, "ADT programs would include the Family Case Management Program and other community-based supervision and support programs carried out by nonprofit organizations with demonstrated expertise in providing such services to keep families together, ensure compliance with immigration court proceedings, and help the nation move toward a more humane and effective immigration system" (Gillibrand 2019).

S. 92: Keep Families Together Act

This bill was introduced in the Senate by Sen. Diane Feinstein on January 31, 2019. There are 41 co-sponsors. Its purpose is to limit the separation of families at or near port of entry. According to the bill, agents or officers of a designated agency shall be prohibited from removing a child from his or her parent of legal guardian, at or near a port of entry or within 100 miles of the border of the United States unless a state court, authorized under state law, has terminated the parents' rights or those of the legal guardian, and has determined that it is in the best interests of the child to be removed from the parents or guardian. The child can also be separated if he or she is a trafficking victim or is at significant risk of becoming a victim of trafficking. If the adult who is accompanying the child is not the parent or legal guardian, the child can be separated. If the child is in danger of abuse or neglect at the hands of a parent or guardian, or is a danger to themselves or others, they can be separated. An agency may not remove a child from a parent or legal guardian solely for the policy goal of deterring individuals from migrating to the United States or for the policy goal of promoting compliance with civil immigration laws. Any separation must be documented in writing and the reason for the separation must be stated, together with stated evidence for the separation. Training will be developed for agents and officers that emphasizes the best interests of the child, childhood trauma, attachment, and child development. This training will facilitate the standardization of the implementation of authorized separations when appropriate (Feinstein 2019).

H.R. 2203: Homeland Security Improvement Act

This bill was introduced by Rep. Veronica Escobar (TX-16) on April 10, 2019. It has 28 co-sponsors. The purpose of this bill is to increase transparency, accountability, and community engagement within the Department of Homeland Security, to provide independent oversight of border security activities, to improve training for agents and officers of U.S. Customs and Border Protection and U.S. Immigration and Customs Enforcement, and for other purposes.

The bill establishes the position of Ombudsman for Border and Immigration Related Concerns within the Department of Homeland Security (DHS). The ombudsman shall establish an independent, neutral, and standardized process to assist individuals in resolving complaints related to U.S. Customs and Border Protection (CBP), U.S. Immigration and Customs and Enforcement (ICE), and related entities, and will make recommendations to DHS to address chronic issues identified in the complaints process. It limits holding in detention to 72 hours, terminates the remain in Mexico and metering policies, and prohibits restraints on women who are pregnant or post-delivery. Oversight includes reports on migrant deaths, review of the use of force, accountability and transparency, and audit and inspection (Escobar 2019a).

Republicans tried to amend this bill by requiring that crimes committed in sanctuary cities by undocumented persons be reported to the Secretary of Homeland Security (Congressional Research Service 2019). The amendment was defeated by a vote of 216–207. H.R. 2203 passed in the House on September 27, 2019, by a vote of 230–174. Next, it goes to the Senate for consideration.

H.R. 2662: Asylum Seeker Protection Act

This bill was introduced by Veronica Escobar (TX-16) on May 10, 2019. The bill has 72 co-sponsors. It was referred to the Committee on the Judiciary. The purpose of this bill is to prohibit funds from being used to implement the Migrant Protection Protocols as announced by the Secretary of Homeland Security on December 20, 2018. It was referred to the House Committee on Judiciary Action and then to the Subcommittee on Immigration and Citizenship Action (Escobar 2019b).

H.R. 2415: The Dignity for Detained Immigrants Act of 2019

This bill was introduced by Rep. Pramila Jayapal (WA-7) on May 20, 2019. It has 157 co-sponsors. H.R. 2415 provides standards for facilities in which aliens in the custody of the Department of Homeland Security are detained, and for other purposes. These standards are no lower than the unannounced inspections by the inspector general of DHS and must take place at least every 12 months. Failure to meet the standards for facilities results in a warning or fine. Continued non-compliance with the standards can lead to the transfer of detainees.

The bill also covers the procedures for the notification and investigation of the death of a person in custody. A report of the results of the investigation will be made available to the public within 60 days of the death. Compensation and attorney's fees are covered under the bill. The reports are not owned by DHS. The bill specifies that no construction or expansion of detention facilities can take place until the plans have been reviewed by the Judiciary Committee. The review must take place to later than 180 days before the start of the construction. For-profit detention centers and the use of jails will be phased out.

Mandatory detention is repealed. No later than 48 hours after being taken into custody, a migrant who has been found to have a credible or reasonable fear of return will receive an initial custody determination from the secretary of Homeland Security. The migrant can be released to await an asylum hearing. If a migrant is required to wear a monitoring device as an alternative to detention, there are no fees for the device beyond operating and maintenance costs.

If the secretary of Homeland Security determines that the release of an alien will not reasonably ensure the appearance of the alien as required or will endanger the safety of any other person or the community, the custody determination under this paragraph will impose the least restrictive conditions for detaining this person. The least restrictive conditions include no detention for vulnerable, including the mentally ill, primary caregivers, and children (persons under the age of 18). An arrested migrant will also be provided with a hearing before an immigration judge no later than 48 hours after being taken into custody. The hearing will determine whether there is probable cause to believe that the person does not have the right to enter or remain in the United States. The burden to establish probable cause shall be on the secretary of Homeland Security (Jayapal 2019).

H.R. 3239: "Humanitarian Standards for Individuals in Customs and Border Protection Custody Act"

This bill was introduced by Rep. Raul Ruiz (CA-36) on June 12, 2019. Rep. Ruiz is a physician. This 20-page bill has 160 co-sponsors and requires U.S. Customs and Border Protection to perform an initial health screening on detainees, and includes other purposes. H.R. 3239 addresses a number of concerns regarding the well-being of border detainees, including water quality, nutrition, hygiene, sanitation, shelter, privacy, psychological assistance for detainees who have experienced sexual violence or other toxic stress, and ensures the physical and mental safety of lesbian, gay, bisexual, transgender, and intersex individuals. Qualifications of medical personnel, guidelines for training of Customs and Border Patrol personnel, transfer procedures from medical facilities, and ethical guidelines of care are also included. The bill requires males and females to be detained separately, and it limits the occupancy capacity of facilities. H.R.3239 has been passed by the House and has been sent on to the Senate (Ruiz 2019).

H.R. 3451: The "Humane Enforcement and Legal Protections for Separated Children Act of 2019," or the "HELP Separated Children Act of 2019"

This bill was introduced by Rep. Lucille Roybal-Allard (CA-40) on June 24, 2019. The 11-page bill had four co-sponsors, Nydia Velázquez (NY-7), Dina Titus (NV-1), David Price (NC-4), and Adriano Espaillat (NY-13). Later 53 others joined. The companion bill in the Senate is S. 2256.

H.R. 3451 stipulates that within two hours of capture, detainees shall be questioned and allowed to make a phone call to arrange for care of their children. Child welfare must also be notified. Children will not be required to translate for their parents, and parents must be allowed to communicate with the child. They are permitted regular phone calls and contact visits with their children. The parent must be told where the child is, and to the extent practicable, the child should be placed near the location of apprehension and near the place of habitual residence. Decisions must be made in the best interests of the child. There will be no impediments, delays, or limits of the obligations of the secretary of Homeland Security, the attorney general, or the secretary of Health and Human Services under the William Wilberforce Trafficking Victims Protection Reauthorization Act, the *Flores* settlement, or Homeland Security Act.

Detention facilities must post information regarding the protections required under this act, and information regarding potential eligibility for parole or release. Absent extraordinary circumstances, individuals who are

13. Seeking Relief Through Congress

detained by the Department of Homeland Security and are parents or legal guardians of children in the United States are permitted regular phone calls and contact visits with their children. They are also provided with contact information for child welfare agencies and family courts in the relevant jurisdictions, and they are given the opportunity to participate fully and, to the extent possible, in person in all family court proceedings, and in any other proceedings that may impact their right to custody of their children. They are also granted free and confidential telephone calls to relevant child welfare agencies and family courts as often as is necessary to ensure that the best interest of their children, including a preference for family unity whenever appropriate, can be considered in child welfare agency or family court proceedings.

The parents will be able to fully comply with all family court or child welfare agency orders impacting the custody of their children. They will be provided access to United States passport applications or other relevant travel document applications for the purpose of obtaining travel documents for their children. They will be afforded timely access to a notary public for the purpose of applying for a passport for their children or executing guardianship or other agreements to ensure the safety of their children. Parents will be granted adequate time and opportunity before removal to obtain passports, birth certificates, travel documents, and other necessary records on behalf of their children if the children will accompany them on their return to or join them in their country of origin. Before leaving the United States, parents and primary caregivers will be able to share information regarding travel arrangements with their consulate, children, child welfare agencies, or other care givers.

Once deported, parents must receive regular phone calls from children, and must be given the child's contact information and the information of welfare agencies that oversee the child. All personnel of the department, cooperating entities, and detention facilities operating under this act will receive mandatory training on the protections required by this act (Roybal-Allard 2019a).

H.R. 3452, the Help Separated Families Act, and S. 2256, the Coordinating Care for Children Affected by Immigration Enforcement Act

H.R. 3452, **the Help Separated Families Act**, was also introduced by Rep. Lucille Roybal-Allard (CA-40) on June 24, 2019. This bill had four co-sponsors, Norma Torres (CA-35), Nydia Velázquez, Dina Titus, and Adriano Espaillat. Later, 47 others joined. This bill will amend part E of title IV of the Social Security Act to ensure that immigration status alone does not disqualify a parent, legal guardian, or relative from being a placement for a foster child. This bill also authorizes discretion to a state, county, or other political subdivision of a state to delay filing for termination of parental rights in foster care cases in which an otherwise fit and willing parent or legal guardian has been deported or is involved in an immigration proceeding, unless certain other conditions have been met. The bill also covers other purposes.

Foreign documents must be accepted. The state is required to accept a foreign consulate identification card or a foreign passport as sufficient identification for purposes of initiating a criminal-records check or a fingerprint-based check. The immigration status of a relative seeking placement of the child with the relative shall not be questioned, except to the extent necessary in determining eligibility for relevant services or programs. The relatives will be made aware that their status will not be questioned. Termination cannot be filed for when a parent is in removal proceedings. Child welfare personnel must speak the language of the child. Authorities must see if the parents want to return with the child. To the greatest extent possible, the privacy and confidentiality of all information gathered in the course of administering the care, custody, and placement of, and follow-up services provided to, a separated child, consistent with the best interest of such child, will be maintained. Other government agencies or persons (other than a parent, legal guardian, or relative caregiver of such child), except that the head of the state agency (or the county or other political subdivision of the state, as applicable) may disclose such information, only after placing a written record of the disclosure in the file of the child (Roybal-Allard 2019b).

S. 2256, the Coordinating Care for Children Affected by Immigration Enforcement Act, was introduced by Sen. Tina Smith (MN) on July 24, 2019. It is a companion bill to H.R.3452. It is co-sponsored by 20 other senators. The purpose of this bill is to protect children affected by immigration enforcement actions (T. Smith 2019).

H.R. 3525: U.S. Border Medical Screening Standards Act

This bill was introduced by Rep. Lauren Underwood (IL-14) on June 27, 2019. Rep. Underwood is a nurse. This bill amends the Homeland Security Act of 2002 to direct the commissioner of U.S. Customs and Border Protection to establish uniform processes for medical screening of individuals interdicted between ports of entry, and for other purposes. Research authorized by this bill focuses on innovative approaches that address gaps in providing comprehensive medical screening for vulnerable populations, particularly children, the elderly, and pregnant women. The bill also creates an interdepartmental electronic health record system. H.R. 3525 was marked up by the Committee on Homeland Security and was ordered to be reported (amended) by voice vote. It passed the House on September 27, 2019, by a vote of 23 to 184 and was referred to the Senate (Underwood 2019).

H.R. 3670: Short Term Detention Standards Act

This bill was introduced by Rep. Elissa Slotkin (MI-08) on July 10, 2019. It is co-sponsored by Rep. Bennie Thompson (MS-2). This bill amends the Homeland Security Act of 2002 that provides only "adequate access to food and water to migrants in short-term U.S. custody" (Sec. 507, 80). H.R. 3670 ensures these individuals access to appropriate temporary shelter, food, and water, sanitation, and personal grooming items. Audits, inspections, including inspections of records, and oversight by members of Congress are authorized. This bill has been passed by the House and has been sent on to the Senate (Slotkin 2019).

S. 2113, the Stop Cruelty to Migrant Children Act, and H.R. 3918, the Stop Cruelty to Migrant Children Act

S. 2113, the Stop Cruelty to Migrant Children Act, was introduced on July 11, 2019, by Sen. Jeff Merkley (OR) and is co-sponsored by 39 other senators. H.R. 3918, which was introduced by Grace Meng (NY-6) in the House of Representatives on July 23, 2019, is the companion bill.

S. 2113 creates non-negotiable standards for the treatment of children in America's care. One provisions of the bill is ending family separation within 100 miles from a border except when authorized by a state court or child welfare agency, or when Customs and Border Protection and an independent child welfare specialist agree that a child is a trafficking victim, is not a child of an accompanying adult, or is in danger of abuse or neglect. Parents of a child that is separated receive a monthly report about the child. The bill sets minimum health and safety standards for children and families at Border Patrol Stations including access to hygiene products, showers, nutritious meals, and prompt medical assessments by trained medical providers. For-profit contractors can no longer operate new Office of Refugee Resettlement (ORR) standard shelters and facilities. Temporary influx facilities must be state-licensed, meet *Flores* standards, and cannot be used to house children indefinitely. The successful Family Case Management Program and other alternatives to family detention are expanded. Roadblocks to placing unaccompanied children with sponsors are removed and the process of moving children out of detention centers and into community-based settings is expedited. Unaccompanied children have access to legal counsel within 72 hours and continue to be placed in a non-adversarial setting for their initial asylum case review. The attorney general will add 75 judges and support staff (Merkley 2019).

H.R. 3918, the Stop Cruelty to Migrant Children Act, was introduced by Rep. Grace Meng (NY-6) on July 23, 2019. It has 33 co-sponsors. The act is designed to protect the health and safety of children in immigration detention, and for other purposes. It is 47 pages in length. The bill states that the federal government is responsible and shall not remove children from parents within 100 miles from the border unless there is a state court order, or it is in the best interests of the child, or if the child is subject to abuse and neglect, or is a danger to self or others, or if the child is a victim of trafficking, or is with a person who is not a parent. Separation cannot be done for purposes of deterrence or to ensure compliance with a policy. Facilities will undergo an annual review. Practices implemented within facilities will be evidenced-based. The presumption of the bill is family unity. If a child is separated from the family, the parent gets a monthly report.

Health and safety protections are determined under the *Flores* settlement. Any rulemaking that supersedes *Flores* is null and void. Prompt medical assessments are required. The maximum number of children detained in a facility is 100. The bill carries a presumption of non-detention. No child shall be delayed or prevented from crossing the border. The bill stipulates that Border Patrol officers are not "asylum officers." Legal information must be available, migrants have the right to counsel, and counsel must have access to migrants. Seventy-five judges who are qualified to hear cases will be added. Support staff will also be provided. Committees in Congress will receive weekly reports of the numbers and age of detained children, and the length of time they have been in the detention care facility. Access to facilities for members of Congress will be mandatory. Some, but not all, aspects of this bill are in H.R. 2203, which has passed the House and has been referred to the Senate (Meng 2019).

H.R. 3777: National Commission to Investigate the Treatment of Migrant Children and Families Act of 2019

This bill was introduced by Yvette Clark (NY-9) on July 16, 2019. The bill establishes a national commission to investigate the treatment of migrant children and families by the Trump administration. The commission will comprise 10 members whose areas of expertise include immigration law, particularly experience representing asylees; public health; civil rights; child welfare; and will include a representative of a humanitarian organization that gives assistance to individuals crossing the southern border, or a local official from a border community on the southern border of the United States.

The commission will examine the handling of migrant families and children apprehended along the United States–Mexico border by U.S. Customs and Border Protection since January 2017. It will determine, evaluate, and report on the evidence developed by all relevant governmental agencies regarding the facts and circumstances surrounding the handling by the Departments of Homeland Security and Health and Human Services of migrant families and children who were apprehended at the southern border since January 2017, and build upon the investigations of other entities. The commission has the authority to hold hearings, receive evidence, and issue subpoenas.

The findings, conclusions, and recommendations of several entities will be built upon. These entities include the Department of Homeland Security Office of Inspector General; the Department of Health and Human Services Office of Inspector General; and other executive branch, congressional, or independent investigations into the treatment of and detention conditions for migrant families and children apprehended at the southern border by the Department of Homeland Security since January 2017. Within 18 months after the date of the enactment of this act, the commission will make a full and complete accounting of the handling of the migrant families and children apprehended at the southern border since January 2017; and will investigate and report to the president and Congress on its findings, conclusions, and recommendations for corrective measures (Clarke 2019). This bill was included in H.R. 2203 and passed the House on September 27, 2019. Next it goes to the Senate for consideration.

H.R. 3868: Help Oversee, Manage, and Evaluate Safe Treatment and Ensure Access Without Delay Act of 2019

This bill, also called the HOMESTEAD Act of 2019, was introduced by Debbie Wasserman Schultz (FL-23) on July 22, 2019. Its purpose is to grant members of Congress access to detention facilities, and it includes other purposes. The members do not have to give notice to enter the facilities. Modifications will not be put in place before the visits. This bill was included in H.R. 2203 and passed the House on September 27, 2019. Next it goes to the Senate for consideration (Wasserman-Schultz 2019).

H.R. 5210, the Refugee Protection Act of 2019, and S. 2936, the Refugee Protection Act of 2019

H.R. 5210, the Refugee Protection Act of 2019, was introduced by Zoe Lofgren (CA-19) on November 21, 2019. Its purpose is to provide for the admission and protection of asylum seekers and other vulnerable individuals, to provide for the processing of refugees and asylum seekers in the Western Hemisphere, and to modify certain special immigrant visa programs, and to provide for other purposes. It has 31 co-sponsors. H.R. 5210 is divided into seven subtitles that include 55 sections. Keeping families together, protections for minors seeking asylum, and assuring a fair day in court for children are all part of the bill. It was passed on to the Committee on the Judiciary, the Committee on Ways and Means, the Budget, and Foreign Affairs, for a period to be subsequently determined by the Speaker, in each case for consideration of such provisions as fall within the jurisdiction of the committee concerned (Lofgren 2019). It was not enacted into law.

S. 2936, the Refugee Protection Act of 2019, is the companion bill to H.R. 5210. It was filed on November 21, 2019, by Patrick Leahy (V) and 15 co-sponsors. The purpose of this bill is to provide for the admission and protection of refugees, asylum seekers, and other vulnerable individuals, to provide for the processing of refugees and asylum seekers in the Western Hemisphere, and to modify certain special immigrant visa programs, and to provide for other purposes. Its short title is "Refugee Protection Act of 2019" (Leahy 2019).

14

Recommendations

14.1 Seeking Freedom

It is difficult to find myself writing the final pages of this book. Nearly every day for the past two years, some occurrence regarding the migrant children and their families has caught my attention and sent me off to discover and record more. With the arrival of the pandemic and the intensification of cruelty toward migrants by the Trump administration, there is even greater need to pay attention. Although the book is ending, the fight for the realization and protection of their human rights will not.

The following is a statement regarding the importance of human rights from the U.S. Department of State:

> The protection of fundamental human rights was a foundation stone in the establishment of the United States over 200 years ago. Since then, a central goal of U.S. foreign policy has been the promotion of respect for human rights, as embodied in the Universal Declaration of Human Rights.... The Department of State works with democratic partners, international and regional organizations, nongovernmental organizations, and engaged citizens to support those seeking freedom [U.S. Department of State 2020].

Unfortunately, at this time some of the words in this statement are not true. Tragically, during the past three years, the United States has, in the most egregious ways, undermined, not supported, "those seeking freedom" at the southern border. During this disgraceful chapter of our history, the U.S. has ripped migrant children away from their families—forced them to suffer unspeakable harm—mocked mothers who cried because they could not comfort their children—made parents suffer the pain of not knowing if their children were alive and safe—burdened parents with the anguish of not knowing where to find their children—ridiculed children who sobbed non-stop because their parents had disappeared—cut off communication between parents and children—forbade caretakers to hug and comfort toddlers—prohibited siblings from hugging and comforting each other—played a part in the suicides of fathers who could not bear the heartache of being unable to protect their children—terrorized extended family members who wanted to help, but could not help for fear that they would be deported or would become targets of the government—marginalized immigrants as terrorists and criminals—treated human beings like animals by incarcerating them in cages—confined children in border stations with freezing cold temperatures—forced people to sleep on concrete floors—threw food at people as if they were dogs—called migrants derogatory names—failed to provide soap and toothpaste for children—dispensed contaminated drinking water to mothers and infants, and toddlers—neglected to offer adequate medical care—enabled the deaths of several children—covered up the circumstances under which children died—sent families back to countries where they were destined to be tortured or to die—continued to churn out policies and practices that would attempt to eliminate migrants from this country—refused to release children and their families from detention facilities even when they were "on fire" with Covid-19.

14.2 Recommendations from Official Places

The law cases and legislation described in Chapters 12 and 13 of this book result from formal systems designed to remedy some of the injury suffered by the migrant families and help ensure that the deplorable treatment they have endured ceases and is never perpetrated by the United States again. In addition, the Young Center for Immigrant Children's Rights (Young Center for Immigrant Children's Rights 2020), Human Rights First (Human Rights First 2020a), and Lee Gelernt, deputy director of the Immigrants' Rights Project, American Civil Liberties Union (Gelernt 2019), have drawn up recommendations to bring an end to the appalling treatment of migrants as well.

Anthony Romero, executive director of the American Civil Liberties Union, has recommended a complete reorganization of the Department of Homeland Security (A. Romero 2020). The Government Accountability Office has questioned the legitimacy of the appointments of the heads of Homeland Security (U.S. Government Accountability Office 2020).

These voices from the courts, government officials, and human rights organizations speak on large stages, and resonate throughout country, the Western Hemisphere, and even the entire world. The following are their recommendations.

Recommendations from the Young Center for Immigrant Children's Rights

- Every government agency must make the best interests of the child a primary consideration in every decision about a child.

All federal agencies must be required to consider children's best interests in every decision, regardless of immigration status or opportunity for legal relief.
- **Congress and agency policy must prohibit family separation in all but the most exceptional cases.** Children must not be separated from parents unless there is evidence that the parent poses an imminent risk to the child's safety.
- **Every decision to temporarily separate a child from a parent must be subject to prompt review by a court with experience in child protection and parental rights—not immigration enforcement officials.** Decisions to separate an immigrant child from a parent should only be made by an independent professional who is culturally sensitive, trained in child welfare, child development, immigration law, and trafficking concerns.
- **Federal agencies (DHS, DOJ, and HHS) should ensure that every child separated from a parent has an attorney and an independent child advocate.** When DHS separates a child and a parent, it should be required to ensure that both parent and child have counsel.
- **Congress must protect the *Flores* settlement and the Trafficking Victims Protection Reauthorization Act (TVPRA).** Before *Flores* and the TVPRA, immigrant children were treated the same as adults; weakening of these protections will undermine the safety of children.
- **The executive branch must end the Remain in Mexico/Migrant Protection Protocols and restore access to asylum** (Young Center for Immigrant Children's Rights 2020).

Human Rights First—Recommendations for the Trump Administration

- **Rescind the Health and Human Services (HHS) interim final rule authorizing the CDC order** and immediately withdraw the CDC order.
- **End MMP and all other policies and practices that violate U.S. asylum and immigration law and U.S. Refugee Protocol obligations,** including the third-country transit asylum ban, turn-backs and orchestrated reductions of asylum processing at ports of entry, and all attempts to send asylum seekers to countries, including El Salvador, Honduras, Guatemala, and Mexico, that do not meet the legal requirements for safe-third-country agreements under U.S. law.

- **Employ effective and humane policies that uphold U.S. laws and treaties and implement measures recommended by public health experts to safeguard asylum seekers, CPB personnel, and public health**, such as implementing social distancing, using appropriate personal protective equipment, providing hand sanitizer, and regularly disinfecting surfaces—steps CBP and the Border Patrol should already be taking.
- **Direct CBP to parole asylum seekers in MPP, who have already been processed by CBP and have pending immigration court cases, into the United States**, and restore timely and orderly processing of asylum seekers and unaccompanied children at ports of entry (Human Rights First 2020a).

Human Rights First—Recommendations for Congress

- Withhold appropriations to DHS and the Department of Justice used to carry out MPP, CDC expulsions, and other forced return programs.
- Adopt the "Asylum Seeker Protection Act" and the "Refugee Protection Act of 2019."
- Hold oversight hearings on MPP and the expulsion of asylum seekers without the required legal processes under the CDC order.
- Request investigations of the claimed justifications and legality of the CDC order by the Offices of Inspector General for DHS and HHS.
- Conduct official visits (when safe, given the Covid-19 pandemic) to Mexican border towns, CBP facilities and Border Patrol stations on the southern border, and immigration courts to monitor the massive human rights violations caused by MPP, the expulsion of asylum seekers and unaccompanied children, and other policies to restrict asylum at the border (Human Rights First 2020a).

Recommendations of Lee Gelernt, Deputy Director, Immigrant's Rights Project American Civil Liberties Union, to the U.S. House Committee on Energy and Commerce Subcommittee on Oversight and Investigations

First, the committee should ensure that HHS account for potentially thousands of families identified in the OIG report. It is not sufficient for the agency to say it is not worth the effort, not when children are at stake.

Second, it is critical that proper procedures and standards be adopted so that separations occur only when there is a genuine reason to believe that the parent is unfit or presents a danger to the child—the traditional child welfare standard. It is not satisfactory or lawful for Customs and Border Protection agents and officers to make unilateral decisions about families.

Third, in the rare instance where separations do occur, HHS and other relevant agencies must develop a database and tracking system, so families can quickly be reunited with their parents.

Fourth, parents who are deported without their children and who were misled or coerced into giving up their own asylum rights should be permitted to return to the United States and given an asylum hearing.

Fifth, funds should be allocated for the families that were separated to assist them with obtaining medical and other assistance for the trauma they suffered and continue to suffer even after reunification (Gelernt 2019).

Call for the Dismantling of the Department of Homeland Security from Anthony Romero, Executive Director, American Civil Liberties Union

Anthony Romero, ACLU executive director, has called for the dismantling of the Department of Homeland Security. Romero states that over the past 20 years, DHS has merged 22 government agencies into an immense department that is powerful but ineffective, due to deficient oversight and management. Romero cites the tragedy of separating of children from their parents at the border, the recent deployment of federal agents to American cities, and surveillance of Black Lives Matter activists as catalysts for his recommendation. Romero suggests restructuring the department into smaller, more efficient federal agencies with diverse leadership, well-defined missions, and distinct responsibilities (A. Romero 2020).

Scrutiny of DHS from the Government Accountability Office

In mid–August 2020, the Government Accountability Office (GAO) reported that Chad Wolf, acting secretary of the Department of Homeland Security, and Ken Cuccinelli, senior official performing the duties of deputy secretary, were not appointed through a valid process (Hesson 2020).

The GAO said that acting assignments have not been valid since Kirstjen Nielsen resigned from the position of secretary of DHS in 2019. Nielsen tried to change the rules regarding temporary appointments so that Kevin McAleenan would fill her position, but she amended the wrong document and set off a chain reaction of proscribed appointments. McAleenan's appointment was not valid, and consequently when he tried to amend the rules to appoint Wolf to the acting post and Cuccinelli as deputy, their appointments were invalid as well (Domonoske 2020).

Acting appointments are typically completed quickly because they circumvent the process of approval by the Senate. This omission eliminates oversight by the legislative branch.

The GAO did not review the consequences of Wolf's and Cuccinelli's service in these positions. The GAO also referred the question of who should be serving as the acting secretary and the senior official performing the duties of deputy secretary to the DHS Office of Inspector General for its review (U.S. Government Accountability Office 2020).

The law case *LLV v. Cuccinelli* is described in Chapter 12 of this book. In that case, Cuccinelli's appointment as acting director of the United States Citizens and Immigration Services (USCIS) was determined to be improper. Asylum directives he implemented while he held that position were found to be invalid. This lawsuit was being appealed. The day before the GAO released their report in August, Trump administration lawyers dropped the appeal (Walerius and Tanvi 2020).

14.3 Finding Resilience in Small Places

In addition to the voices on the large stages, there are also those consistent voices in small places that make a difference for migrants who are suffering every day. There are also the voices of the migrants themselves, who tell their stories and encourage each other to go forward. I close this book with two of those voices: Martha Iskyan, the volunteer for Refugee Aid who was the translator on our trip to the shelters in Mexicali, Mexico, and a child from the Hosanna shelter in Mexicali, Mexico.

Martha wrote the following piece about her work and the resilience of people in times of high stress and loss:

> I have been a Red Cross volunteer for the past 20 years—a mental health disaster volunteer. In the beginning I would be sent out to help folks affected by floods, hurricanes, tornadoes, and other natural calamities or mass shootings, for example, the shooting in Las Vegas. For the past 5 years, I have been involved as a facilitator and trainer of workshops designed to alleviate suffering for our military personnel and their families in a program called "Service to the Armed Forces." Our team travels to different bases or anywhere the military commanders want us to go, and we give workshops on communication, anger management, depression, taking care of children, and providing caregiving for adults. The caregiving workshop is especially helpful for persons taking care of wounded members. There is also a mind-body workshop that has been very popular. Now with the Covid-19 pandemic, we have been able to turn these workshops into virtual sessions.
>
> I have always been interested in wanting to aid those that are in need, and I am a

14. Recommendations 223

huge advocate of our immigrants and their families. Being involved in Refugee Aid, with the sorting and distribution of needed supplies for families stranded at the Mexican border, has been gratifying, but since the border has closed, I feel helpless that I am not able to do more.

Since I speak Spanish and live in Arizona, where there is a large Spanish-speaking population, I help out with translating for the Red Cross, as well as for Refugee Aid. The Red Cross often responds to house fires and, unfortunately, most persons affected are Spanish-speaking families. We provide them with monetary help as well as information about where to go to get back on their feet after a fire. We also do condolence calls after a family member passes away as a result of a fire, or nowadays with the passing of Covid-19 victims.

Over the years, a revelation to me has been how very resilient people are in times of high stress and loss. The objective of our aid is to help clients through the most difficult times and simultaneously give them the resources necessary to become independent [M. Iskyan, personal communication, July 2, 2020].

Little has been written about the resilience of the asylum seekers in this time of stress and loss because the emphasis has been placed on the hardship they have suffered. The sheer survival of the migrant families attests to their resilience. They have withstood each traumatic event only to be faced with the challenge of the next. Tragically, during the past three years, the United States has, in the most egregious ways, undermined, not supported, the people seeking freedom at the southern border.

The asylum seekers from Northern Triangle of Central America are not terrorists, or criminals, or animals. Many are children. They are mostly women. Many women are pregnant. They are small in stature but enormously powerful in strength and spirit. They have strong bonds and understand the importance of being together and helping each other. They find their greatest joy in being together. They care about each other. The men protect their children. If they are homeless and have to walk the streets, they form groups and shelter each other. They are vigilant and make sure their children are safe. They have deep love for each other. The children like to go to school, read books, learn, and play.

The Trump administration has treated migrant families cruelly in a relentless attempt to separate families and deport parents. Those I met who were detained in Mexico have faith that together, they can find a way to a better life. At the Hosanna shelter, a large sheet of paper with a hand-painted Christmas tree was displayed on one of the cement walls. White paper ornaments adorned the tree. A child's message of joy and hope for the holiday season or the coming year was written on each ornament. Although Christmas had been celebrated nearly three months prior to my visit, the tree was still on the wall. The messages reflected the spirit of caring for each other within the community. In their messages they asked for the following:

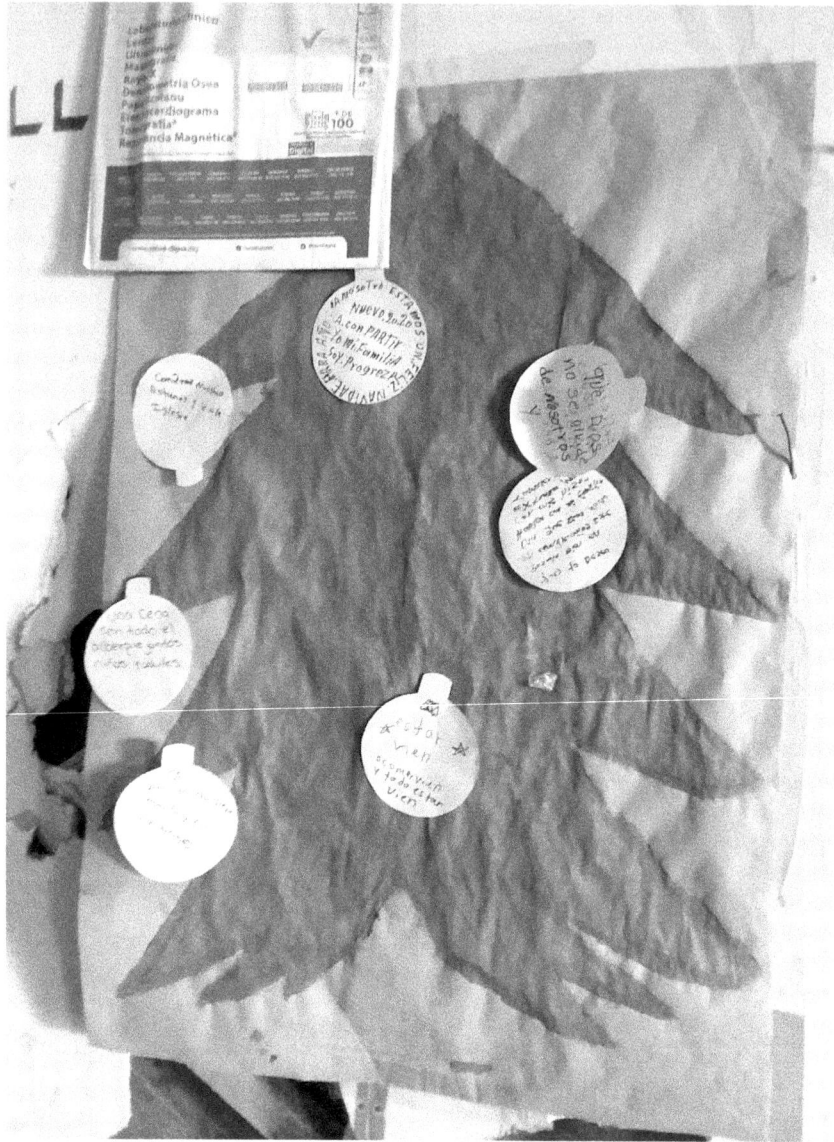

Christmas tree with wishes for the new year (author's photograph).

- To be well, to eat well, and all to be well,
- A dinner with all of the Albuquerque shelter together, children and adults,
- For me, I would like to have fun with friends,
- That God does not forget us and happiness to all in the Albuquerque.

14. Recommendations

In the fourth statement, I discovered the second epigraph for the beginning of this book. For me, it reflects the deep faith in God and love and solidarity the migrants from Central America have for each other. Despite merciless treatment by our government, many seekers of asylum and safety still believe in their dream of finding a better life in America.

May we all work to make that dream a reality.

Jo-Anne Wilson-Keenan
August 17, 2020

The State of Things Today

I completed the manuscript for this book in late summer of 2020, but the plight of migrant children and their families continued. Against the backdrop of the Covid-19 pandemic, over 70,000 people hoping to gain asylum in the U.S. were forced to remain at the southern border.

Jennifer Nagda, policy director at the Young Center for Immigrant Children's Rights, reported that between March and September 2020, the Department of Homeland Security detained children in hotels rather than in safe, state-licensed programs. She stated, "The children had no access to Child Advocates, to attorneys, or to any of the protections guaranteed to them under federal law. They were supervised by unknown adults with no experience in child development and trauma" (Nagda 2020). Children as young as age ten were left alone with these adults. Over 600 of children had been detained in border hotels in 2020, instead of being placed in state-licensed programs.

Nagda argued, however, that ORR had the capacity to process these children in their centers (Yucatan Times, 2020). Health precautions such as safe distancing, wearing masks, and using hand sanitizer could have been employed to maintain the children's safety.

On September 4, 2020, Judge Dolly Gee, of the United States District Court of Central California, wrote that the conditions under which the children were detained in the hotels "are not adequately safe and do not sufficiently account for the vulnerability of unaccompanied minors in detention." She ruled, "DHS shall cease placing minors at hotels by no later than September 15, 2020" (Jenny L. Flores, et al. v. William P. Barr, et al., 2020).

By November 2020, under the CDC order Title 42, 200,000 migrants were expelled at the border. This number included at least 8,800 unaccompanied children (Williams, 2020).

In November, U.S. District Judge Emmet Sullivan issued a preliminary injunction ordering the Department of Homeland Security to stop expelling the unaccompanied migrant children. The order pertained only to this group of children. He also denied a request by the Justice Department to stay the order pending an appeal (Williams, 2020). Therefore, the government could not continue deporting the children although they did file an appeal and the case continued to be litigated (Carranza, 2020).

By the end of the year, the number of children who were separated from their parents had risen to over 5,400. At least 611 were missing, 500 of whom children are still missing today. According to the ACLU, this number may an underestimated number.

Despite the hardships, humanitarian work continues.

Mary Jo Forman Miller, CEO of Refugee Aid says:

> Refugee Aid pivoted and began sending food and supplies to the shelters in Mexicali, MX when the Remain in Mexico policy began. In response to Covid, Refugee Aid began distributing food in the Phoenix area through pop-up food banks managed by the Latino churches who had hosted asylum seeking families in 2019. Refugee Aid sincerely values their close relationship with these churches and deeply admires the love, compassion and humanitarian aid that the churches provide to their communities. Refugee Aid is now working to support both their church partners and the Welcome Center, which is busy now and in need of assistance. Many hands, much love, much work [M.J. Forman Miller, personal communication March 4, 2021].

In October 2020, *The Young Center for Immigrant Children's Rights* released a 99-page report that reimagines how the federal government can adjudicate an unaccompanied or separated child's request to remain permanently in the United States. The report is titled *Reimagining Children's Immigration Proceedings: A Roadmap for an Entirely New System Centered Around Children*. It develops "a framework for a new system, built around the need and capacities of children." The report endeavors to "reimagine the way in which the federal government adjudicates an unaccompanied child's request to remain permanently in the United States." There are seven guiding principles included. The first is that the primary focus of every decision made about a child considers the child's best interests.

Another principle emphasizes many of the rights that have been examined in this book. It reads:

> All children placed in immigration proceedings have the same rights, including having the right to express their own wishes, to safety, to liberty, to be protected from family separation, to develop, to maintain their identity, to have their best interests considered in all decisions, to be treated with dignity and respect, and to have a fair opportunity to seek protection from harm." Many of these rights have been examined in this book [Young Center for Immigrant Children's Rights, 2020 b].

In October 2020, Sarah Richie, Director of Communications for the Kino Border Initiative wrote *Lifting Up the Voices of Children*. In this article, she explains the importance of the *Convention on the Rights of the Child*. Sara states:

In 1989, the United Nations adopted the Convention on the Rights of the Child (CRC), which recognized countries' obligation to protect children and their rights, regardless of their immigration status or that of their parents. The CRC paved the way for nations to be held accountable to high standards of treatment of vulnerable populations under the age of 18 and was recognized as 'the first significant steps toward creating a world in which any child—even the most vulnerable separated immigrant child—can be aided to reach his or her full potential.' The United States played a fundamental role in the drafting of the CRC, which one United Nations member nation has yet to ratify.

Richie also presents the consequences of the failure of the U.S. to ratify the CRC.

The U.S. government's refusal to ratify the CRC has ethical repercussions within the international community. Seeing the U.S., a driving force in the drafting of the CRC, refuse to ratify it sends a message that it is acceptable to shirk moral responsibility and emboldens other nations to follow suit. Not only has the US refused to accept moral leadership, it has set an abhorrent precedent for the treatment of children in recent years. Since 2017, we have witnessed and documented the Trump Administration's series of attacks on the immigrant population, during which children have been used as political pawns of family separations, subjected to detainment in clandestine hotels, and rapidly expelled without proper review, to name a few examples [Richie 2020].

From the time of the 2020 presidential election to the end of Trump's term, migrant families continued to live under his harsh treatment. He refused to admit defeat resulting in an insurrection at the Capitol on January 6.

On January 20, 2021, Joseph R. Biden became the president of the United States. On that day, he sent the U.S. Citizenship Act to Congress "to restore humanity and American values to our immigration system" (Biden, 2021).

President Biden nominated Alejandro Mayorkas as secretary of homeland security. Mayorkas is a DHS veteran and designed the Deferred Action for Childhood Arrivals (DACA) program. In the first weeks of his administration, Biden issued several executive actions undoing the policies of former president Trump had established. The administration understands that change will take time. The following are a few of Biden's major actions:

Executive Order—"Creating a Comprehensive Regional Framework to Address Root Causes of Immigration Throughout North and Central America, and to Provide Safe and Orderly Processing of Asylum Seekers at the United States Border"—The Trump administration designed 96 asylum-related policies. President Biden's executive order requires the secretary of homeland security to review some of former President Trump's 96 policies. Then the process of creating new rules can begin. Further purposes of this order are to create both a comprehensive plan for getting at the causes of migration and an entirely new system of processing asylum seekers. Accomplishing of these goals will take an extensive period of time (Libowsky & Oehlke, 2021).

"Executive Order on the Establishment of Interagency Task Force in the Reunification of Families"—On February 2, President Biden signed this executive order. The secretary of homeland security will lead the task force. Other members will include the secretaries of state, and health and human services, the attorney general and other government leaders. The executive director of the Task Force will be Michelle Brané, the former director of the Migrant Rights and Justice Program at the Woman's Refugee Commission. The following are some of the functions of the Task Force:

> Identifying all children who were separated from their families at the United States-Mexico border between January 20, 2017, and January 20, 2021, in connection with the operation of the Zero-Tolerance Policy;
> To the greatest extent possible, facilitating and enabling the reunification of each of the children with their families by;
> providing recommendations regarding provision of additional services and support to the children and their families, including trauma and mental health services;
> providing recommendations regarding reunification of any additional family members who were separated, such as siblings, where there is compelling humanitarian interest to do so;
> providing recommendations to the President concerning the exercise of any Presidential authorities necessary to reunite the children with their families as appropriate and consistent with applicable law [Biden, Executive Order on the Establishment of Interagency Task Force on the Reunification of Families, 2021].

Executive Order—Migrant Protection Protocols—On January 20, 2021, President Biden announced that asylum seekers would no longer be placed in this holding program in Mexico. On February 19, the first asylum group of 25 seekers were allowed to cross over the San Ysidro Port of Entry in California. Others are following. Some of these asylum seekers have waited nearly two years to enter the U.S. (Libowsky & Oehlke, 2021).

The orders of the new president have inevitable shortcomings, yet they are the first steps in reversing the changes to immigration policies made by President Trump:

> …Biden's early immigration executive actions span a wide range of issues and address many of the changes the Trump administration made through his abuse of executive authority. The executive actions are best understood as an undoing of Trump's policies rather than as new policies on their own. The actions are nuanced, thoughtful and pragmatic, and they have the potential to serve as a guidepost for more sustained, lasting reform [Libowsky & Oehlke].

And so the next chapter for those seeking asylum in the U.S. begins.

Appendix

1. **Convention on the Rights of the Child [UN General Assembly 1989a]** —Complete text with Preamble and 54 Articles—15 pages in length—Reprinted with permission of The United Nations—first mentioned on p. 14 in main text.

2. CRC UN General Assembly. (1990, March 7). [**UN General Assembly 1989b]** *Convention on the Rights of the Child.* UN, Treaty Series, Vol. 1577, p.3 https://treaties.un.org/pages/ViewDetails.aspx?src=IND&mtdsg_no=IV-11&chapter=4&lang=en. Reprinted with permission of the United Nations.

3. **Memorandum for the Secretary Kirstjen Nielsen, April 23, 2018,** [McAleenan 2018] requesting her signature on one of three options regarding family separation—Redacted copy of memorandum to Department of Homeland Security Secretary, Kirstjen Nielsen from Kevin K. McAleenan, Commissioner, U.S. Customs and Border Patrol, L. Francis Cissna, Director, U.S. Citizenship and Immigration Services, and Thomas (last name and position redacted)—5 pages in length—reprinted with permission of Project On Government Oversight and Open the Government—first mentioned on p. 41 in main text.

4. From Project On Government Oversight (POGO) and Open the Government (OTG), "New document shows Nielsen signed off on family separation policy," [Project on Government Oversight and Open the Government 2018b] Reprinted with permission of Project on Government Oversight and Open the Government.

5. **Executive Order of Donald J. Trump,** June 20, 2018, "Affording Congress an Opportunity to Address Family Separation"—3 pages in length—public domain—First mentioned on p. 57 in main text

6. **Email, July 11, 2018, from Acting Chief,** Law Enforcement Directorate, U.S. Border Patrol Headquarters [Project on Government Oversight 2018]—1 page in length—reprinted with permission of Project On Government Oversight and Open the Government—first mentioned on p. 67 in main text.

7. From CBP Email dated July 11, 2018. Re: NTW/WA for FMUA's, retrieved from Project on Government Oversight (POGO) FOIA: [Project on Government Oversight 2018] https://www.documentcloud.org/documents/4936571-FOIA-Release-7-11-Emeail.html The guide to the terminology written by Katherine Hawkins can be found linked in this email. Reprinted with

permission of the Project on Government Oversight (POGO) and Open the Government (OTG). Guide to terminology written by Katherine Hawkins in email of July 11, 2018, reprinted with permission of Project On Government Oversight and Open the Government.

    8. **Notice to Appear**—Redacted copy—from the U.S. Department of Homeland Security—3 pages in length—public domain—first mentioned on p. 157 in the main text

Chapter Notes

Preface

1. CRC UN General Assembly. (1989 November 20). *Convention on the Rights of the Child.* UN, Treaty Series, Vol. 1577, p. 3: https://treaties.un.org/pages/ViewDetails.aspx?src=IND&mtdsg_no=IV-11&chapter=4&lang=en. Reprinted with permission of the United Nations.

2. ICCPR UN General Assembly. (1966 December 16). *International Convention on Civil and Political Rights.* United Nations, Treaty Series, vol. 999, p. 171: https://treaties.un.org/Pages/ViewDetails.aspx?chapter=4&clang=_en&mtdsg_no=IV-4&src=IND. Reprinted with permission of the United Nations.

3. Refugees UN General Assembly. (1951, July 28). *The Convention Relating to the Status of Refugees.* UN, Treaty Series, vol. 189, p. 137: https://treaties.un.org/Pages/showDetails.aspx?objid=080000028003002e. Reprinted with permission of the United Nations.

4. Torture UN General Assembly. (1984 December 10). *Convention Against Torture and Other Cruel, Inhuman or Degrading Treatment or Punishment.* UN, Treaty Series, vol. 1465: https://treaties.un.org/pages/ViewDetails.aspx?src=IND&mtdsg_no=IV-9&chapter=4&lang=en. Reprinted with permission of the United Nations.

5. Discrimination UN General Assembly. (1966, March 7): *International Convention on the Elimination All Forms of Racial Discrimination.* Retrieved from UN, Treaty Series, Vol. 660, p.195: https://treaties.un.org/Pages/ViewDetails.aspx?src=IND&mtdsg_no=IV-2&chapter=4&clang=_en. Reprinted with permission of the United Nations.

Chapter 1

1. From Anthony W. Fontes, "Migrants' stories: Why they flee," *The Conversation*, April 9, 2019. Retrieved from The Conversation: https://theconversation.com/migrants-stories-why-they flee-114725. Reprinted with permission of Anthony W. Fontes.

2. 94 Stat. 102—Refugee Act of 1979—Content Details—STATUTE—94—Page 102: https://www.govinfo.gov/app/details/STATUTE-94/STATUTE-94—Pg 102.

3. Human Rights First, "The Flores Settlement and Family Incarceration: A Brief History and Next Steps," October 30, 2018: https://www.humanrightsfirst.org/resource/flores-settlement-and-family-incarceration-brief-history-and-next-steps. Reprinted with permission of Human Rights First.

4. Https://www.justice.gov/human trafficking/keylegislation.

Chapter 2

1. From Kay McGowan and Fay Givens, *The Indian Schools: The Survivors' Story* [Video Production], 2011. Culture Unplugged: https://www.cultureunplugged.com/documentary/watch-online/play/54410/Indian-School-A-Survivor-s-Story. Information reprinted with permission of Kay McGowan and Fay Givens.

2. From Warren Petoskey, *Dancing My Dream*, Read the Spirit Books, Canton, Michigan, 2009. Reprinted with permission of Warren Petoskey 2009.

3. From The Young Center for Immigrant Children's Rights, "More than 200

experts in child welfare, juvenile justice oppose government plans to take children from parents at border." January 23, 2018: https://www.theyoungcenter.org/stories/2018/1/16/experts-oppose-plans-to-take-children-from-parents-at-border. Reprinted with permission of The Young Center for Immigrnat Children's Rights.

4. From Project On Government Oversight (POGO) and Open the Government (OTG), "New document shows Nielsen signed off on family separation policy," September 25, 2018: https:www.pogo.org/press/release/2018/new-documents-show-nielsen-signed-off-on-family-separation-policy/ Reprinted with permission of Project on Government Oversight and Open the Government.

5. Letter from Project On Government Oversight (POGO) and Open the Government (OTG), to Senate Committee on Homeland Security and Government Affairs, October 2, 2018: https://docs.pogo.org/letter/2018/HSGAC-letter-10-2-18-Final-4.pdf?mtime=20181002170133. Reprinted with permission of Project on Government Oversight and Open the Government.

Chapter 3

1. From CBP Email dated July 11, 2018. Re: NTW/WA for FMUA's, retrieved from Project on Government Oversight (POGO) FOIA: https://www.documentcloud.org/documents/4936571-FOIA-Release-7-11-Emeail.html. The guide to the terminology written by Katherine Hawkins can be found linked in this email. Reprinted with permission of the Project on Government Oversight (POGO).

Chapter 4

1. From Young Center for Immigrant Children's Rights Staff, "Working for immigrant children in custody and across the border in times of COVID-19," Webinar transcript: https://static1.squarespace.com/static/597ab5f3bebafb0a625aaf45/t/5e97754c13775b6404892267/1586984268891/2020_04_15+Final+Webinar+Transcript-Young+Center.pdf. Reprinted with permission of the Young Center for Immmigrant Children's Rights.

Chapter 5

1. From Sondra Crosby, MD and George J. Annas, JD, MPH, "POV: Child detention at the border is torture," *BU Today* July 18, 2019: www.bu.edu/articles2019/child-detention-at-border-is-torture. Reprinted with permission of Sondra Crosby, MD.

2. From Jaana Juvonen, & Jennifer Silvers, "Separating children from parents at the border isn't just cruel: It's torture.": *UCLA Newsroom*, May 20, 2018, https://newsroon.ucla.edu/stories/separating-children-from-parents-at-the-border-isnt-just-cruel-its-torture. Reprinted with permission of UCLA Media Relations.

Chapter 8

1. From Justin Rohrlich, "U.S. border officers die by suicide 30% more often than other cops," *Quartz*. January 1, 2012: https://qz.com/1738901/us-border-officers-die-by-suicide-30-percent-more-often-than-other-cops. Reprinted courtesy of Quartz at QZ.com.

Chapter 9

1. Michael E. Hayden, "Emails confirm Miller's twin obsessions: Migrants and crime," Southern Poverty Law Center: Hatewatch, November 25, 2019: https://www.splcenter.org/hatewatch/2019/11/25/emails-confirm-millers-twin-obsessions-immigrants-and-crime. Reprinted with permission from Michael E. Hayden.

2. From Human Rights First, "Orders from above: Massive human rights abuses under Trump administration return to Mexico policy," October 2019. Report written by Eleanor Acer, Kennji Kuzuka, and Rebecca Gendelman: https://www.humanrightsfirst.org/sites/default/files/hrordersfromabove.pdf. Reprinted with permission from Human Rights First.

The Florence Immigrant and Refugee Rights Project, email communications, 11–22–2019. Reprinted with permission from The Florence Project.

Chapter 11

1. Ignatian Solidarity Network; Kino Border Initiative. (2020 April 2). Witness

from the Border. igsol.net/fb. Reprinted with permission from Ignatian Solidarity Network; Kino Border Initiative.

2. From Human Rights First, "Pandemic as pretext: Trump administration exploits COVID-19, expels asylum seekers and children to escalating danger," May 2020. Report written by Kennji Kizuka, Eleanor Acer, & Rebecca Gendelman: https://www.humanrightsfirst.org/sites/default/files/PandemicAsPretextFINAL.pdf. Reprinted with permission of Human Rights First.

Chapter 12

1. Civil Rights Litigation Clearinghouse, *Flores v. Barr*, May 27, 2020 (University of Michigan, Ann Arbor): https://www.clearinghouse.net/detail.php?id=9493. Reprinted with permission of Professor Margo Schlanger.

2. Civil Rights Litigation Clearinghouse, *J.S.R. v. Sessions/ V.F.B. v. Sessions*, May 14, 2020 (University of Michigan, Ann Arbor): https://www.clearinghouse.net/detail.php?id=1666. Reprinted with permission of Professor Margo Schlanger.

3. Civil Rights Litigation Clearinghouse, *Ms. J.P. v. Sessions*, May 14, 2020 (University of Michigan, Ann Arbor): https://www.clearinghouse.net/detail.php?id=16667. Reprinted with permission of Professor Margo Schlanger.

4. Civil Rights Litigation Clearinghouse, *Innovation Law Lab et al. v. Nielson et al.*, April 19, 2020 (University of Michigan, Ann Arbor): https://www.clearinghouse.net/detail.php?id=171118. Reprinted with permission of Professor Margo Schlanger.

5. Civil Rights Litigation Clearinghouse, *Kiakombua v. McAllenan*, March 16, 2020, (University of Michigan, Ann Arbor): https://www.clearinghouse.net/detail.php?id=17238. Reprinted with permission of Professor Margo Schlanger.

6. Civil Rights Litigation Clearinghouse. *Padilla v. U.S. Immigration and Customs Enforcement*, June 1, 2020 (University of Michigan, Ann Arbor): https://www.clearinghouse.net/detail.php?id=16635. Reprinted with permission of Professor Margo Schlanger.

Bibliography

Acevedo, N. 2019. Why are migrant children dying in custody? NBC News, March 29. https://www.nbcnews.com/news/latino/why-are-migrant-children-dying-u-s-custody-n1010316.
ACLU. 2019. A.I.I.L v. Sessions. October 3. https://www.aclu.org/cases/aiil-v-sessions.
ACLU of DC. 2020. Make the road New York v. McAleenan—challenge to Trump administration expansion of "expedited removal" for immigrants. June. https://www.acludc.org/en/cases/make-road-new-york-v-mcaleenan-challenge-trump-administration-expansion-expedited-removal.
Ainsley, J. 2018. Former ICE director: Some migrant family separations are permanent. NBC News, June 19. https://www.nbcnews.com/storyline/immigration-border-crisis/former-ice-director-some-migrant-family-separations-are-permanent-n884391.
Ainsley, J. Edwards. 2017. Despite Trump vow to end catch and release, he is still freeing thousands of migrants. Reuters, June 6. https://www.reuters.com/article/us-usa-immigration-detention-idUSKBN18X1G4.
Ainsley, J., and Soboroff, J. 2020. Trump cabinet officials voted in 2018 White House meeting to separate migrant children, say officials. NBC News, August 20. https://www.nbcnews.com/politics/immigration/trump-cabinet-officials-voted-2018-white-house-meeting-separate-migrant-n1237416.
American Civil Liberties Union. 2014. ICCPR update. April. https://www.aclu.org/sites/default/files/assets/faq_iccpr_updated_april_2014.pdf.
_____. 2019. Memo in support of motion to enforce preliminary injunction, case no. 18-cv-00428-DMS-MDD. July 30. https://www.aclu.org/legal-document/ms-l-v-ice-memo-support-motion-enforce-pi.
American Immigration Council. 2020. Policies affecting asylum seekers at the border. January 29. https://www.americanimmigrationcouncil.org/research/policies-affecting-asylum-seekers-border.
American Immigration Lawyers Association. 2016. ICE factsheet on the Family Case Management Program. January 8. https://www.aila.org/infonet/ice-fact-sheet-family-case-management-program.
Amnesty International Publications. 2012. Convention on the Rights of the Child. Retrieved February 6, 2012: http://www.amnestyusa.org.
AP News. 2018. Desert detention camp for migrant kids still growing. November 27. Retrieved from Snopes.com: https://www.snopes.com/ap/2018/11/27/desert-detention-camp-for-migrant-kids-still-growing/.
Associated Press. 2018a. Children separated from parents at U.S. border held in cages in Texas warehouse. AP News, June 18. Retrieved from *The Telegraph*: https://www.telegraph.co.uk/news/2018/06/18/children-separated-from-parents-us-border-held-cage-texas-warehouse/.

_____. 2018b. A sprawling tent city for migrant teens in TX, costs soar and staff is hired without fingerprint checks. *Los Angeles Times,* November 27. https://www.latimes.com/nation/la-na-migrant-teen-detention-camp-checks-20181127-story.html.

_____. 2019. South West Key looks to reopen 2 shelters for immigrant children. *Mohave Daily News,* August 18. http://www.mohavedailynews.com/news/southwest-key-looks-to-reopen-shelters-for-immigrant-children/article_cbf6e84e-c23f-11e9-8485-3788e1e64dac.html.

Aweis, D. 2015. The President: "Advancing and protecting children's rights advances and protects Somalia's future." January 20. Retrieved from Somalia: https://www.unicef.org/somalia/media_16042.html.

Azmy, B., Kadidal, S., Wells Dixon, J., and Schwartz, G. 2018a. *D.J.C.V. v. U.S. Immigration and Customs Enforcement.* October 4. Retrieved from Center for Constitutional Rights: https://ccrjustice.org/home/what-we-do/our-cases/djcv-v-us-immigration-and-customs-enforcementAzmy.

_____. 2018b. *Ms. Q. v. U.S. Immigration and Customs Enforcement.* October 24. Retrieved from Center for Constitutional Rights: https://ccrjustice.org/home/what-we-do/our-cases/ms-q-v-us-immigration-and-customs-enforcement.

Azmy, B., Schwartz, G., and Guisado, A. 2019. *East Bay Sanctuary Covenant v. Barr.* July 16. Retrieved from Center for Constitutional Rights: https://ccrjustice.org/home/what-we-do/our cases/east-bay-sanctuary-covenant-v-barr.

Bachelet, M. 2019. Bachelet appalled by conditions of detention in the U.S. July 8. Retrieved from UN Human Rights Office of the High Commissioner: https://www.ohchr.org/EN/NewsEvents/Pages/DisplayNews.aspx?NewsID=24800&LangID=E.

Bailey, A.C. 2020. 1619 Project: Slave auction sites. *New York Times Magazine,* February 16. https://www.nytimes.com/interactive/2020/02/12/magazine/1619-project-slave-auction-sites.html.

Bajak, F. 2017. ICE shutters helpful family management program amid budget cut. *Christian Science Monitor,* June 9. https://www.csmonitor.com/USA/Foreign-Policy/2017/0609/ICE-shutters-helpful-family-management-program-amid-budget-cuts.

Baker, K., Kulish, N., and Ruiz, R. 2018. He's built an empire, with detained migrant children as the bricks. *New York Times,* December 2. https://www.nytimes.com/2018/12/02/us/southwest-key-migrant-children.html.

Barnes, R., and Miroff, N. 2020. Supreme Court agrees with Trump administration on limits for asylum seekers. *Washington Post,* June 25. https://www.washingtonpost.com/politics/courts_law/supreme-court-agrees-with-trump-administration-on-limits-on-asylum-seekers/2020/06/25/695b3b74-b6e8-11ea-a510-55bf26485c93_story.html.

BBC News. 2019. U.S. border: Calls for inquiry after teen dies in detention. BBC News, May 22. https://www.bbc.com/news/world-us-canada-48503072.

Berger, J. 2017. DHS secretary orders immigration agent hiring surge, end to "catch and release." Fox News, February 21. https://www.foxnews.com/politics/dhs-secretary-orders-immigration-agent-hiring-surge-end-to-catch-and-release.

Biden, J. R. 2021. *Executive Order on the Establishment of Interagency Task Force on the Reunification of Families.* Retrieved from Briefing Room: https://www.whitehouse.gov/briefing-room/presidential-actions/2021/02/02/executive-order-the-establishment-of-interagency-task-force-on-the-reunification-of-families/.

_____. 2021. *Fact Sheet: President Biden Sends Immigration Bill to Congress as Part of His Commitment to Modernize our Immigration System.* Retrieved from The White House Briefing Room: https://www.whitehouse.gov/briefing-room/statements-releases/2021/01/20/fact-sheet-president-biden-sends-immigration-bill-to-congress-as-part-of-his-commitment-to-modernize-our-immigration-system/.

Blitzer, W. 2017. The Situation Room. CNN Transcripts, March 6. http://transcripts.cnn.com/TRANSCRIPTS/1703/06/sitroom.01.html.

BlueMeanie, A. 2019. New allegations of child abuse in Yuma migrant detention center. Blog for Arizona, July 10. https://blogforarizona.net/new-allegations-of-child-abuse-in-yuma-migrant-detention-center/).

Boston Globe Editorial. 2020. America closes its doors on the world. *Boston Globe,* June 26, p. A10.

Bouvier, J. 1856. *A Law Dictionary, Adapted to the Constitution and Laws of the United States.*

Braine, T. 2020. Forget politics: family separation is torture, doctors say. *New York Daily News,* February 25. https://www.nydailynews.com/news/world/ny-physicians-for-human-rights-family-separation-torture-20200226-4842bpscyjbwb4lss04ln77aa a.

Brown, D.L. 2018. "Barbaric": America's cruel history of separating children from their parents. *Washington Post,* May 31. https://www.washingtonpost.comost/news/retropolis/wp/2018/05/31/barbaric-americas-cruel-history-of-separating-children-from-their-parents/).

Brown, R. 2018. Former ICE head: Separated kids may never see parents again. *New York Post,* June 19. https://nypost.com/2018/06/19/former-ice-head-separated-kids-may-never-see-parents-again/.

Bruinius, H. 2018. Family Separation: Evangelicals add their voices to opposition. *Christian Science Monitor,* June 18. https://www.csmonitor.com/USA/Justice/2018/0618/Family-separation-Evangelicals-add-their-voices-to-opposition).

Burke, G., and Mendoza, M. 2018. U.S. waived FBI checks on staff at growing teen migrant camp. AP News, November 28. https://apnews.com/0c62b088c27147b0a6055d1e8394a3af.

Burnett, J. 2018. Transcript: White House Chief of Staff John Kelly's interview with NPR. NPR, May 11. https://www.npr.org/2018/05/11/610116389/transcript-white-house-chief-of-staff-john-kellys-interview-with-npr.

Bush, L. 2018. Laura Bush: Separating children from their parents at the border "breaks my heart." *Washington Post,* June 17. https://www.washingtonpost.com/opinions/laura-bush-separating-children from their-parents-at-the-border-breaks-my-heart/2018/06/17/f2df517a-7287-11e8-9780-b1dd6a09b549_story.html.

Cabrera, A. 2018. Democratic lawmakers angry with what they saw in South Texas. CNN, June 18. http://lite.cnn.com/en/article/h_5175601433ba4b8b18225eaf2910f05b.

Canadian Civil Liberties Association. 2015. Summary: International Covenant of Civil and Political Rights (ICCPR). October 15. https://ccla.org/summary-international-covenant-on-civil-and-political-rights-iccpr/.

Carranza, R. 2020. *U.S. judge orders Trump administration to stop expelling unaccompanied migrant children.* Retrieved from azcentral.: http://www.azcentral.com/story/news/politics/immigration/2020/11/18/judge-orders-u-s-stop-expelling-migrant-children/3766468001.

Castro, J. 2019. CHC Chair Castro's remarks following investigation into Felipe Gomez Alonzo's death. Joaquin Castro Press Release. January 8. https://castro.house.gov/media-center/press-releases/chc-chair-castro-remarks-following-investigation-felipe-gomez-alonzo-s.

Castro Press Conference. 2019. CHC Chair Castro remarks following investigation into Felipe Gomez Alonzo's death. Joaquin Castro, Congressman for the 20th District of Texas. January 7. https://castro.house.gov/media-center/press-releases/chc-chair-castro-remarks-following-investigation-felipe-gomez-alonzo-s.

Castro Press Release. 2018. Members of Congress: Systemic failures contributed to Jakelin Caal's death. Joaquin Castro, Congressman for the 20th District of Texas.

December 19. https://castro.house.gov/media-center/press-releases/members-congress-systemic-failures-contributed-jakelin-caal-s-death.

Centers for Disease Control and Prevention. 2020a. Quarantine and Isolation. March 20. https://www.cdc.gov/quarantine/order-suspending-introduction-certain-persons.html. The complete text of the order is available on the linked PDF file.

———. 2020b. Quarantine and Isolation. May 19. https://www.cdc.gov/quarantine/order-suspending-introduction-certain-persons.html. The complete text of the order is available in the linked PDF file.

Chapin, A. 2019. This is why so many children are dying in Border Patrol custody. HuffPost, May 22. https://www.huffpost.com/entry/why-children-are-dying-in-border-patrol-custody_n_5ce497cfe4b0547bd12ec053.

Chapman, M. 2018. GOP candidate: Child separation is fine because kids cry at daycare, too. *American Independent,* June 20. https://americanindependent.com/michael-grimm-republican-candidate-family-separation-children/.

Civil Rights Litigation Clearinghouse. 2020a. *Flores v. Barr.* May 27. https://www.clearinghouse.net/detail.php?id=9493. Reprinted with the permission of Professor Margo Schlanger.

———. 2020b. *J.S.R. v. Sessions.* May 14. https://www.clearinghouse.net/detail.php?id=16665. Reprinted with permission of Professor Margo Schlanger.

———. 2020c. *Ms. J.P. v. Sessions.* May 14. https://www.clearinghouse.net/detail.php?id=16667. Reprinted with permission of Professor Margo Schlanger.

———. 2020d. *Innovation Law Lab et al. v. Nielson et al.* April 19. https://www.clearinghouse.net/detail.php?id=171118. Reprinted with permission of Professor Margo Schlanger.

———. 2020e. *Kiakombua v. McAllenan.* March 16. https://www.clearinghouse.net/detail.php?id=17238. Reprinted with permission of Professor Margo Schlanger.

———. 2020f. *Padilla v. U.S. Immigration and Customs Enforcement.* June 1. https://www.clearinghouuse.net/detail.php?id=16635. Reprinted with permission of Professor Margo Schlanger.

Clarke, Y. 2019. H.R. 3777: National Commission to Investigate the Treatment of Migrant Families Act of 2019. July 16. Retrieved from Congress.gov: https://www.congress.gov/bill/116th-congress/house-bill/3777.

CNN Newsource. 2019. Guatemalan boy died of flu and a bacterial infection while in U.S. custody, autopsy shows. CNN, April 3. https://www.kjrh.com/news/national/guatemalan-boy-died-of-flu-and-a-bacterial-infection-while-in-us-custody-autopsy-shows).

Cohen, E., and Bonifield, J. 2019. CBP will not vaccinate migrants against flu. CNN, August 20. https://www.msm.com/en-us/news/us/cbp-will-not-vaccinate-migrants-against-flu/ar-AAG4Med.

Committee Hearing on the Judiciary, U.S. Senate (Serial J115-1), 115th Cong. 2017. Committee Hearing on the Nomination of the Hon. Jeff Sessions to Become Attorney General of the U.S. January 17. https://www.congress.gov/115/chrg/CHRG-115shrg28637/CHRG-115shrg28637.htm.

Committee on the Judiciary. 2018. Oversight of Immigration Enforcement and Family Reunification Efforts, remarks by Sen. Dick Durbin. July 31. https://www.judiciary.senate.gov/imo/media/doc/07-31-18%20Grassley%20Statement.pdf.

Committee on Oversite and Reform. 2019. Full Committee Hearing of Acting Secretary of Homeland Security Kevin K. McAllenan. July 18. Retrieved from: https://republicans-oversight.house.gov/hearing/full-committee-hearing-acting-secretary-of-homeland-security-kevin-k-mcaleenan/.

Common Dreams. 2018. Barbara Lee urges UN to probe Trump's human rights abuses at border as violations of human rights law. June 21. https://www.commondreams.org/

news/2018/06/21/barbara-lee-urges-un-probe-trumps-human-rights-abuses-border-violation-international.
Congressional Research Service. 2019a. H.R. 2003: Homeland Security Improvement Act. September 25. Retrieved from GovTrack: https://www.govtrack.us/congress/bills/116/hr2203/summary.
_____. 2019b. Unaccompanied alien children: An overview. October 9. fas.org/sgp/crsl/homesec/R43599.pdf.
Conley, J. 2018. "Shut this place down": Children drugged and given forced injections at Texas detention facility, lawsuit says. Common Dreams News, June 21. https://www.commondreams.org/news/2018/06/21/shut-place-down-children-drugged-and-given-forced-injections-texas-detention.
Cordero, C.F., Li Feldman, H., and Keitner, C. 2020. The law against family separation. Retrieved from Georgetown University Law Center: https://scholarship.law.georgetown.edu/cgi/viewcontent.cgi?article=3252&context=facpub.
Cornell Law School Legal Information Institute. n.d. 8 U.S. legal code § 1325 improper entry by an alien. https://www.law.cornell.edu/uscode/text/8/1325.
Crosby, S., and Annas, G. 2019. POV: Child detention at the border is torture. BU Today, July 18. www.bu.edu/articles2019/child-detention-at-border-is-torture. Reprinted with permission of Sondra Crosby, MD.
Cullinane, S. 2018. Inside Border Protection's processing detention center: Chain link fences and thermal blankets. CNN Politics, June 18. https://www.cnn.com/2018/06/18/politics/immigration-mcallen-border-patrol-photos/index.html.
Cummings, E., and Meadows, M. 2018. Letter requesting data on separated children. July 5. Retrieved from Congress of the United States, House of Representatives, Committee on Oversight and Government Reform: https://oversight.house.gov/sites/democrats.oversight.house.gov/files/documents/Meadows-Cummings%20Letter%20Requesting%20Info%20on%20Separated%20Children.pdf.
Danelius, H. 1984. Convention against torture and other cruel, inhumane or degrading treatment or punishment. December 10. Retrieved from Audiovisual Library of International Law: http://legal.un.org/avl/ha/catcidtp/catcidtp.html.
de Vogue, A., and Alvarez, P. 2020. Supreme Court rules asylum seeker cannot challenge removal. CNN, June 25. https://www.cnn.com/2020/06/25/politics/asylum-request-thuraissigiam-supreme-court/index.html.
Department of Homeland Security et al. v.Thuraisigium, 19-161 U.S. (U.S. Court of Appeals for the Ninth Circuit June 25, 2020).
Derysh, I. 2018. Kirstjen Nielsen blames family of seven-year-old girl who died in Border Patrol custody. Salon, December 4. https://www.salon.com/2018/12/14/kirstjen-nielsen-blames-family-of-seven-year-old-girl-who-died-in-border-patrol-custody/.
Desjardins, L., Barajas, J., and Bush, D. 2018. "My son is not the same": New testimony paints bleak picture of family separation. July 6. Retrieved from PBS News Hour: https://www.pbs.org/newshour/politics/my-son-is-not-the-same-new-testimony-paints-bleak-picture-of-family-separation.
Diaz, D. 2017. Kelly: DHS is considering separating undocumented children from their parents at the border. CNN. March 7. https://www.cnn.com/2017/03/06/politics/john-kelly-separating-children-from-parents-immigration-border/index.html.
Dickerson, C. 2018a. Hundreds of immigrant children have been taken from parents at border. *New York Times*, April 20. https://www.nytimes.com/2018/04/20/us/immigrant-children-separation-ice.html.
_____. 2018b. Migrant children moved under cover of darkness to a Texas tent city. *New York Times,* September 30. https://www.nytimes.com/2018/09/30/us/migrant-children-tent-city-texas.html.
_____. 2019. Migrant children are entitled to toothbrushes and soap, Federal Court

rules. *New York Times,* August 15. http://www.nytimes.com/2019/08/15/us/migrant-children-toothbrushes-court.html.

Dinan, S. 2019a. Democrats visit border station where migrant boy died, demand better care. *Washington Times,* January 7. https://www.washingtontimes.com/news/2019/jan/7/congressional-hispanic-caucus-democrats-visit-border.

———. 2019b. DHS chief restarts program to delay deporting sick illegals. *Washington Times,* September 19. https://www.washingtontimes.com/news/2019/sep/19/kevin-mcaleenan-dhs-chief-restarts-program-delay-d.

———. 2019c. Ken Cuccinelli hits Congress' failure to pass migrant bill: "If you cared enough to pass a law." *Washington Times,* September 30. https://www.washingtontimes.com/news/2019/oct/30/ken-cuccinelli-blasts-congress-failure-pass-immigr/.

DNYUZ. 2019. Lawsuit seeks information on John Kelly's ties to company housing migrants. July 30. https://dnyuz.com/2019/07/30/lawsuit-seeks-info-on-john-kellys-ties-to-company-housing-migrants/).

Domonoske, C. 2020. Government watchdog says Homeland Security leaders were not legitimately appointed. NPR, August 14. https://www.npr.org/2020/08/14/902537541/government-watchdog-says-homeland-security-leaders-were-not-legitimately-appoint.

Driver, A. 2018. 13,000 migrant children in detention: America's horrifying reality. CNN, October 1. https://www.cnn.com/2018/10/01/opinions/13000-migrant-children-horrifying-reality-driver/index.html.

El Ministerio de Relacionas Exteriores de Guatemala. 2018. Communicado Oficial Gobierno de la Republica de Guatemala. December 25. https://www.minex.gob.gt/noticas/Notica.aspx?id=28104.

Elfrink, T. 2018. ICE handcuffs immigrant kids on their 18th birthdays, drags them to jail. *Miami New Times,* August 23. https://www.miaminewtimes.com/news/ice-handcuffs-immigrants-on-18th-birthday-at-homestead-childrens-center-sends-them-to-jail-10651093.

EPA. N.d. Summary of the Administrative Procedure Act. https://www.epa.gov/laws-regulations/summary-administrative-procedure-act#:~:text=(1946),on%20notices%20of%20proposed%20rulemaking.

Escobar, V. 2019a. H.R. 2203: Homeland Security Improvement Act. April 10. Retrieved from congress.gov: https://www.congress.gov/bill/116th-congress/house-bill/2203/text.

———. 2019b. H.R. 2662: Asylum Seeker Protection Act. June 26. Retrieved from Congress.gov: https://www.congress.gov/bill/116th-congress/house-bill/2662/all-info.

Federal Writers Project. 1941. Slave narratives: A folk history of slavery in the United States from interviews with former slaves, vols. 1, 5,13. Retrieved from Library of Congress: https://www.loc.gov/collections/slave-narratives-from-the-federal-writers-project-1936-to-1938/articles-and-essays/.

Feinstein, D. 2019. S. 92: Keep Families Together Act. January 13. Retrieved from congress.gov: https://www.congress.gov/bill/116th-congress/senate-bill/292/text.

Fernandez, M. 2018. Inside the former Walmart that is now a shelter for 1,500 migrant children. *New York Times,* June 14. https://www.nytimes.com/2018/06/14/us/family-separation-migrant-children-detention.html.

Flores, A. 2019. The Trump administration is canceling English classes, soccer, and legal aid for unaccompanied immigrant children. Buzzfeed, June 6. https://www.buzzfeednews.com/article/adolfoflores/trump-administration-ending-legal-aid-classes-immigrant.

Flores, B.D. 2018. Twitter post, May 30. Retrieved from Catholic News Service: https://www.catholicnews.com/services/englishnews/2018/bishops-across-us-condemn-separation-detention-of-migrant-children.cfm.

Flynn, M. 2019. Detained migrant children got no toothbrush, no soap, no sleep. It's no problem, government argues. *Washington Post*, June 21. Retrieved from the Texas Tribune: https://www.texastribune.org/2019/06/21/detained-migrant-children-no-toothbrush-no-soap/.

Fontes, A.W. 2019. Migrants' stories: Why they flee. The Conversation, April 9. https://theconversation.com/migrants-stories-why-they flee-114725. Reprinted with permission of Anthony W. Fontes.

Frazee, G. 2019. A look inside the facilities where migrant families are detained. PBS News Hour, August 26. https://www.pbs.org/newshour/nation/new-trump-rules-would-detain-families-longer-this-is-where they would-stay.

Fredrick, J. 2019. Metering at the border. NPR, June 29. https://www.npr.org/2019/06/29/737268856/metering-at-the-border.

Frej, W. 2018. Franklin Graham blasts Trump's immigrant family separations at the border. Huffpost, June 14. https://www.huffpost.com/entry/franklin-graham-blasts-trump-border_n_5b223db7e4b09d7a3d7a7c16.

Frerichs, J. 2017. U.S. interventions have destabilized Central America. Progressive Voices of Iowa. October 10. https://progressivevoicesofiowa.com/2017/10/10/us-interventions-have-destabilized-central-america.

Fritze, J. 2019. Trump used words like "invasion" and "killer" to discuss immigrants at rallies 500 times: USA Today analysis. *USA Today*, August 8. https://www.usatoday.com/story/news/politics/elections/2019/08/08/trump-immigrants-rhetoric-criticized-el-paso-dayton-shootings/1936742001/.

Gammage. 2017. Army begins unearthing remains of children who died at Carlisle Indian School. *Philadelphia Inquirer*, August 8. https://www.inquirer.com/philly/news/army-begins-unearthing-remains-of-children-killed-at-carlisle-indian-school-20170808.html.

Gee, J.D. 2018. United States District Court of Central California Civil Minutes—General. July 9. https://www.aila.org/File/Related/14111359ac.pdf.

Gelernt, L. 2019. Written testimony of Lee Gelernt, deputy director, Imigrants' Rights Project American Civil Liberties Union. February 7. Retrieved from U.S. House Committee on Energy and Commerce Subcommittee on Oversight and Investigations: https://docs.house.gov/meetings/IF/IF02/20190207/108846/HHRG-116-IF02-Wstate-GelerntL-20190207-U1.pdf.

Gerstein, J. 2018. 17 states sue Trump over family separations. Politico, June 18. https://www.politico.com/story/2018/06/26/states-sue-donald-trump-family-separations-676377.

Giartelli, A. 2019. Activists turned away after showing up to Border Patrol detention facility with flu vaccines. *Washington Examiner*, December 10. https://www.washingtonexaminer.com/news/activists-turned-away-after-showing-up-to-border-patrol-detention-facility-with-flu-vaccines.

Gillibrand, K. 2019. Gillibrand, Senate colleagues introduce legislation to require alternatives to detention for asylum seekers, migrant children, and families entering the country. June 21. https://www.gillibrand.senate.gov/news/press/release/gillibrand-senate-colleagues-introduce-legislation-to-require-alternatives-to-detention-for-asylum-seekers-migrant-children-and-families-entering-the-country.

Gomez, A. 2019. Thousands of migrant children report they were sexually assaulted in U.S. custody. *USA Today*, February 26. https://www.usatoday.com/story/news/politics/2019/02/26/thousands-migrant-children-report-sexual-assaults-us-custody-border-detain/298884002.

Gomez, L. 2019. Southwest Key seeks to reopen 2 shuttered Arizona facilities. *Arizona Mirror*, August 13. https://www.azmirror.com/2019/08/13/southwest-key-seeks-to-reopen-2-shuttered-arizona-facilities.

Gonzalez, D. 2018. Toddler dies after leaving migrant detention center, prompting 40M claim against Eloy. *Arizona Republic*, August 28. https://www.azcentral.com/story/news/politics/immigration/2018/08/28/mariee-juarez-dies-after-leaving-detention-center-family-sues-eloy/1126840002/.

Gonzales, R. 2019. ACLU: Administration is still separating migrant families despite court order to stop. Nevada Public Radio, July 30. https://knpr.org/npr/2019-07/aclu-administration-still-separating-migrant-families-despite-court-order-stop.

Gore, D. 2018. Nielsen's rhetoric on family separations. FactCheck.org, June 20. https://www.factcheck.org/2018/06/nielsens-rhetoric-on-family-separations/.

Government Accountability Office. 2018. Unaccompanied children: Agency efforts to reunify children separated from parents at the border. October 9. https://www.gao.gov/reports/GAO-19-163/.

Grabell, M., and Sanders, T. 2018. Immigrant youth shelters: "If you're a predator, it's a gold mine." ProPublica, July 27. https://www.propublica.org/article/immigrant-youth-shelters-sexual-abuse-fights-missing-children.

The Guardian (U.S. edition). 2015. Arizona sheriff's office mishandling of rape case results in $3.5m settlement. April 8. https://www.theguardian.com/us-news/2015/apr/08/arizona-phoenix-sheriff-joe-arpaio-rape-case-settlement.

Guidos, R. 2018. Update: Bishops across the U.S. condemn separation, detention of children. Catholic News Service, June 19. https://www.catholicnews.com/services/englishnews/2018/bishops-across-us-condemn-separation-detention-of-migrant-children.cfm.

Haag, M. 2018. 2 Workers at Arizona migrant children's centers are charged with sexual abuse. *New York Times*, August 3. https://www.nytimes.com/2018/08/03/us/sexual-abuse-arizona-migrant-children.html.

Hayden, M.E. 2019. Emails confirm Miller's twin obsessions: Migrants and crime. Southern Poverty Law Center: Hatewatch, November 25. https://www.splcenter.org/hatewatch/2019/11/25/emails-confirm-millers-twin-obsessions-immigrants-and-crime. Reprinted with permission from Michael E. Hayden.

Henderson, C. 2020. The EU just updated its guest list—and U.S. travelers still can't visit. July 16. Retrieved from the Points Guy: https://thepointsguy.com/news/americans-wont-be-welcome-in-europe/.

Hennessy-Fiske, M. 2018. "Prison-like" migrant youth shelter is understaffed, unequipped for Trump's zero-tolerance policy, insider says. *Los Angeles Times*, June 14. https://latimes.com/nation/la-na-border-migrant-shelter-20180614-story.html.

———. 2019. Six migrant children have died in U.S. custody. *Los Angeles Times*, May 24. https://www.latimes.com/nation/la-na-migrant-child-border-deaths-20190524-story.html.

Hesson, T. 2020. Top Trump Homeland Security appointments improper, U.S. government watchdog says. Reuters, August 14. https://www.reuters.com/article/us-trump-immigration/top-trump-homeland-security-appointments-improper-u-s-government-watchdog-says-idUSKCN25A1YN.

House Committee on Oversight and Reform. 2019. Staff Report: Child separation by the Trump administration. July. https://oversight.house.gov/sites/democrats.oversight.house.gov/files/2019-07-2019.%20Immigrant%20Child%20Separations-%20Staff%20Report.pdf.

House of Representatives Committee on Oversight and Reform. 2019. Oversight Committee approves 1st subpoenas of the 116th Congress—and they are bipartisan. February 26. https://oversight.house.gov/news/press-releases/oversight-committee-approves-first-subpoenas-of-the-116th-congress-and-they-are.

House of Representatives Subcommittee on Oversight, Investigations—Committee on Energy and Commerce. 2019. Examining the failures of the Trump administration's inhumane family separation policies. February 7. https://energycommerce.house.

gov/committee-activity/hearings/hearing-on-examining-the-failures-of-the-trump-administration-s-inhumane.https://energycommerce.house.gov/sites/democrats.energycommerce.house.gov/files/documents/HIF038.020%20-%20OI%20-%20 Hrg%20-%202019%20Feb%2007%20-%20UNEDITED.pdf.

Houshayer, S. 2018. Family separation in harmful to children's health. Families USA, June 19. https://www.familiesusa.org/resources/family-separation-is-harmful-to-childrens-health/.

Howell, T. J. 2018. Rep. Ted Lieu plays tape of crying children from House floor. *Washington Times,* June 22. https://www.washingtontimes.com/news/2018/jun/22/ted-lieu-plays-tape-crying-child-house-floor.

Hsu, S.S. 2020. Federal judge strikes down Trump asylum rule targeting Central Americans. *Washington Post,* July 1. https://www.washingtonpost.com/local/legal-issues/us-judge-strikes-down-trump-asylum-rule-targeting-central-americans/2020/07/01/96e57616-bb4a-11ea-bdaf-a129f921026f_story.html.

Human Rights First. 2018. The Flores settlement and family incarceration: A brief history and next steps. October 30. https://www.humanrightsfirst.org/resource/flores-settlement-and-family-incarceration-brief-history-and-next-steps. Reprinted with permission of Human Rights First.

———. 2019. Orders from above: Massive human rights abuses under Trump administration return to Mexico policy. October. https://www.humanrightsfirst.org/sites/default/files/hrfordersfromabove.pdf. Reprinted with permission from Human Rights First.

———. 2020a. Pandemic as pretext: Trump administration exploits COVID-19, expels asylum seekers and children to escalating danger. May. https://www.humanrightsfirst.org/sites/default/files/PandemicAsPretextFINAL.pdf. Reprinted with permission.

———. 2020b. Press release: The second Trump asylum ban has been defeated in court. July 1. https://www.humanrightsfirst.org/press-release/second-trump-asylum-ban-has-been-defeated-court.

Humanium. (n.d.). Rights of the child. https://www.humanium.org/en/child-rights/.

Hunter. 2018. The Trump team has been very clear: Child separation is intended as a "deterrent." Daily Kos, June 19. https://www.dailykos.com/stories/2018/6/19/1773493/-The-Trump-team-has-been-very-clear-Child-separation-is-intended-as-deterrent-to-refugees.

Ignatian Solidarity Network; Kino Border Initiative. 2020. Witness from the border. April 2. igsol.net/fb. Reprinted with permission.

Inter-American Court on Human Rights. 2014. Advisory opinion: Rights and guarantees of children in the context of migration and/or in need of international protection; paras. 154–160. August 19. http://www.corteidh.or.cr/docs/opiniones/seriea_21_eng.pdf.

Jackson, A. 1833. Fifth speech to Congress. Library of Congress. December 3. https://www.loc.gov/resource/maj.01085_0275_0278/?sp=1.

Jayapal, Pramila. 2019. H.R. 2415: The Dignity for Detained Immigrants Act of 2019. May 20. Retrieved from Congress.gov: https://www.congress.gov/bill/116th-congress/house-bill/2415/text.

Jenny L. Flores, et al. v. William P. Barr, et al., CV 85-4544-DMG (AGRx) (United States District Court Central District of California September 4, 2020).

Johnson, A. 2018. Judge orders many migrant children removed from Texas facility said to use psychotropic drugs. NBC News, July 30. https://www.nbcnews.com/news/us-news/judge-orders-most-migrant-children-removed-texas-facility-uses-psychotropic-n895966.

Jordan, M. 2018. "A breaking point": Second child's death prompts new procedures for border agency. *New York Times,* December 26. https://www.nytimes.com/2018/12/26/us/felipe-alonzo-gomez-customs-border-patrol.html.

_____. 2019. U.S. must provide mental health services to families separated at the border. *New York Times*, November 6. https://www.nytimes.com/2019/11/06/us/migrants-mental-health-court/html/.

Jordan, M., and Fernandez, M. 2018. Judge rejects long detentions of migrant families, dealing Trump another setback. *New York Times*, July 9. https://www.nytimes.com/2018/07/09/us/migrants-family-separation-reunification.html.

Juvonen, J., and Silvers, J. 2018. Separating children from parents at the border isn't just cruel: it's torture. UCLA Newsroom, May 22. https://newsroon.ucla.edu/stories/separating-children-from-parents-at-the-border-isnt-just-cruel-its-torture. Reprinted with permission of UCLA Media Relations.

Karanth, S. 2019. Civil rights groups call for Trump to fire Stephen Miller over white nationalism. HuffPost, November 19. https://www.huffpost.com/entry/civil-rights-groups-call-trump-fire-stephen-miller-white-nationalism_n_5dd3565be4b082dae8130241.

Karlin-Smith, S. 2018. Health secretary: "No reason" why separated families can't find children. Politico, June 26. https://www.politico.com/story/2018/06/26/azar-separated-families-673186.

Kates, G., and Donaghue, E. 2019. "I have spent a lot of time crying": Migrant children describe life at Homestead shelter. CBS News, May 31. https://www.cbsnews.com/news/migrant-children-describe-life-at-homestead-shelter-in-court-filing/.

Khalid, A. 2017. The controversial immigration program Trump's AG pick wants to bring back. Daily Dot, January 10. https://www.dailydot.com/layer8/what-is-operation-streamline-immigration-program-jeff-sessions.

Kim, S.M. 2018. Trump warns against admitting unaccompanied migrant children: "They're not innocent." *Washington Post*, May 23. https://www.washingtonpost.com/politics/trump-warns-against-admitting-unaccompanied-migrant-children-theyre-not-innocent/2018/05/23/e4b24a68-5ec2-11e8-8c93-8cf33c21da8d_story.html.

Kirby, J. 2018. The 2,300 migrant kids already separated from their families won't immediately be reunited with parents. Vox, June 20. https://www.vox.com/2018/6/20/17486446/family-separation-reunification-trump-executive-order-immigration.

Koerner, C. 2019. Kids describe in their own words the dire conditions inside a border detention center. BuzzFeed News, June 27. https://www.buzzfeednews.com/article/claudiakoerner/children-border-detention-conditions-immigrants-hungry.

Kraft, C. 2018. AAP statement opposing separation of children at the border. American Academy of Pediatrics. May 8. https://www.aap.org/en-us/about-the-aap/aap-press-room/Pages/StatementOpposingSeparationofChildrenandParents.aspx.

Kumpf, K. 2019. Why it's time to shut down Homestead detention center. American Friends Service Committee. June 12. https://www.afsc.org/blogs/news-and-commentary/why-its-time-to-shut-down-homestead-detention-center.

Lach, E. 2018. A closeup of the government's new tent camp for migrant kids. *New Yorker*, June 19. https://www.newyorker.com/news/dispatch/a-closeup-of-the-governments-new-tent-camp-for-migrant-kids.

Leahy, P. 2019. S. 2936: Refugee Protection Act of 2019. November 21. Retrieved from Congress.gov: https://www.congress.gov/116/bills/s2936/BILLS-116s2936is.pdf.

Lee, B. 2018. Congresswoman Barbara Lee: UN observers to investigate family separations on the U.S. border. June 20. https://lee.house.gov/imo/media/doc/UN%20Letter.pdf.

Leekley, S., & Leekley, J. (1978). *Moments: The Pulitzer Prize Photographs*. New York: Crown Publishers, Inc.

Levin, B. 2019. The Trump administration is deporting kids with cancer. *Vanity Fair*, August 27. http://www.vanityfair.com/news/2019/08/medical-deferred-action-deportations.

Levinson, D. 2018. Memorandum to Lynn Johnson, assistant secretary, Administration

for Children and Families. November 27. Retrieved from Office of the Inspector General: https://oig.hhs.gov/oas/reports/region12/121920000.pdf.
LexisNexis. 2020. *TVPRA Victory-Ramirez v. ICE*. July 2. Retrieved from https://www.lexisnexis.com/legalnewsroom/immigration/b/insidenews/posts/tvpra-victory-ramirez-v-ice.
Libowsky, S., and Oehlke, K. 2021. *President Biden's Immigration Actions: A Recap*. Retrieved from Lawfare: https://www.lawfareblog.com/president-bidens-immigration-executive-actions-recap.
Little, B. 2011. Government boarding schools once separated Native American children from families. History.com, November 1. https://www.history.com/news/government-boarding-schools-separated-native-american-children-families.
Lofgren, Z. 2019. H.R. 5210: The Refugee Protection Act. November 21. Retrieved from Congress.gov: https://www.congress.gov/116/bills/hr5210/BILLS-116hr5210ih.pdf.
Lydgate, J. 2010. Assembly-line justice. January. Retrieved from Berkeley Law: https://www.law.berkeley.edu/files/Operation_Streamline_Policy_Brief.pdf.
Madan, M.O. 2019. All children have been removed from Homestead detention center. They're not coming back. *Miami Herald*, August 3. https://www.miamiherald.com/news/local/immigration/article233488172.html.
Marquette, C. 2019. Catholic nuns, priests protesting migrant children's treatment arrested on Capitol Hill. RollCall.com, July 18. https://www.rollcall.com/news/congress/dozens-protesting-migrant-child-treatment-arrested-in-russell.
Martinez, S. 2018. Today's migrant flow is different. *The Atlantic*, June 26. https://www.theatlantic.com/international/archive/2018/06/central-america-border-immigration/563744/.
McAleenan, K. 2018. Memorandum for the secretary of Homeland Security. Decision on increasing immigration violation prosecutions. April 23. Retrieved from United States Department of Homeland Security: https://www.documentcloud.org/documents/4936568-FOIA-9-23-FamilySeparation-Memo.html.
McDonnell, P.J. 2019. Death at the border: 4 from Guatemala, 3 of them children, succumb to heat in Texas. *Los Angeles Times*, July 8. https://www.latimes.com/world/la-fg-guatemala-migrants-20190708-story.html.
McGowan, K., and Givens, F. 2011. *The Indian Schools: The Survivors' Story*. Motion picture. Retrieved from Culture Unplugged: https://www.cultureunplugged.com/documentary/watch-online/play/54410/Indian-School—A-Survivor-s-Story. Information reprinted with permission of Kay McGowan and Fay Givens.
Mekelburg, M. 2019. No migrant children remain at Tornillo tent shelter as it heads toward closure, official says. *USA Today*, January 12. https://www.usatoday.com/story/news/nation/2019/01/12/tornillo-shelter-no-migrant-children-closed-border-us/mexico/2558537002/.
Mendez, J.E. 2015. Report of the Special Rapporteur on torture and other cruel, inhuman or degrading treatment or punishment. March 5. Retrieved from United General Assembly: https://drive.google.com/file/d/129HhNvkXxpTCGJZ0JYzy47P-qDL0gWYL/view.
Mendoza, M., and Fenn, L. 2018. Detaining immigrant kids is now a billion-dollar industry. Associated Press, July 17. https://apnews.com/289b015df6e94ac6b2a35c28b11365b5.
Meng, G. 2019. H.R. 3918: The Stop the Cruelty to Migrant Children Act. July 23. Retrieved from congress.gov: https://www.congress.gov/bill/116th-congress/house-bill/3918/text?r=6&s=1.
Merchant, N. 2018. Hundreds of children wait in Border Patrol facility in Texas. Associated Press, June 18. https://apnews.com/9794de32d39d4c6f89fbefaea3780769.
Merkley, J. (@SenJeffMerkley). 2018. "I was barred entry. Asked repeatedly to speak

to a supervisor—he finally came out and said he can't tell us anything. Police were called on us. Children should never be ripped from their families & held in secretive detention centers." Twitter.com, June 3. https://twitter.com/SenJeffMerkley/status/1003444959905746944.

Merkley, J. 2019a. *America Is Better Than This: Trump's War Against Migrant Families.* New York: Twelve.

———. 2019b. S. 2113: Stop Cruelty to Migrant Families Act. July 7. Retrieved from congress.gov: https://www.congress.gov/bill/116th-congress/senate-bill/2113/text.

Miller, M.E., Brown, E., and Davis, A.C. 2018. Inside Casa Padre, the converted Walmart where the U.S. is holding nearly 1,500 immigrant children. *Washington Post,* June 14. https://www.washingtonpost.com/local/inside-casa-padre-the-converted-walmart-where-the-us-is-holding-nearly-1500-immigrant-children/2018/06/14/0cd65ce4-6eba-11e8-bd50-b80389a4e569_story.html.

Millich, G. 2012. Survivors of Indian boarding schools tell their stories. WKAR, February. https://www.wkar.org/post/survivors-indian-boarding-schools-tell-their-stories#stream/0.

Miroff, N. 2018. Hours before her collapse in U.S. custody, a dying migrant child's condition went unnoticed. *Washington Post,* December 4. https://www.washingtonpost.com/world/national-security/hours-before-her-collapse-in-us-custody-a-dying-migrant-childs-condition-went-unnoticed/2018/12/14/1c454d18-ffb8-11e8-862a-b6a6f3ce8199_story.html.

———. 2019. Under secret Stephen Miller plan, ICE to use data on migrant children to expand deportation efforts. *Washington Post,* December 20. https://www.washingtonpost.com/immigration/under-secret-stephen-miller-plan-ice-to-use-data-on-migrant-children-to-expand-deportation-efforts/2019/12/20/36975b34-22a8-11ea-bed5-880264cc91a9_story.html.

Miroff, N., and Dawsey, J. 2019. The adviser who scripts Trump's immigration policy. *Washington Post,* August 17. https://www.washingtonpost.com/graphics/2019/politics/stephen-miller-trump-immigration/?wpisrc=nl_most&wpmn=1.

Miroff, N., Dawsey, J., and Armus, T. 2020. Trump administration working out details of suspending immigration during coronavirus crisis, plans to close off the United States to a new extreme. *Washington Post,* April 21. https://www.msn.com/en-us/news/us/trump-says-he-will-issue-order-to-suspend-immigration-during-coronavirus-crisis.

Moore, R. 2019. DHS inspector general finds "no misconduct" in deaths of two Guatemalan children. *Washington Post,* December 20. https://www.washingtonpost.com/immigration/dhs-inspector-general-finds-no-misconduct-in-deaths-of-two-guatemalan-migrant-children/2019/12/20/505c0814-2387-11ea-a153-dce4b94e4249_story.html.

Moore, R., and Sacchetti, M. 2019. Toddler who died after being taken into custody at the Mexican border suffered multiple diseases. *Washington Post,* July 14. https://www.washingtonpost.com/immigration/toddler-who-died-after-being-taken-into-custody-at-the-mexican-border-suffered-multiple-diseases/2019/07/02/5fda6674-9d03-11e9-9ed4-c9089972ad5a_story.html.

Moore, R., Schmidt, S., and Jameel, M. 2019. Inside the cell where a sick 16-year-old boy died in Border Patrol care. ProPublica., December 5. https://www.propublica.org/article/inside-the-cell-where-a-sick-16-year-old-boy-died-in-border-patrol-care.

Mosenbergen, D. 2019. Doctors demanding flu vaccines for migrant children arrested in California. HuffPost, December 11. https://www.huffpost.com/entry/doctors-flu-vaccine-migrant-children-cbp-protest_n_5df06771e4b01e0f29567e4e.

Nagda, J. 2020. *UPDATE: Court rules against children's detention in hotels.* Retrieved from The Young Center: https://connect.xfinity.com/appsuite/v=7.10.3-6.20200722.054552/print.html?print_1599854606858.

Nathan, D. 2019. U.S. border officials use fake addresses, dangerous conditions, and mass trials to discourage asylum-seekers. Intercept, October 4. https://theintercept.com/2019/10/04/u-s-border-officials-use-fake-addresses-dangerous-conditions-and-mass-trials-to-discourage-asylum-seekers/.

National Archives UK. (n.d.). What was it like to be a child slave in America in the Nineteenth Century? https://www.nationalarchives.gov.uk/documents/education/childhood-slavery-contextual-essay.pdf.

National Immigrant Justice Center. 2018. Garcia Ramirez et al. v. ICE et al. August 30. https://immigrantjustice.org/court_cases/garcia-ramirez-et-al-v-ice-et-al.

National Immigration Forum. 2018. Trafficking Victims Protection Reauthorization Act safeguards children. May 23. https://immigration forum.org/article/trafficking-victims-protection-reauthorization-act-safeguards-children/.

National Indian Child Welfare Association. 2020. About ICWA. January. https://www.nicwa.org/about-icwa/.

Nielsen, K. (@SecNielsen). 2018. "We do not have a policy of separating families at the border. Period." Twitter, June 18. https://twitter.com/secnielsen/status/1008467414235992069?lang=en.

Nielsen, K., and Harris, K. 2018. Video of senate hearing. May 18. Retrieved from YouTube.com: https://www.youtube.com/watch?v=ljdWqGqqN-8&ab_channel=MediaBuzz.

Nowak, M. 2019a. Press conference: Global study on children deprived of liberty. November 18. Retrieved from UN Web TV: http://webtv.un,org/watch/global-study-on-children-deprived-of-liberty-press-conference-geneva-18-november-2019/6105423168001/.

———. 2019b. The United Nations global study on children deprived of liberty. November. Retrieved from Omnibook: https://omnibook.com/view/e0623280-5656-42f8-9edf-5872f8f08562.

Office of the Inspector General. 2019. Management alert—DHS needs to address dangerous overcrowding and prolonged detention of children and adults in the Rio Grande Valley (redacted). July 2. https://www.oig.dhs.gov/sites/default/files.assets/2019-07/OIG-19-51-Jul19.pdf.

Office of the Inspector General, U.S. Department of Health and Human Services. 2019. Separated children placed in Office of Refugee Resettlement care. *OEI-BL-18-00511*. February 7. https://oig.hhs.gov/oei/reports/oei-BL-18-00511.pdf.

Office of Inspector General, U.S. Department of Homeland Security. 2015. Streamline: Measuring its effect on illegal border crossing. May 15. https://www.oig.dhs.gov/assets/Mgmt/2015/OIG_15-95_May15.pdf.

———. 2018. Special review—Initial observations regarding family separation issues under the zero tolerance policy. September 27. https://www.oig.dhs.gov/sites/default/files/assets/2018-10/OIG-18-84-Sep18.pdf.

———. 2019. DHS lacked technology needed to successfully account for separated migrant families. November 25. https://www.oig.dhs.gov/sites/default/files/assets/2019-11/OIG-20-06-Nov19.pdf.

Office of Refugee Resettlement. 2015a. Children entering the U.S. unaccompanied. December 20. https://www.acf.hhs.gov/orr/resource/children-entering-the-united-states-unaccompanied.

———. 2015b. ORR Guide: Children entering the United States unaccompanied. January 30. https://www.acf.hhs.gov/orr/resource/children-entering-the-united-states-unaccompanied.

———. 2019a. Children entering the United States Unaccompanied: Guide to terms. January 8. https://www.acf.hhs.gov/orr/resource/children-entering-the-united-states-unaccompanied-guide-to-terms.

———. 2019b. Children entering the U.S. unaccompanied, Section 7. September 18.

http://acf.hhs.gov/orr/resource/children-entering-the-united-states-unaccompanied-section-7#7.1.

Ortega, B. 2019. With asylum seekers blocked from reaching safe haven in U.S., volunteers take help south to them. CNN, October 22. https://www.cnn.com/2019/10/22/us/asylum-center-ice-inv/index.html.

Ortiz, A., and Levenson, M. 2019. D.H.S. inspector general finds "no misconduct" by officials in deaths of two migrant children. *New York Times*, December 21. https://www.nytimes.com/2019/12/21/us/border-children-deaths-dhs.html.

Oster, M. 2019. Jewish streams call on Trump to fire Stephen Miller for supremacist views. *Jerusalem Post*, November 25. https://www.jpost.com/Diaspora/Jewish-streams-call-on-Trump-to-fire-Stephen-Miller-for-supremacist-views-608922.

Owens, C., Kight, S.W., and Stevens, H. 2019. Thousands of migrant youth suffered sexual abuse in U.S. custody. Axios, February 26. https://www.axios.com/immigration-unaccompanied-minors-sexual-assault-3222e230-29e1-430f-a361-d959c88c5d8c.html.

Petoskey, W. 2009. *Dancing My Dream*. Canton, MI: Read the Spirit. Reprinted with permission of Warren Petoskey.

Poole, S. 2018. "Tender age" shelters: A new way to describe kidnapping. *Guardian*, June 20. https://www.theguardian.com/us-news/shortcuts/2018/jun/20/tender-age-shelters-a-new-way-to-describe-the-kidnapping-of-children.

Pingree, C. 2019. Press release: Pingree leads letter signed by 100+ members of Congress demanding Stephen Miller's immediate firing. November. https://pingree.house.gov/news/documentsingle.aspx?DocumentID=3175.

Project on Government Oversight. 2018. CBP email dated July 11, 2018 re: NTW/WA for FMUA's from POGO FOIA. July 11. https://www.documentcloud.org/documents/4936571-FOIA-Release-7-11-Emeail.html. The guide to the terminology written by Katherine Hawkins can be found linked in this email. Reprinted with permission of the Project on Government Oversight (POGO).

Project on Government Oversight and Open the Government. 2018a. Letter from POGO and OTG to Senate Committee on Homeland Security and Government Affairs. October 2. https://docs.pogo.org/letter/2018/HSGAC-letter-10-2-18-Final-4.pdf?mtime=20181002170133.

———. 2018b. New document shows Nielsen signed off on family separation policy. September 25. https:www.pogo.org/press/release/2018/new-documents-show-nielsen-signed-off-on-family-separation-policy/. Reprinted with permission of Project on Government Oversight and Open the Government.

Pullella, P. 2018. Exclusive: Pope criticizes Trump administration policy on migrant family separation. Reuters, June 20. https://in.reuters.com/article/pope-interview/exclusive-pope-criticises-trump-administration-policy-on-migrant-family-separation-idINKBN1JG0YA.

Pūra, Dainius. n.d. Cf.A/HRC/38/36, para. 58. UN Human Rights Commission.

Refugee International. 2018. President Trump's executive order and the *Flores* settlement explained. June 28. https://www.refugeesinternational.org/reports/2018/6/28/trumps-executive-order-and-the-flores-settlement-explained-bswdt.

Reichlin-Melnick, A. 2020. What you need to know about Trump's proposal to eliminate the U.S. asylum system. Immigrationimpact.com, July 11. http://immigrationimpact.com/2020/06/11/end-asylum-trump/13.Xv9DQyhKiUl.

Resettlement Division of Unaccompanied Children's Services. n.d. Power Point presentation. www.slideserve.com/thane/office-of-refugee-resettlement-division-of-unaccompanied-children's-s-services.

Richie, S. 2020. *Lifting Up the Voices of Children*. Retrieved from Kino Border Initiative : https://www.kinoborderinitiative.org/lifting-up-the-voices-of-children/.

Rohrlich, J. 2019. U.S. border officers die by suicide 30% more often than other cops. Quartz, October 31. https://qz.com/1738901/us-border-officers-die-by-suicide-30-percent-more-often-than-other-cops. Reprinted courtesy of Quartz at QZ.com.

Romero, A. 2020. Dismantle the Department of Homeland Security. Its tactics are fearsome. ACLU News and Commentary, August 13. https://www.aclu.org/news/immigrants-rights/dismantle-the-department-of-homeland-security-its-tactics-are-fearsome/.

Romero, D. 2020. Government must release migrant children in detention centers because of coronavirus, judge orders. NBC News, June 26. https://www.nbcnews.com/news-us/government-must-release-migrant-children-detention-centers-because-coronavirus-judge-n1232328.

Romero, S., Kanno-Youngs, K., Fernandez, M., Borunda, D., Montes, A., and Dickerson, C. 2019. Hungry, scared, and sick: Inside the migrant detention center in Clint, Tex. *New York Times*, July 9. https://www.nytimes.com/interactive/2019/07/06/us/migrants-border-patrol-clint.html.

Romo, V. 2018. Hispanic caucus calls for investigation into migrant child's death. NPR, December 18. https://www.npr.org/2018/12/18/678035538/hispanic-caucus-calls-for-investigation-into-migrant-childs-death.

Roosevelt, E. 1958a. *On My Own*. New York: Dell.

———. *Speech to the UN, tenth anniversary of the adoption of the Universal Declaration of Human Rights*. New York, NY: United Nations.

Rosenberg, E. 2018. "Gut-wrenching" recording captures sounds of crying children separated from parents at the border. *Washington Post*, June 19. https://washingtonpost.com/news/post-nation/wp/2018/06/18/a-secret-recording-captures-the-sounds-of-crying-children-separated-from-parents-at-the-border/.

Roybal-Allard, L. 2019a. H.R. 3451: Humane Enforcement and Legal Protections for Separated Children Act of 2019. June 24. Retrieved from congress.gov: https://www.congress.gov/bill/116th-congress/house-bill/3451/text.

———. 2019b. H.R. 3452: The Help Separated Families Act. June 24. Retrieved from congress.gov: https://www.congress.gov/bill/116th-congress/house-bill/3452/text.

Ruiz, R. 2019. H.R. 3239. Humanitarian Standards for Individuals in Customs and Border Protection Custody Act. June 12. Retrieved from congress.gov: https://www.congress.gov/bill/116th-congress/house-bill/3239.

Sacchetti, M. 2018. Top homeland security officials urge criminal prosecution for parents crossing the border with children. *Washington Post*, April 26. https://www.washingtonpost.com/local/immigration/top-homeland-security-officials-urge-criminal-prosecution-of-parents-who-cross-border-with-children/2018/04/26/a0bdcee0-4964-11e8-8b5a-3b1697adcc2a_story.html.

———. 2019a. Trump administration cancels English classes, soccer, legal aid for unaccompanied child migrants in U.S. shelters. *Washington Post*, June 5. https://www.washingtonpost.com/immigration/trump-administration-cancels-english-classes-soccer-legal-aid-for-unaccompanied-migrants-in-us-shelters-/2019/06/05/df2a0008-8712-11e9-a491-25df61c78dc4-story_html.

———. 2019b. Federal judge blocks Trump administration from detaining migrant children for indefinite period. *Washington Post*, September 27. https://www.washingtonpost.com/immigration/federal-judge-blocks-trump-administration-from-detaining-migrant-children-for-indefinite-periods/2019/09/27/49a39790-e15f-11e9-b199-f638bf2c340f_story.html.

Sakelaris, N. 2019a. Migrant children to House panel: Trump is cutting life-saving program. United Press International, September 11. https://www.upi.com/Top_News/U.S./2019/09/11/Migrant-children-to-House-panel-Trump-is-cutting-life-saving-program/3731568216724/.

_____. 2019b. Trump administration to lift limits on detention for migrant families. United Press International, August 21. https://www.upi.com/Top_News/U.S./2019/08/21/Trump-administration-to-lift-limits-on-detention-for-migrant-families/4461566395021/.

Sanders, S., and Nielsen, K. 2018. Press briefing by Press Secretary Sarah Sanders and Department of Homeland Security Secretary Kirstjen Nielsen. Whitehouse.gov. June 18. https://www.whitehouse.gov/briefings-statements/press-briefing-press-secretary-sarah-sanders-department-homeland-security-secretary-Kirstjen-nielsen-061818.

Santas, R. 2019. There's only 1 baby left at the largest family detention center in U.S., ICE says. *Vice,* March 5. https://www.vice.com/en/article/kzdkaa/ice-released-12-babies-in-texas-but-5-are-still-detained.

Schwartz, M. 2019. Inside the deportation courts. *New York Review of Books,* October 10. https://www.nybooks.com/articles/2019/10/10inside-the-deportation-courts/.

Sears, B. 2019. Your brain on hugs. December 30. https://www.askdrsears.com/topics/parenting/child-rearing-and-development/your-brain-on-hugs.

Senate and House of Representatives of the United States of America. 1978. Public Law 95–608. November 8. https://www.govinfo.gov/content/pkg/STATUTE-92/pdf/STATUTE-92-Pg3069.pdf.

Sessions, J. 2018a. Memorandum for prosecutors along southwest border. April 6. Retrieved from Office of the Attorney General: https://www.justice.gov/opa/press-release/file/1049751/download.

_____. 2018b. Attorney General Sessions delivers remarks to Association of State Criminal Investigative Agencies: 2018 spring conference. May 7. Retrieved from the United Stated Department of Justice: https://www.justice.gov/opa/speech/attorney-general-sessions-delivers-remarks-association-state-criminal-investigate.

Shamdasani, R. 2018. Press briefing note on Egypt, United States, and Ethiopia. June 5. Retrieved from United Nations Human Rights Office of the High Commissioner: https://www.ohchr.org/EN/NewsEvents/Pages/DisplayNews.aspx?NewsID=23174&LangID=E.

Shear, M., Goodnough, A., and Haberman, M. 2018. Trump retreats on separating families, but thousands remain apart. *New York Times,* June 20. https://www.nytimes.com/2018/06/20/us/politics/trump-immigration-children-executive-order.html.

Shear, M., and Haberman, M. 2020. Trump's temporary halt to immigration is part of a broader plan, Stephen Miller says. *New York Times*, April 24. https://www.nytimes.com/2020/04/2020/us/politics/coronavirus-trump-immigration-stephen-miller.

Sheridan, P.H. 1869. Nice day for genocide: Shocking quotes on Indians by U.S. leaders, part 2. Indian Country Today. https://indiancountrytoday.com/archive/nice-day-for-a-genocide-shocking-quotes-on-indians-by-u-s-leaders-pt-2-itTXslul5EKc694gf4DLfA.

Sholtis, B. 2019. Remains of students at Carlise Indian School returned to families. WHYY, July 11. https://whyy.org/articles/remains-of-students-at-carlisle-indian-school-returned-to-families/.

Silva, D. 2019. Family of Salvadoran migrant dad, child who drowned say he "loved his daughter so much." NBC News, June 26. https://www.nbcnews.com/news/latino/family-salvadoran-migrant-dad-child-who-drowned-say-he-loved-n1022226.

Sims, C. 2019. *Team of Vipers: My 500 Extraordinary Days in the Trump White House.* New York: Thomas Dunne.

Slotkin, E. 2019. H.R. 3670: Short Term Detention Standards Act. July 10. Retrieved from Congress.gov: https://www.govtrack.us/congress/bills/116/hr3670.

Smith, K. 2019. 12 detained babies have been released from ICE custody in Dilley, Texas. CBS News, March 4. https://www.cbsnews.com/news/immigrant-children-detained-12-babies-released-from-ice-custody-detention-center-dilley-texas-2019-03-04/.

Smith, S. 2018. Evangelical leaders rebuke Donald Trump for separating immigrant children from families at border. *Christianity Today,* June 5. https://www.christiantoday.com/article/evangelical-leaders-rebuke-donald-trump-for-separating-immigrant-children-from-families-at-border/129568.htm.

Smith, T. 2019. S. 2256: Coordinating Care for Children Affected by Immigration Enforcement Act. July 24. Retrieved from Congress.gov: https://www.congress.gov/bill/116th-congress/senate-bill/2256/text.

Soboroff, J. 2018. Surge of children separated at border floods facility for undocumented immigrants. NBC News, June 14. https://www.nbcnews.com/news/us-news/surge-children-separated-border-floods-facility-undocumented-immigrants-n883001.

———, 2019. Emails show Trump administration had "no way to link" separated migrant children to parents. NBC News, May 1. https://www.nbcnews.com/politics/immigration/emails-show-trump-admin-had-no-way-link-separated-migrant-n1000746.

———. 2020. *Separated: Inside an American tragedy.* New York: Custom House.

Soboroff, J., and Ainsley, J. 2019. Migrant kids in overcrowded Arizona border shelter allege sexual assault, retaliation from U.S. agents. NBC News, July 9. https://www.msn.com/en-ca/lifestyle/lifestylegeneral/migrant-kids-in-arizona-report-sex-assault-retaliation-from-border-agent-ar-AAE67xv.

Speckhard, D. 2018. The U.S. helped cause the problems many migrants face in their own countries: We should help fix them. *Baltimore Sun,* May 1. https://www.baltimoresun.com/opinion/op-ed/bs-ed-op-0502-caravan-wall-20180501-story.html.

Sripom, B. 2016. What is the importance of human touch for all young children? Quora, July 22. https://www.quora.com/What-is-the-importance-of-human-touch-for-all-young-children.

Stanton, J. 2018. The incoming head of the Congressional Hispanic Caucus called on the Customs and Border Patrol chief to resign. BuzzFeedNews, December 18. https://www.buzzfeednews.com/article/johnstanton/joaquin-castro-kevin-mcaleenan-resign-border-protection.

Stevenson, A. 1962. Remarks at Eleanor Roosevelt's memorial service. Hyde Park, New York.

Stewart, E. 2018. Sarah Sanders on immigrant family separation: "It is very biblical to enforce the law." Vox, June 14. https://www.vox.com/2018/6/14/17465662/sarah-sanders-family-separation-bible-sessions.

Stobbe, M. 2019. U.S. health officials link childhood trauma to adult illness. Associated Press, November 5. https://apnews.com/bf647b36c0a64e4b935b96426d5baf86.

Taylor, D. 2018. Why did a little Guatemalan girl die after crossing the U.S. border? *The Guardian,* December 17. https://www.theguardian.com/us-news/2018/dec/17/guatemalan-girl-jakelin-caal-maquin-death-crossing-us-border.

Thompson, G. 2018. Listen to children who've just been separated from their parents at the border. ProPublica, June 18. https://www.propublica.org/article/children-separated-from-parents-border-patrol-cbp-trump-immigration-policy.

Tillett, E. 2018. Sen. Jeff Merkely denied entry into one migrant detention facility, claims he saw kids caged in another. CBS News, June 4. https://www.cbsnews.com/news/senator-jeff-merkley-barred-brownsville-texas-detention-center-refugee-children-2018-06-04/.

Totenberg, N. 2020. Supreme Court sides with Trump administration in asylum cases. NPR, July 25. https://www.npr.org/2020/06/25/883312496/supreme-court-sides-with-trump-administration-in-deportation-case.

Trib Live: *The Washington Post.* 2018. Democrats denounce Border Patrol station conditions. TRIB Live. December 18. https://archive.triblive.com/news/world/democrats-denounce-border-patrol-station-conditions/.

Tribe, L.H. 2019. Democrats are debating a dangerous false choice for impeachment. *Washington Post*. December 5. https://www.washingtonpost.com/opinions/2019/12/05/democrats-are-debating-dangerous-false-choice-impeachment/.
Trump, D. (@realDonaldTrump). 2019. "The Fake News Media, in particular the Failing @nytimes, is writing phony and exaggerated accounts of the Border Detention Centers. First of all, people should not be entering our Country illegally...." Twitter, July 7. https://deadline.com/2019/07/president-donald-trump-tweetstorm-the-sunday-edition-39-1202642675/.
Tutu, D. M. 2001. Foreword. In C. Castle, *For Every Child*. New York: Phyllis Fogelman Books.
Twenty-six Jewish Organizations. 2018. Letter to Attorney General Sessions and Secretary Nielsen. June 12. Retrieved from Anti-Defamation League: https://www.adl.org/sites/default/files/documents/jewish-orgs-letter-sessions-nielsen-family-separations-2018-06-12.pdf.
Ulloa, J. 2020. Court protects DACA, for now. *Boston Globe*, June 19, pp. A1, A6.
UN General Assembly. 1951. *The Convention Relating to the Status of Refugees*. UN, Treaty Series, vol. 189, July 28, p. 137. https://treaties.un.org/Pages/showDetails.aspx?objid=080000028003002e. Reprinted with permission of the United Nations.
_____. 1966a. *International Convention on Civil and Political Rights*. United Nations, Treaty Series, vol. 999, December 16, p. 171. https://treaties.un.org/Pages/ViewDetails.aspx?chapter=4&clang=_en&mtdsg_no=IV-4&src=IND. Reprinted with permission of the United Nations.
_____. 1966b. *International Convention on the Elimination All Forms of Racial Discrimination*. UN, Treaty Series, vol. 660, March 7, p. 195. https://treaties.un.org/Pages/ViewDetails.aspx?src=IND&mtdsg_no=IV-2&chapter=4&clang=_en. Reprinted with permission of the United Nations.
_____. 1984. *Convention Against Torture and Other Cruel, Inhuman or Degrading Treatment or Punishment*. UN, Treaty Series, vol. 1465, December 10. https://treaties.un.org/pages/ViewDetails.aspx?src=IND&mtdsg_no=IV-9&chapter=4&lang=en. Reprinted with permission of the United Nations.
_____. 1989a. *The United Nations Convention on the Rights of the Child*. November 20. Retrieved from UNICEF: https://downloads.unicef.org.uk/wp-content/uploads/2010/05/UNCRC_united_nations_convention_on_the_rights_of_the_child.pdf?_ga=2.210446930.634554858.1579377424-1623028791.1579377424.
_____. 1989b. *Convention on the Rights of the Child*. UN, Treaty Series, vol. 1577, November 20, p. 3. https://treaties.un.org/pages/ViewDetails.aspx?src=IND&mtdsg_no=IV-11&chapter=4&lang=en. Reprinted with permission of the United Nations.
UN Human Rights Council. 2010. Report of the Working Group on Arbitrary Detention, Para 60. January 15. Retrieved from Office of the High Commission on Human Rights: https://www2.ohchr.org/english/bodies/hrcouncil/docs/13session/A.HRC.13.30_AEV.pdf.
UN Secretary General. 2014. *Report of the UN Secretary General on international migration and development, A/68/190*. Para. 78. New York: United Nations.
Underwood, L. 2019. H.R. 3525: U.S. Border Medical Screening Standards Act. June 27. Retrieved from congress.gov: https://www.congress.gov/bill/116th-congress/house-bill/3525/text.
UNHRC (United Nations High Commission on Refugees). 1981. Note on family reunification. August 13. Retrieved from ¶ 2, UN Doc. EC/SCP/17.
_____. 2015. State parties to the 1951 convention relating to the status of refugees and 1967 protocol. April. https://www.unhcr.org/protect/PROTECTION/3b73b0d63.pdf.
_____. 2020a. Central American refugee crisis. July. https://www.unrefugees.org/emergencies/central-america/.

———. 2020b. What is a refugee? August. https://www.unrefugees.org/refugee-facts/what-is-a-refugee/.
UNICEF. 2012. Human rights and children. April 2. https://www.unicef.org/policyanalysis/rights/index_62016.html.
———. 2016. A summary of the rights under the Convention on the Rights of the Child. December. https://www.unicef.org/montenegro/en/reports/summary-rights-under-convention-rights-child.
———. 2020. Four principles of the Convention on the Rights of the Child: Four principles that together form a new attitude toward children. August 7. https://www.unicef.org/armenia/en/stories/four-principles-convention-rights-child.
———, n.d. *What Is the Convention on the Rights of the Child?* https://www.unicef.org/child-rights-convention/what-is-the-convention.
United Nations. 2020a. Chapter IV: Human Rights: International Convention on Civil and Political Rights. Retrieved from United Nations Treaty Collection: https://treaties.un.org/Pages/ViewDetails.aspx?chapter=4&clang=_en&mtdsg_no=IV-4&src=IND.
———. 2020b. Human rights. Retrieved from United Nations: https://www.un.org/en/sections/issues-depth/human-rights/.
U.S. Customs and Border Protection. 2015. National standards on transport, escort, detention, and search. October. https://www.cbp.gov/sites/default/files/assets/documents/2017-Sep/CBP%20TEDS%20Policy%20Oct2015.pdf.
———. 2019. Customs and Border Protection (CBP) employee suicide report. September 11. https://www.documentcloud.org/documents/6534877-Suicide-Summary-20190911-1.html.
U.S. Department of Health and Human Services. 2018a. Fact Sheet: Unaccompanied alien children sheltered at Tornillo Land Port of Entry (LPOE), Tornillo, Texas. December 26. https://www.hhs.gov/sites/default/files/Unaccompanied-Alien-Children-Sheltered-at-Tornillo-Fact-Sheet.pdf.
———. 2018b. Separated children placed in Office of Refugee Resettlement Care. December. https://www.oig.hhs.gov/oei/reports/oei-BL-18-00511.asp.
U.S. Department of Justice. 2020. A guide to disability rights: Rehabilitation act. February 24. https://www.ada.gov/cguide.htm#:~:text=The%20Rehabilitation%20Act%20prohibits%20discrimination,employment%20practices%20of%20Federal%20contractors.
U.S. Department of State. 2020. Policy issues: Human rights and democracy. July. https://www.state.gov/policy-issues/human-rights-and-democracy/.
U.S. Government Accountability Office. 2018. Unaccompanied children—agency efforts to reunify children separated from parents at the border. October. https://www.gao.gov/assets/700/694918.pdf.
———. 2020. Decision: Department of Homeland Security B-331650. August 14. https://www.gao.gov/assets/710/708830.pdf.
U.S. Supreme Court. 2020. No. 18-587 [U.S. Jun 18, 2020]
Vazquez, M. 2018. Dem senator accuses Trump administration of "cruel" effort against immigrant children. CNN, June 4. https://www.cnn.com/2018/06/04/politics/jeff-merkley-immigration-center-unaccompanied-minors/index.html.
Vieux, H. 2020. The second Trump asylum ban has been defeated in court. Human Rights First, July 1. https://www.humanrightsfirst.org/press-release/second-trump-asylum-ban-has-been-defeated-court.
VOA News. 2019. Major Texas border station closed for flu outbreak after teen death. Voice of America, May 22. https://www.voanews.com/usa/major-texas-border-station-closed-flu-outbreak-after-teen-death.
Walerius, R., and Tanvi, M. 2020. GAO says Wolf, Cuccinelli appointments at DHS invalid. Rollcall, August 14. https://www.rollcall.com/2020/08/14/gao-says-wolf-cuccinelli-appointments-at-dhs-invalid/.

Wallace, D. 2019. Lack of flu shots for migrants at CBP detention centers a concern, critics say. Fox News, August 21. https://www.foxnews.com/health/border-patrol-immigration-officials-do-not-administer-flu-influenza-shots-detention-centers.
Warren, E., Blumenthal, R., Klobacher, A., Booker, C.A., Harris, K.D., Wyden, R., ... Merkley, J.A. 2019. Letter to Kevin McAleenan, Acting Secretary, U.S. Department of Homeland Security and Alex Azar, Secretary, U.S. Department of Health and Human Services. September 6. Retrieved from United States Senate: https://www.warren.senate.gov/imo/media/doc/2019.09.06%20Letter%20to%20DHS%20HHS%20re%20flu%20vaccines%20for%20detained%20immigrants.pdf.
Warren, E., and Jayapal, P. 2019. Letter to chief executive officer of Caliburn, Jim Van Dusen. June 6. Retrieved from Congress of the United States: https://www.warren.senate.gov/imo/media/doc/2019.06.05%20Letter%20to%20Caliburn%20International%20re-%20John%20Kelly%20Appointment.pdf.
Wasserman-Schultz, D. 2019. H.R. 3868: Help Oversee, Manage, and Evaluate Safe Treatment Without Delay Act of 2019. July 22. Retrieved from Congress.gov: https://www.congress.gov/bill/116th-congress/house-bill/3868?s=1&r=1.
WebMD. 2019. CBP won't vaccinate migrants against flu. August 21. https://www.webmd.com/cold-and-flu/news/20190821/cbp-wont-vaccinate-migrants-against-flu.
White, J. 2019. Statement of Jonathan White, commander, U.S. Public Health Service Commissioned Corps, U.S. Department of Health and Human Services. February 7. Retrieved from U.S. House Subcommittee on Energy and Commerce Subcommittee on Oversight and Investigations: https://docs.house.gov/meetings/IF/IF02/20190207/108846/HHRG-116-IF02-Wstate-WhiteJ-20190207-U1.pdf.
Williams, J. (2020). *S appeals judge's order barring expulsions of migrants.* Retrieved from The Hill: https://the hill.com/latino/527673-us-appeals-judges-order-barring-expulsions-of-migrant-children.
Wilson-Keenan, J.-A. 2015. *From Small Places: Toward the Realization of Literacy as a Human Right.* Rotterdam, The Netherlands: Sense.
Wolf, C. (@SpoxDHS). 2019. "Of course Border Patrol isn't going to let a random group of radical activists show up and start injecting people with drugs." Twitter, December 10. https://twitter.com/SpoxDHS/status/1204495969439625216.
Woltjen, M. 2020. The White House is quietly deporting children. *New York Times,* June 22. https://www.nytimes.com/2020/06/22/opinion/coronavirus-children-border-deportation.html.
Wyden, R., and Warren, E. 2018. Letter to Alex M. Azar II, secretary, U.S. Department of Health and Human Services. October 17. https://www.wyden.senate.gov/imo/media/doc/101818%20Letter%20to%20Azar%20OIG%20Report%20Child%20Separation.pdf.
Wyrich, A. 2019. 27 Senators call on Trump to fire Stephen Miller. Daily Dot, December 9. https://www.dailydot.com/layer8/27-senators-call-on-trump-to-fire-stephen-miller/.
Young Center for Immigrant Children's Rights. 2018a. More than 200 experts in child welfare, juvenile justice oppose government plans to take children from parents at border. January 23. https://www.theyoungcenter.org/stories/2018/1/16/experts-oppose-plans-to-take-children-from-parents-at-border. Reprinted with permission of the Young Center for Immigrant Children's Rights.
_____. 2018b. Urgent appeals from experts in child welfare, juvenile justice, and child development to halt any plans to separate children from parents at the border. January 16. https://static1.squarespace.com/static/597ab5f3bebafb0a625aaf45/t/5a5e55cf0d9297a44bbb8d3e/1516131791958/2018_01_16+Child+Welfare+Juvenile+Justice+Opposition+to+Parent-Child+Separation+Plan.pdf.
_____. 2018c. Young Center for Immigrant Children's Rights commends child welfare

expert's overwhelming opposition to parent-child separation. June 7. https://www.theyoungcenter.org/stories/2018/6/7/540-orgs-protest-separation.

_____. 2018d. Renewed appeal from experts in child welfare, juvenile justice and child development. June 7. https://static1.squarespace.com/static/597ab5f3bebafb0a625aaf45/t/5b196fbf70a6ade9adfb3377/1528393664012/REV_2018_06_07_Child+Welfare+Juvenile+Justice+Opposition+to+Parent+Child+Separation+%281%29.pdf.

_____. 2019. Human consequences of immigration policy changes. An update from the field. Webinar transcript. December 10. https://static1.squarespace.com/static/597ab5f3bebafb0a625aaf45/t/5df9268cd31f9e2dc867b64a/1576609421330/2019_12_10+Young+Center+Webinar+Transcript-Final.pdf. Reprinted with permission of the Young Center for Immigrant Children's Rights.

_____. 2020. Family separation is not over: How the Trump administration continues to separate children from their parents to serve its political ends. June. https://www.theyoungcenter.org/stories/2020/6/25/the-young-center-for-immigrant-childrens-rights-releases-report-on-family-separation.

_____. (2020). *Reimagining Children's Immigration Proceedings: A Roadmap for an Entirely New System Centered around Children*. Chicago, Illinois: The Young Center for Immigrant Children's Rights.

_____. (2020b). *Reimagining Children's Immigration Proceedings: A Roadmap for an Entirely New System Centered around Children*. Retrieved from Young Center for Immigrant Children's Rights: https://theyoungcenter.org/reimagining-childrens-immigration proceedings.

Young Center Staff. 2020. Working for immigrant children in custody and across the border in times of COVID-19. April 14. Retrieved from Squarespace.com: https://static1.squarespace.com/static/597ab5f3bebafb0a625aaf45/t/5e97754c13775b6404892267/1586984268891/2020_04_15+Final+Webinar+Transcript-Young+Center.pdf.

YourTango Experts. 2018. The harmful effects of toxic stress on you and your children. PsychCentral. July 8. https://psychcentral.com/blog/the-harmful-effects-of-toxic-stress-on-you-your-children/.

Yucatan Times. 2020. U.S. is swiftly deporting migrant children at the border. *Yucatan Times*, March 20. https://www.theyucatantimes.com/2020/03/u-s-is-swiftly-deporting-migrant-children-at-the-border/.

_____. (2020). U.S. is swiftly deporting migrant children at the border. Yucatan Times. Retrieved from The Yucatan Times: https://www.theyucatantimes.com/2020/03/u-s-is-swiftly-deporting-migrant-children-at-the-border/.

Zak, D. 2020a. Legislative bulletin. National Immigration Forum. June 12. https://immigrationforum.org/article/legislative-bulletin-friday-june-12-2020/.

_____. 2020b. The Trump administration's proposed changes to the U.S. asylum system. National Immigration Forum. June 18. https://immigration forum.org/article/the-trump-administrations-proposed-changes-to-the-u-s-asylum-system.

Zero to Three. 2016. Trauma and toxic stress. March 7. https://psychcentral.com/blog/the-harmful-effects-of-toxic-stress-on-you-your-children/.

Index

Numbers in **_bold italics_** indicate pages with illustrations

Acer, Eleanor xi
Administration for Children and Families (ACF) 100, 103, 108
Administrative Procedure Act 1, 74, 179, 187–188, 197–198, 201, 203
African American Research Collaborative 27
Aguilar Ochoa, Neily Yoseli 124
Ainsley, Julia 45
Al Otro Lado Inc., et al. v. John F. Kelly, et al., Nielson 195–196
Albence, Matthew 69
Albright, Madeline 16
Alito, Justice Samuel 183
Alonzo-Gomez, Felipe 120, 122
American Academy of Pediatrics 47, 54, 114, 125, 144
American Civil Liberties Union 2, 48, 66–67, 126, 137, 176, 179, 187–189, 194, 198, 200, 202–203, 218, 220–221
American Immigration Council's Dilley Pro Bono Project 116
Anishinaabemowin 31
Annas, George xii, 84
Antelope Wells Border Crossing 79, 80, 118–119
Anti-Corruption and Public Integrity Act 112
Apostle Paul 56
Arizona Department of Health and Safety 51
Arpaio, Sheriff Joe 99
Autonomous University of Baja California, Mexicali, Mexico 163
Ayoub-Rodriquez, Dr. Lisa 125
Azar, Alex M. II 46, 63–64, 69, 70, 144, 189

Bachelet, Michelle 82, 83
Barr, AG William P. 70, 184–185, 199–200, 202
Belous, Laura 80
Bernfield, Jim xi
Blumenthal, Sen. Richard 207
Book of Obadiah 56
Border Protection Standards 75–79
Boston Globe 170

Brané, Michelle 79
Brian, Danielle xiii, 42, 45
Broward Transitional Center 109–110
Brown, Rep. Anthony 206
Budd, Jenn 127
El Buen Pastor 150–**_151_**
Bush, Laura 54
Bush administration 32

CA and 19 other states v. Homeland Sec. et al. 186–187
Caal, Jakelin 117–118, 120, 122
Caal, Nery Gilberto 117–118
Calexico, California x, 155–156, 166
Caliburn International Corporation 110–112
Campbell, Craig x, 153–155, 166
Canada 20, 171–172
Cancian, Maria 103
Caritas/Catholic Charities x, **_156_**, 166
Carlisle Indian Industrial School 30–32, 107, 189
Carroll, Fr. Sean xii, 169
Carvalho, Alberto 109
Casa Padre 6, 49, 50, 52, 123
Casa Phoenix 51
Castro, Rep. Joaquin 80, 118, 121, 126
Catholic Day of Action for Detained Children 55
CDC order (Title 42), 171, 173- 176, 219–220
Center for Human Rights and Constitutional Law 55, 184
Centers for Disease Control and Prevention (CDC) 75, 106, 144–145, 171–176, 185, 219–220
Chavez-Duenas, Nayeli 102
Chemerinsky, Erwin 75
Chicas Perez, Briseyda 124
Chicas Perez, Denilsen 124
Child Protective Services (CPS) 96, 99–100
Children entering the United States unaccompanied 89–101; cultural services 90–91; educational services 89; medical services 91–92; protection from

victimization 92–94; requirements for care providers and staff 95–10
Christian Science Monitor 56
Cicilline, Rep. David 50
Cissna, L. Francis xiii, 43
Citizens for Responsibility and Ethics in Washington 110
Ciudad Juarez, Mexico 123, 136
Clark, Rep. Yvette 214
Clint Border Patrol Station 79, 81–82, 126
Committee on Statelessness and Related Problems 59
Comprehensive Health Services 110–112
Conference of Plenipotentiaries 18, 59
Congressional Hispanic Caucus 118
Convention Against Torture and Other Inhuman or Degrading Treatment and Punishment 1, 6, 18, 84–85, 177, 201
Convention on the Rights of the Child 1, 4, 6, 14–17, 19, 35, 39–41, 48, 53, 58–59, 63, 72, 80–81, 86, 103–104, 116–117, 141, 145, 166, 174
Convention Relating to the Status of Refugees 6, 18, 40, 143, 155, 174, 176, 178, 198
Cordova-Valle, Darlyn Cristabel 122
Cortez Masto, Sen. Catherine 114, 207
COVID-19 xii, 6, 30, 167–168, 170–177, 184–186, 195, 198, 218, 222, 223
credible fear 76, 175, 177, 180, 182–183, 198, 203–204
Cristabel, Darlyn 117, 122
Crosby, Sandra xii, 84
Cuccinelli, Ken 131, 142–143, 204–205, 221–222
Cummings, Rep. Elijah E. 10, 66, 70, 128

Danaher, Dr. Fiona 142
Dancing My Dream, xi, 30
Daniels, Judge George 143
Davidson, Antar 113
DCJV v. ICE et al 190–191
Deferred Action for Childhood Arrivals (DACA) 133, 182
de León Gutiérrez, Juan 123
"deleted family units" 62, 63
Department of Family and Protective Services 50
Department of Homeland Security et al. v. Regents of the University of California et al. 182
Desai, Neha 109
Desjardins, Lisa 74
Division of Unaccompanied Children Services (DUCS) 45, 87
DNA testing 65, 188
Doctors for Camp Closures 145
Driver, Alice 105–106, 117
Durbin, Sen. Dick 62
Dutch, Rep. Ted 101

East Bay Sanctuary v. Barr 199–201
18th Street gang 11

El Paso Times 81
El Salvador 11, *12*, 16, 48, 117, 124, 134–135, 190–191, 194, 219
Escobar, Rep Veronica 119, 208
Espacio Amiable 162
Espaillat, Rep. Adriano 114, 210–211
Estrella del Norte shelter 113
Evangelical Immigration Table 56
Executive Office for Immigration Review (EOIR) 21, 87, 174

Fabian, Sarah B. 58
Faith in Action 55
Faith in Public Life 55
Families Belong Together 145
Family Case Management Program (FCMP) 34, 207, 213
family separation policy 47, 62, 75, 133, 188, 191
family units (FMUAs) 44, 60, 66, 72–73
Federal Writers' Project 28
Feinstein, Sen. Diane 207
Fernandez, Henry 27
Fields, John W. 28
Fifth Amendment 74, 188, 195
Fitzgerald, Thomas 69
Flake, Sen. Jeff 33
Florence Immigrant and Refugee Rights Project xii, 80, 137, 169
Flores, Bishop Daniel E. 55
Flores Settlement Agreement 5, 17, 19–22, 33–34, 36, 45, 55, 57–58, 71, 82,
Flores v. Barr 86, 184
Flores v. U.S. et al. 183–184
Flowers, Mary Miller 65
flu vaccine 25, 122, 143–144
Fontes, Anthony W. xi, 12, 14
Forman Miller, Mary Jo ix–x, 147, 168
Fortuna, Lisa 102
Fourth Amendment 195
Fray, Julie 56
Freedom of Information Act (FOIA) xiii, 1, 42–43, 59
Fresco, Leon 34
Friedman, Marla 127
From Small Places: Toward the Realization of Literacy as a Human Right 3

Garcia, Sylvia 119
Garcia-Siller, Archbishop Gustavo 55
Garlic, Delia 29
Gee, Dolly M. 20, 57–58, 82, 104, 142, 184–186
Gelernt, Lee 218, 220
Gendelman, Rebecca xi
General Assembly of the United Nations 18–19, 35
Gidley, Hogan 119
Gillibrand, Sen. Kristen 207
Givens, Fay x, 30
González, Vincente 50,

Index

Government Accountability Office (GAO) 1, 38, 65, 67, 218, 221–222
Grace v. Barr 202
Graham, Rev. Franklin 56
Grassley, Sen. Chuck 62
Green, Rep. Al 80, 119
Greenberg, Mark 106
Grimm, Michael 115
Guantanamo Bay 84
The Guardian 114
Guatemala 6, 11–14, 16–17, 48, 79, 117–118, 120–125, **130**, 136–137, 153, **159**, 160, 169, 176, 194, 219
Guatemalan Foreign Ministry 120, 121
Guterres, Sec. Gen. António 53

Harbury, Jennifer 114
Harris, Kamala 41, 43, 133
Hawkins, Katherine xiii, 60
Hayden, Michael xii, 131–132
Health and Human Services Office of the Inspector General 100, 189
Helping with All My Heart 150, **152**, **153**
Hernandez Vasquez, Carlos 123–124
las hieleras 5, 80
Homan, Thomas 43
Homeland Security Act of 2002 75, 210, 212–213
Homestead Detention Center 105, 109–112, 114, 184
Honduras 11, 16, 48, 102, 109, 134, 136, 142, 150, 160, 169, 190, 194, 219
Hosanna shelter **22**, **23**, **157–159**, 222–223, **224**
House Energy and Commerce Subcommittee on Oversight and Investigations 68–69, 220
House Homeland Security Committee 124
House Judiciary Committee 69
House Oversight Committee 10
H.R. 532, Alternatives to Detention Act 206–207
H.R. 2203: Homeland Security Improvement Act 208
H.R. 2415: The Dignity for Detained Immigrants Act of 2019 209
H.R. 2662: Asylum Seeker Protection Act 208
H.R. 3239: Humanitarian Standards for Individuals in Customs and Border Protection Act 210
H.R. 3451: The "Humane Enforcement and Legal Protections for Separated Children Act of 2019" 210
H.R. 3452: The Help Separated Families Act 211–212
H.R. 3525: U.S. Border Medical Screening Standards Act 212–213
H.R. 3670: Short Term Detention Standards Act 213
H.R. 3777: National Commission to Investigate the Treatment of Migrant Families Act of 2019 214–215

H.R. 3868: Help Overseee, Manage, and Evaluate Safe Treatment and Ensure Access Without Delay Act of 2019 (HOMESTEAD Act of 2019) 215
H.R. 3918; The Stop Cruelty to Migrant Children Act 213–214
H.R. 5210: The Refugee Protection act of 2019 216
Hull, Aaron 82
Human Rights First xi, 2, 20, 36, 134–137, 173, 175, 200–201, 218, 220
Hurd, Rep. Will 105

Illegal Immigrant Reform and Immigrant Responsibility Act (IIRAIRA) 2, 11, 182
Immigration and Customs Enforcement (ICE) 1, 21,34, 42–43, 58, 62, 64, 69, 71, 77, 109, 117, 146–150, 155, 185–187, 189, 193, 203, 208
Immigration and Nationality Act (INA) 2, 196, 198, 201, 203–204
Implementing Bilateral and Multilateral Asylum Cooperation Agreement Under the Immigration and Nationality Act (ACA Rule) 196
Indian Child Welfare Act 32
Indian Industrial School, Mt Pleasant, MI 30
Indian Schools, The Survivor's Story (motion picture) x–xi, 30
Innovation Law Lab et al. v. Nielson et al. 198–199
Inter-American Court of Human Rights 40
International Bill of Rights 18
International Convention on the Elimination of All Forms of Racial Discrimination (ICERD) 1, 6–7, 19, 35, 86
International Covenant on Civil and Political Rights (ICCPR) 1, 6, 17–18, 49, 139, 140
International Rescue Committee (IRC) 155
Iskyan, Howard x, 149
Iskyan, Martha x, 149, 156, 222

Jackson, Andrew 29
Janet Reno, Attorney General of the United States, et al. (1996) 33, 183
Jayapal, Rep. Pramila 110, 114, 209
Johannsen, Dr. Bert 125
Johnson, Sen. Ron xiii, 42–43
JP et al. v. Sessions et al. 75
Juarez, Mariee 117
Justice for Our Neighbors of East Texas 108
Juvonen, Jaana xii, 85

Kagan, Justice Elena 183
Karnes Federal Residential Center 184–186
Kelly, John F. 34–36, 38, 46, 110–112, 131, 195–196
K'iche 79
Kiel, Doug 32
Kino Border Initiative xii, 26, 169–170, 173
Kizuka, Kennji xi

Kraft, Dr. Colleen 47, 114
Kronstadt, Judge John A. 75, 193, 194

LBGTQI youth 93, 94
Leahy, Rep. Patrick 216
Lee, Rep. Barbara 53
Lee Jackson, Rep. Sheila 50
Level 4 threat risk 134
Liddell, Chris 46
Lieu, Rep. Ted 114
Linton, Dr. Julie 125
L.L.M. v. Cuccinelli 204
Lofgren, Rep. Zoe 216
Lordsburg Border Patrol Station 79, 80, 118
Luján, Rep. Ben Ray 118

Magaz, Fernando 103
Make the Road et al. v. McAleenan et al. 202–203
Make the Road New York, African Services Committee, Catholic Diocese et al. v. Citizenship and Immigration Services 196–198
Malecki, Eva 56
Mara Salvatrucha 11
Maria M. Kiakombua et al v. Customs and Border Protection 201–202
Markey, Sen. Edward 207
Marlow, Dr. Ryan 108
Marriott, Brian 57
Martinez, Reyna x, 156, **162**
Martinez, Sofia 11
Martinez Ramirez, Valeria 124
Matamoros, Mexico 134–138, 168
Maxwell, Ann 68, 69
McAleenan, Kevin xiii, 10, 43, 66, 131, 142, 144, 172, 202–203, 221
McAllen, Texas (Ursula Border Station) 52, 79, 144
McCaskill, Sen. Claire xiii, 42–43
McGhan, Don 46
McGowan, Kay x, 30–31
Mendez, Juan 84
Meng, Rep. Grace 213
Merkley, Sen. Jeff 6, 10, 50, 52–53, 79, 125–126, 207, 213
Metering 25, 120–121, 125, 133, 175, 208
Mexicali, Mexico ix–x, **12**, 136, 155–156, 160, 163, 166, 168, 222
Miami-Dade School System 109
Migrant Protection Protocols (MPP, Remain in Mexico) 25, 133–138, 167, 171, 173–174, 199–200, 208, 219–220
Migrant Stories: Why They Flee xi
Miller, Stephen xii, 45–46, 131–133, 145, 170–172
Miranda Aquilar, Juana Anastasia 124
Morgan, Mark 173
Ms. J.P. et al. v. Sessions et al. 193–194
Ms. L. v. ICE 66, 187–189
Ms. Q and J v. ICE 189–191
Murzda, Katy 116

Nagda, Jennifer 175
Nasada, Fr. Sam **162**
Nathan, Debbie 138
National Immigration Forum 177
Never Again Action 145
New York Times 5, 38, 50–51, 81, 105–106, 138, 171
New York Times Review of Books 138
Nielsen, Kirstjen xiii, 9, 36, 38, 41–46, 54, 62–63, 70, 119, 131
Ninth Circuit Court of Appeals 20, 82, 137, 183, 185, 194, 196, 198–200, 204
Nogales, Arizona xii, 169
Nogales, Sorona, Mexico xii, 26, 169–170
Northern Triangle of Central America ix, 5–6, 11, 54, 83, 223
Nowak, Manfred 72, 84
Nuevo Laredo, Mexico 134–136, 138

Obama administration 33–34, 58, 106, 120
Office of Management and Budget 1, 73
Office of Refugee Resettlement 1, 21, 24, 38, 41–42, 45, 54, 63, 65, 67, 71, 75, 87, 88–91, 93, 95–103, 105–108, 112, 116, 143, 175, 185–186, 213
Office of the Inspector General: Department of Health and Human Services 68, 100; Department of Homeland Security 1, 63–65, 73, 121
100 Angels 151
Open the Government xiii, 42–45, 59
Operation Streamline 32–33, 39
Option 3 43–44
Orders from Above: Massive Human Rights Abuses under the Trump Administration Return to Mexico Policy 134–135
Orellana, Nolbiz 109

Pacheco, Levian 103
Padilla v. ICE 203–204
Palazzo, Nicholas 66
Pallone, Rep. Frank, Jr. 69
Pandemic as Pretext: Trump Administration exploits Covid-19, expels asylum seekers and children to escalating danger xi, 173, 175
Paso del Norte 120, 123
Petoskey, Warren xi, 30–32
Phoenix airport 147–148, **148**, 152–153, **154**, 166
Phoenix bus station x, 147–148, 153, 166
Phoenix Welcome Center 155
Physicians for Human Rights 85
Pocan, Rep. Mark 50
Pompeo. Mike 46
Pope Francis 55
Port Isabel, Texas 71
La Posada x, **12–13**, **25**, **129**, **160**, 160–161, **161–165**, 166
Post, Dianne ix, 7, 27, 29, 32, 34, 42, 52, 58, 90, 99, 105, 139, 155, 174, 176–179, 184, 186–196, 198–205

Index

Pratt, Capt. Richard Henry 29, 30
Price, Rep. David 210
Project on Government Oversight (POGO) xiii, 42–45, 59–60
ProPublica 102, 114–115, 123
Public Charge 25, 143, 197
Pūras, Dainius 116, 125

Q'eqchi 118

Ramirez v. ICE 192–193
Ramirez Vasquez, Wilmer Josue 123, 125
Redfield, Dr. Robert 171
refoulement 18, 83, 177, 198–199
Refugee Aid ix, x, 6, 26, 102, 147–149, 153, 155–156, 162, 164, 166, 168, 222
Report of the Special Rapporteur on the right of everyone to the enjoyment of the right to the highest attainable standard of physical and mental health 125
Report of the Special Rapporteur on torture and other cruel or degrading treatment or punishment 84, 125
Reyes Sopon, Yequelin Mereidy 124
Reynosa-Gonzalez, Dalila 108
Riley, Jason 132
Rio Grande Valley 82
Rivera Reyes, Marleny Mereidy 124
Romero, Anthony 218, 221
Rood, John 46
Roosevelt, Eleanor 14–15, 164–165
Rosenbaum, Mark 75
Rosenberg, Lisa xiii, 43, 45
Rowe, Katie 29
Roybal-Allard, Rep. Lucille 210–211
Rudd, John 29
Ruiz, Rep. Raul 118–119, 210

S. 92: Keep Families Together Act 207–208
S. 1894: Alternatives to Detention Act of 2019 206–207
S. 2113: The Stop Cruelty to Migrant Children Act 213–214
S. 2256: The Coordinating Care for Children Affected by Immigration Enforcement Act 210–212
S. 2936: The Refugee Protection Act of 2019 216
S. Gloria x, 149–154, 166
Sabraw, Judge Dana 58, 66, 187–188, 203
Sanchez, Jennifer 51
Sanchez, Dr. Juan 50–51, 105
Sanders, Sarah Huckabee 56
Sandweg, John 58
Save the Children 162
Schey, Peter 58
Schlanger, Margo xi
Schwartz, Madeleine 138–139, 178
Senate Committee on Homeland Security and Governmental Affairs xiii, 41
Senate Finance Committee 63, 69,

Senate Judiciary Committee 36, 62
Sessions, AG Jeff 33, 38–39, 49, 54, 56, 65, 67–68, 75, 131, 187, 191–194
Sexual Abuse Significant Incident Report (SA/SIR) 99–100,
Shamdasani, Ravina 47–48
Shiloh Treatment Center 103–104
Short, Marc 46,
Silvers, Jennifer xii, 85
Sisters of Mercy of the Americas 55
Slotkin, Rep. Elisa 213
Smith, Rep. Adam 209
Smith, Sen. Tina 212
Soboroff, Jacob 6, 45
Solis, Bishop Oscar 55
Sotomayor, Justice Sonia 183, 198
South Texas Family Residential Center (Dilley) 116, 184–185
The Southern Baptist Convention 56
Southern Poverty Law Center xii, 2, 131, 133, 195, 198, 200
Southwest Key 49–51, 103, 105, 113, 123, 195
Sparling, Deirdre x, 102, 130, 148
Special Review—Initial Observations Regarding Family Separation Issues Under the Zero-Tolerance Policy 63
Supreme Court 137, 180, 182–183, 197–201
Sutton, Katie 29

Tamaulipas, Mexico 134, 137
Tamayo Madueño, Altagracia x, 160–161, *162*, 164
Tender age shelters 114
Texas Health and Human Services Commission 50
Thompson, Rep. Bennie 124
Thuraissigiam, Vijayakumar 182, 183
Title 42 183
Titus, Rep. Dina 210–211
Tornillo tent city 71, 103, 105–109, 114, 117, 175
Torres, Rep. Norma 211
torture 1, 4, 6, 18, 24, 55, 84–86, 134, 136–137, 168, 177, 183, 191, 195–196, 201, 206, 218
toxic stress 47, 74–75, 109, 210
Trafficking Victims Protection Reauthorization Act (TVPRA) 2, 17, 19–22, 45, 110, 141, 174, 193, 210, 219
Transit Ban 25, 141, 200
trauma 4–5, 24, 28, 31, 36–37, 54–56, 72, 75, 84, 93, 102, 113, 125–126, 136, 191, 193, 195, 207, 221, 223
Tribe, Lawrence 128
Trump, Donald 22, 34, 53, 57, 68, 72, 82, 129, 132, 167, 171, 189
Tutu, Archbishop Desmond 4–5
26 Jewish organizations 54

Unaccompanied Alien Children (UAC) 1, 19, 21–22, 60, 73, 78, 87–88, 92, 97–98, 186
Underwood, Rep. Lauren 212
United Nations 1, 48, 53

United Nations Children's Fund (UNICEF) 1, 4, 16
United Nations General Assembly 15–19
UN Global Study on Children Deprived of Liberty 39, 72, 84, 108, 113, 115
United Nations High Commissioner for Refugees 1, 18, 40, 162
United States Citizens and Immigration Services (USCIS) 204–205, 222
U.S. Citizenship and Immigration Services (USCIS) xiii, 43, 142, 144, 222
U.S. Constitution 19, 37, 58, 128, 182–184, 188, 190–192, 195, 197, 200–201, 203–204
U.S. Court of Appeals for the Ninth Circuit 20, 82, 137, 183, 185, 188, 194, 196, 198–200, 204,
U.S. Customs and Border Protection (CBP) xiii, 1, 24, 42–43, 62, 64–66, 71–73, 76–77, 81, 88, 105, 120, 123, 125–127, 135–137, 143–145, 147, 172–173, 175, 176, 183, 185, 195, 201, 208, 210, 212–213, 215, 220–221
U.S. Department of Health and Human Services (HHS) 1, 34, 37, 41–42, 45–46, 50–51, 57, 60, 62, 68–70, 73, 75, 80, 87, 100, 102–103, 106–107, 112, 117, 141, 143, 144–146, 188–189, 194, 219–221; Office of the Inspector General 68, 100, 215
U.S. Department of Homeland Security (DHS) 1, 5, 9, 10, 32,34, 36, 38–39, 41–45, 47, 49, 51, 53–54, 59, 62–65, 67–69, 73, 75, 83, 87, 99, 110–112, 118, 121–122, 131, 134–137, 144–145, 173–174, 182,-183, 185, 192, 194–195, 199, 204, 208–209, 211, 215, 218–222; Office of the Inspector General 63- 65, 73, 83,137, 215
U.S. District Court for the Central District of California 20, 109
U.S. Department of Justice (DOJ) 32, 34, 39, 47, 51, 85, 87, 101, 111, 181, 186, 219–220
U.S. District Court for the Central District of California 20, 109

U.S. Refugee Act of 1980 18, 201
U.S. Senate Committee on Oversight and Reform 70
Universal Declaration of Human Rights 1,14, 17, 48, 217
unsanitary conditions 10, 82, 84
Ursula Border Station (McAllen, Texas) 52, 79

Van Hollen, Sen. Chris 50
Vazquez, Marta x, *150*, 166
Vela, Rep. Filemon, Jr. 50
Velazquez, Rep. Nydia 210–211
Vieux, Henry 201

Wall Street Journal 132
Warren, Elizabeth 63, 110, 144
Washington Post 27, 42, 114, 123, 128, 145–146, 171–172
Washington Times 114
Wasserman Schultz, Rep. Debbie 215
Weber, Mark 141, 146
Welch, Rep. Peter 50
Weslaco Border Patrol Station 123
White, Cmdr. Jonathan 68, 102, 189
Williams, Joanna xii, 169
Wolf, Chad 131, 221
Wolfe, Kenneth 57
Woltjen, Maria 5, 168, 174
Woman's Refugee Commission 79
Wyden, Ron 63

Young Center for Immigrant Children's Rights xii, 65, 168, 174–175, 218
Youngstown site 51
Yuma Border Patrol Station 79, 80, 102

Zaccaro, Ray 52
zero-tolerance policy xiii, 9, 10, 24, 32–33, 38–39, 44–45, 48–49, 53–55, 63–65, 67–68, 71–75, 94, 111, 113, 121, 128, 131–132, 190–191

www.ingramcontent.com/pod-product-compliance
Ingram Content Group UK Ltd.
Pitfield, Milton Keynes, MK11 3LW, UK
UKHW041930140426
5217IPUK00014B/411